EDINBURGH DAYS,
or Doing What I Want to Do

Books by Sam Pickering

Essay Collections
A Continuing Education
The Right Distance
May Days
Still Life
Let It Ride
Trespassing
The Blue Caterpillar and Other Essays
Living to Prowl
Deprived of Unhappiness
A Little Fling and Other Essays
The Last Book
The Best of Pickering
Indian Summer

Travel
Walkabout Year
Waltzing the Magpies

Literary Studies
The Moral Tradition in English Fiction, 1785–1850
John Locke and Children's Books in Eighteenth-Century England
Moral Instruction and Fiction for Children, 1749–1820

Teaching
Letters to a Teacher

EDINBURGH DAYS

or Doing What I Want to Do

SAM PICKERING

The University of South Carolina Press

© 2007 University of South Carolina

Published by the University of South Carolina Press
Columbia, South Carolina 29208

www.sc.edu/uscpress

Manufactured in the United States of America

16 15 14 13 12 11 10 09 08 07   10 9 8 7 6 5 4 3 2 1

Library of Congress Cataloging-in-Publication Data

Pickering, Samuel F., 1941–
    Edinburgh days, or, Doing what I want to do / Sam Pickering.
        p. cm.
    ISBN-13: 978-1-57003-691-0 (cloth : alk. paper)
    ISBN-10: 1-57003-691-8 (cloth : alk. paper)
    1. Pickering, Samuel F., 1941– —Homes and haunts—Scotland—Edinburgh.
2. Edinburgh (Scotland)—Description and travel. 3. Pickering, Samuel F., 1941–
—Travel—Scotland. I. Title. II. Title: Edinburgh days. III. Title: Doing what
I want to do.
    DA890.E3P53 2007
    941.3'4086092—dc22
    [B]

                                                              2006038877

This book was printed on a Glatfelter recycled paper with 20 percent postconsumer
waste content.

CONTENTS

INTRODUCTION

I got to the dentist's office early and, sitting down, looked at my fellow patients. Across the room a large woman sagged into a stuffed chair, the June number of *Connecticut Magazine* balanced on her diaphragm like a screen, on the cover of the issue the phrase "Summer Times" brighter than noon, beneath the words fat hunks of watermelon, red as sunburn. The woman looked inert, and the arms of the chair pushed the flesh along her flanks up over her stomach, kneading it into yeasty folds. Suddenly the woman sat upright and, leaning forward, stared at the rug. Quickly she hoisted herself out the chair, took two steps, raised her right foot then lowered it, grinding the ball into the rug, her heel wagging back and forth like a tail. "I killed that spider," she said, glancing around the room searching for approval. "Spider, hell!" I said, "You killed God!" "What?" the woman said, rocking backward. "You killed God," I repeated. "After what you did, you better go home and pray for forgiveness. Who knows what will happen if you go through that door?" I said, pointing toward the door that separated the reception room from the dentists' offices, for good measure adding, "Certainly God doesn't know what will happen. He's dead."

At that moment Donna appeared and said, "Sam." I stood and sauntered through the door. I met Jim in the hall. "Sam," Jim said, "What are you up to? I heard a commotion in the waiting room and was concerned until I remembered you had an appointment to have your teeth cleaned." "Jim," I said, "I've been worried about you. You look tired, and because I am kind and sweet I've been chasing away patients so you can take a vacation."

Later, as I left the office, Jim said, "It's always a treat to see you, Sam." "The time has come for me to leave Storrs—again," I thought, the scrubbing having not simply polished my molars but also given me leisure enough to gnaw at my character. I'd been back in Connecticut for nine days, having spent the previous four and a half months in Scotland. Tornados of pollen swirled though eastern Connecticut, and I stayed in bed my first three days at home, my sinuses hot air balloons, a high temperature heating them and making them swell, rising behind my nose and pushing my eyes out, turning them into goggles.

The first day out of the house I went to the Memorial Day parade in Mansfield Center. Every year the high school and middle school bands play martial music, the players strutting, banging drums, lifting their legs high with the "field artillery." Parents amble beside Cub and Brownie Scouts. Coaches try to marshal second and third grade baseball players into squads. The players are wonderfully undisciplined, always skipping out of lineups to hug parents and talk to classmates. Aging veterans throw peanuts and candy from the windows of antique cars. Packs of dogs gambol along, slobbering but not barking or sniffing one another rudely. Vicki and I never miss the parade. We stand beside the road and talk to friends while sipping coffee and eating chocolate doughnuts.

This year I felt out of sorts, in part because I recognized few people, our children having graduated from teams and schools. Instead of following marchers into the new cemetery on the hill, I lingered in the old graveyard, the death's heads on the eighteenth-century stones more familiar than most townsfolk. Below a rise I found a golf ball, a Pinnacle 4. The thought of someone's practicing chip shots amid rows of leaping boards cheered me, and I turned and strolled up Cemetery Road to the new graveyard. Red-winged blackbirds called raucously from the marsh, and an oriole snapped over the road, black and orange feathers slapping like a flag. "A good day," I thought, the sky soft as tissue and the sun light and promising. I was wrong. The weather had seduced me into optimism. Instead of climbing the hill in the center of the graveyard and listening to speeches, I walked around the field. A ring of yellow iris circled the marsh, and a wood thrush sang in the woods. I smiled and listened to the bird. But then I came across a new grave on a spit of land at the western lip of the cemetery, that of a boy killed in Iraq, a high school classmate of my son Edward. Grass had not sprouted, and the grave was brown. At the back of the grave stood nine small American flags, all limp and unbudded, wrapped around thin black sticks. At the foot of the grave friends had placed votive offerings, a bottle of Killian's Irish Red Ale, a tin of Copenhagen snuff, a blue cigarette lighter, the word NAVY stamped on it in white, and then a homemade ashtray, the sort children make for parents in the fifth grade.

To the left of the ashtray sat a small teddy bear, one of a collection of bears sold by the post office. Printed on a heart-shaped card stapled to the bear was "HERO." Sewed onto the bear's left breast was an American flag. The bear had sat for weeks in the rain, and watermarks had risen over his legs, stretching along his back and across his belly in dark lines. A woman strode down the hill and stood beside me. "His mother comes here every day," she said. "No," I whispered under my breath. I almost said, "Don't forgive them for what they have done, Lord," thinking about the people in Washington who had forced heartache upon little towns all over America. Instead I walked silently away, hunched over, swallowing my words before they sliced out of mouth into handle and blade.

As I drove home from the dentist's office, I ached to return to Edinburgh. There I'd be alone and could escape the silliness of my character and sadness of America. Of course I stayed in Storrs. The next morning I roamed woods and fields above the Fenton River. In lowlands the fragrance of white clover turned air into honey, European skippers flickering over the blossoms, glittering like orange crystals. Female garter snakes dozed in the sun gravid with young. A fire-rimmed tortoiseshell butterfly patrolled wetlands beside the beaver pond, and red-spotted purples puddled the sandy edges of a road. That night I opened a box of books and showed Vicki my favorite places in Edinburgh.

Two years ago I applied to be a fellow at the Institute for Advanced Studies in the Humanities at the University of Edinburgh. I intended to write a book on nature writers. In my application I said I planned to stay in Scotland for eight months. The fellowship was low on money but high on amenities, among other things supplying acquaintances, a university identity, and an office looking into a court blowsy with cherry blossoms in the spring. The institute occupied an eighteenth-century building in Hope Park Square, facing the Meadows, once a shallow lake but now a park, host to dog walkers, footballers, cricketers, joggers, spooning couples, a playground of children, and occasionally weedy alcoholics. The dean and provost at the University of Connecticut having agreed to give me a semester off with pay, I planned to fly to Edinburgh two days after Christmas and stay until the last week of August, the stay interrupted once, for Edward's graduation from Middlebury College in Vermont.

Plans are as fragile as good intentions. I didn't leave Connecticut until January 9, and I returned on May 19, the shifting dates of doctors' appointments and of a court case warping the struts under my plan. Moreover, I jettisoned my project. The previous May, after his junior year at college, Edward told me he wanted to write an honors paper on eighteenth-century English literature. He mentioned several topics, all of which seemed hackneyed. Earlier in the year he took a course on the pastoral in which he wrote about Gilbert White, an eighteenth-century divine and naturalist, famously known as the author of *The Natural History of Selborne*. For a decade I'd collected books in which nineteenth-century writers described ramblings in field and forest. As Edward talked, I looked at a shelf and counted the books, twenty-eight in all. "Why not write about Gilbert White?" I asked Edward. "Boy, that's a good idea," Edward said. "I'd really like that." "Would you?" I said. "You bet," Edward answered.

"Wait a minute," I said, turning on the computer. I selected a folder entitled "Dad" and deleted a file containing the beginning of my project, ninety pages I'd written about nature writers. Edward and I talked for an hour. "Start with White and talk to teachers at Middlebury," I advised him. "Then read some of these books and follow hunches," I said, pointing to the books on the shelf. I didn't discuss the project with Edward again, except to ask about his progress, a matter of pages not ideas, believing that conversation with me would not only give him an unfair advantage over his classmates but would also influence the course of his writing, making the project mine, not his. "Did you tell Edward that you deleted your book?" Vicki asked later. "No," I said. "Gee," Vicki said, "that was probably your last book." "Maybe," I said, "but so what? I've written nineteen books. One more doesn't matter." "Well, then, what will you do in Edinburgh?" Vicki asked. "Who knows?" I said. "I'll find something."

I went to Edinburgh alone. When my stay shrank from eight to four and a half months, Vicki decided to remain in Storrs, observing that we'd have difficulty finding someone to live in the house for a semester. Additionally she noted that since Edward and Eliza were still in college having a parent nearby made good sense. "You never know with children," Vicki said. Lastly she stayed home to take care of Penny, our Jack Russell terrier. Penny had suddenly aged, flesh melting from her spine, her legs stiffening and back curving up like the rim of a bicycle wheel, knobby and bony with spokes.

To say wives care more for dogs than husbands is a truth often thought but rarely expressed. Although old dogs yelp more, they aren't as cantankerous as aging husbands. They don't slam doors and growl. They don't tell the same stories year after year, dinner after dinner, salad through dessert. Dogs are devoted and trail after their mistresses, feet pattering and tails wagging. Although they might have an occasional accident on the kitchen floor, they do not raid the refrigerator, knock over glasses of milk, or scatter clothes around the bedroom. Rarely do their opinions drive companions "around the bend" or cause "the yips." Moreover, the fragrance of a ten-year-old dog is sweeter than that of a husband of twenty-five years, or so I explained when people asked why Vicki did not accompany me to Edinburgh.

Despite not going to Scotland, Vicki spent days packing my bags, sending me off with a mall of supplies, these stored into two suitcases and a backpack. At the airport the clerk at the check-in counter attached orange labels with "HEAVY" stamped on them to both bags, one weighing 37 kilos, the other, 29. Among the racks of clothing, I carried twenty-two pairs of socks: seven "everyday," four dress, two argyle, four hiking, and five running. In the bags lay seven pairs of trousers, two each of khakis, corduroys, and gray flannels plus a single pair of blue jeans. I carried eight neckties, two sweaters, two scarves, two pairs of gloves, nine pairs of underpants, a fleece, a "shirt jacket" from L. L. Bean, seven short-sleeved shirts, and eleven long-sleeved shirts, two of these last white, four colored dress, four button-down flannels, and one button-down, "lighter weight plaid." Vicki also packed running clothes: shorts, a baseball hat, two shirts, a jacket, and long sweatpants for cold weather. I took six pairs of shoes: two pairs for everyday walking, one each for dress and running, a pair of hiking boots, and slippers to pad around in during evenings in my flat.

Vicki crammed a pharmacy of toiletries into the suitcases, including four toothbrushes, two packets of floss, toothpaste, cough drops, two pairs of nail clippers, tweezers, a hairbrush, Q-tips, sunscreen, a pillbox, aspirin, antibiotics, saline spray, vitamins, braces for my neck and ankle, Band-Aids, a ChapStick, on and on through ounces to kilos. When I unpacked the bags I discovered a sewing kit, stain remover, a wooden shoe shine kit, an umbrella, a water bottle, scissors, salt and pepper, a laundry bag, even a shopping list. On a note card measuring 5 x 8 inches, Vicki listed 102 items I might buy at a grocery or drugstore. Instead of rummaging through my flat before going shopping in order to paste together a list of things to purchase, all I had to do was consult the note card.

Aside from passport, wallet, and extra eyeglasses for both reading and walking, I added little to the bags other than a guidebook describing British birds, a handful of ballpoint pens, and two reporter's notebooks, 4 x 10 inches. I am peculiar about money and often pay debts before being billed. In the pocket of my jacket I stuffed £2,000 so I could pay my first month's rent as soon as I arrived, this being £600, or $1,140. The institute arranged a flat for me in a house in Newington, an attractive, affluent district a mile and a half south of central Edinburgh. Houses in Newington were stone, usually three or four stories high, most built in the late nineteenth century and smacking of both Georgian and Victorian architecture. Although small, often no bigger than carpets, yards in front of the houses had been manicured so that they bloomed throughout the year. Behind the houses stretched bigger gardens, narrow and long, shaped like one of my notebooks, the margins bushy with shrubs and flower beds.

Before going to Scotland I knew little about Edinburgh. Forty years ago when I was a student in Cambridge, I spent a summer escorting twenty-four American girls through Europe. I met the group in London. After four days we traveled to Edinburgh—by train, I think. We stayed in Edinburgh two or three days before sailing across the North Sea to Bergen, Norway. All I remember about the experience was that one night I drank too much and after climbing part of the way up Arthur's Seat, the remnants of an ancient volcano on the eastern side of the city, I tumbled down a mild slope, rolling over rocks, tearing the trousers of my brown suit, and losing my eyeglasses. When I arrived in Edinburgh this January, the only tourist site familiar to me was the monument to Sir Walter Scott on Princes Street. And I suspect I recognized the monument not because memory picked the lock on a door closed forty years ago, but because I had recently seen a photograph of the monument in a magazine, probably *National Geographic.*

In truth I may have applied to the institute because of envy and its consort, spite, rather than because of curiosity, intellectual or geographical. For the last decade and a half I wrote a book a year. During this time I applied for many grants, some national, others local. While people who'd written one or two books plucked funds off foundations as easily as picking apples off the ground, I couldn't win a grant no matter how I stretched. In the long run rejection promotes humility and is good for one's character. In the short run rejection irks, and so I applied to the institute in part because I was tired of watching people whose writings I did not admire stacking fellowships atop each other like suitcases and each semester setting off for places overseas far from the classroom.

Rancor and modest intention serve thought, and pleasure, better than high seriousness, the nitrogen content in this last often wilting spontaneity. Because I wasn't committed to a project, I roamed Edinburgh and pages sprouted through my days. "My Edinburgh" grew by happenstance, the paragraphs mirrors reflecting not simply landmarks in the city but also the meanderings of mind and mood. I think consistency weakness, not strength, the resort of the timid and the small minded. Accordingly the chapters in this book grew not in response to a plan but to my amblings. Although I have revised the book, I've let some inconsistencies stand. Moreover, I have not lopped chapters into agreeable topiary, preferring not to hide sour garden clippings behind hedges thick with deceptive "acceptable" words. Also, the book is a collection of essays, pausing for a moment then abruptly cantering forward like the actual, not fictional, doings of days.

Although a person can slip the leash of family for a moment, he cannot escape himself. Lurking weightless in my luggage was the baggage of many books: interests, patterns of writing, and, most prominently, Carthage, Tennessee, a real town but on my pages an imaginary country place whose inhabitants ferret me out, no matter my location, and whose doings inevitably interrupt my narratives.

Readers will discover that I am not a carouser, perhaps not even sociable. In hopes of being transformed by "learning experiences," romantic youth drinks deep and tipples into illness and feverish observation. I have lived long. Books have taught me more than wine. At night I wander pages, not streets. I am also opinionated, so much so that my family often thinks me an embarrassment. Last Thursday when snared by a woman who subjects me to a litany of questions about writing whenever she catches me, I emended something Harold Nicolson wrote seventy years ago, bringing the remarks up to date. "Don't drink or take drugs. Intoxication is advisable only when one comes to a difficult or moving passage, say, the arrangement of parts during fornication." "Why did you say that?" Vicki asked me later. I didn't answer.

Oh, well, despite setting out for Scotland with modest intentions and no expectations, optimism is hard to smother, especially for an American, and I have hopes for this book. I hope readers are entertained. I want them to smile often and laugh out loud once or twice. I hope that occasionally readers will pause and ponder, at times because my words intrigue, other times because my words irritate. I hope that the Edinburgh I depict is alluring enough to make people visit Scotland. I loved my months in Edinburgh, and in May if I had not been so worn out from stuffing belongings back into my suitcases and carting them to the airport for the trip home, I would have wept when my plane left the ground, bound for New England.

Up from Boston

I FLEW FROM BOSTON TO LONDON on Virgin Atlantic. The flight was a children's excursion. Classrooms raced around the terminal as if they were at recess, all the students enrolled in foreign study programs in Britain. Clots of students were so thick I felt like a hall monitor. No aisle seats were available when I checked my bags. "Ask again before you board," the woman at the counter said, seating me in row 48. I followed the woman's instructions. "Yes," the clerk at the gate said, "there is one aisle seat free, 62F. If you don't mind seating near the rear of the plane, you can have it." I took the seat. Alas, the clerk was mistaken. 62F was the middle seat in a center row of three seats, located at the back of the plane at the point where the aircraft narrowed to a caret. I was the lone adult in a toddler's pool of splashing babies, all sinking under backpacks, camping gear, and computer bags. On my left sat a girl from Boston College; on my right a boy from Wheaton. Traffic jams of wires wrapped their heads, heavy metal and hip-hop throbbing and honking. To get into my seat I climbed over roundabouts of carry-on luggage. Once the flight took off the student in front of me slammed her seat back, locking me in place. Not once during the flight did I leave my seat. I was stiff as a corpse when the plane landed in Britain. My feet cramped; the veins behind my knees pumped themselves into fists, and disks along my back clattered.

Virgin Atlantic left Boston late. When the plane's wheels lifted off the ground, the flight was forty-four minutes and eleven seconds behind schedule. Consequently, after the flight reached London, I ignored the pain racketing along my back and through my knees and scampered through Heathrow to British Midland. I need not have hurried, as my flight on British Midland departed eighty-four minutes and thirty-nine seconds behind schedule. At Heathrow I pushed into lines, my hearing not sharp enough to distinguish mutterings from the general airport hubbub. In fact I let other harried travelers nip ahead of me. "God bless you," a woman said, racing to catch a flight to Cyprus. Flying Virgin Atlantic was not a serene experience. The airline neglected to book me on British Midland. Because I had a valid ticket, however, a clerk found a place for me on the plane, an aisle seat on the last row, 34D. While waiting for the flight to be called, I went to the lavatory and brushed my teeth. While I stood in front of the sink, a toilet behind me overflowed, a wave of water gushing frothy from beneath the door and sweeping over my shoes, soaking my socks.

The flight to Edinburgh was bumpy. The plane sloshed about so much that the girl next to me wept. In verse, poets are often compared to harps. As the winds of life blow through the poet's mind, he transforms them into stanzas, ordered and usually zephyrous in tone. The winds of Scotland are not poetic. They carom around stone buildings, breaking quatrains, and pushing people about, turning walks into free verse and broken lines.

I have now spent three days in Edinburgh. The first night I slept fitfully. I went to bed at 6:00, then woke up at 8:00, 10:12, 12:00, 1:26, 3:14, and 4:40. Finally I got up at 7:22, ate breakfast, then walked to the Institute for Advanced Studies, counting my steps on the way, 1,629 from the door of my flat to the entrance of the institute. Yesterday in Armchair Books, a border collie mounted me. "A traditional Gaelic greeting, I presume," I said to the man running the store. When he did not respond, I forged ahead, saying, "This is unexpected but extremely pleasant, a treat that makes me eager to make the acquaintance of the two-legged and kilted." When the man remained silent, I started laughing, thrusting the dog aside and sliding onto the floor into a fit of giggling.

At Armchair I bought a secondhand copy of *Duty*, a book written at the end of the nineteenth century by Samuel Smiles, a British moralist and social critic, best known today as the author of *Self-Help*. Almost whistling, I strolled back to my flat and brewed a pot of English breakfast tea, and treating myself to two McVitie's Plain Chocolate Digestives,

I stretched out on the couch in my sitting room and read the first four chapters of *Duty*. Afterward I prepared dinner, hard-boiling an egg and spreading butter and cheddar cheese over two slices of toast. I dipped the egg into Bundh Pasanda sauce. Usually the sauce is drizzled over chicken, but dollops go nicely with hunks of egg. After dinner I read more Smiles. "Man does not live for himself alone," Smiles stated at the beginning of *Duty*. "He lives for the good of others as well as himself. Every one has his duties to perform—the richest as well as the poorest. To some life is pleasure, to others suffering. But the best do not live for self-enjoyment, or even fame. Their strongest motive is hopeful useful work in every good cause."

"That's the ticket," I thought. "I'll write a self-help book that will better the lives of the dreary multitude as well as filling my suitcases with gold." I decided to call the book *The Blissful Foxtrot: Fifty-five Steps to Jesus, Sexual Satisfaction, Drug and Gambling Free Days, Literacy, and Winning Life's Lotteries, Even Those You Did Not Enter.* Before falling asleep I hammered step 41 together: "If weaned, do not fly Virgin Atlantic." I sleep well after good work, and I did not get out of bed until 7:45 the next morning. "Step 12," I said, slipping into my slippers, "A good sleep means a good day." During breakfast I read two more chapters of Smiles, after which I composed step 55, "Never write a self-help book." On Blacket Place the wind growled, bending trees into creaks and grunts. Walking was difficult. Still I counted steps to the entrance of the institute, this time following a different route. I took 1,606 steps, reducing the trek by 1.41 percent—a sign, I thought, of bright days to come.

Invisible

"DEAR INVISIBLE MAN," the note began. I'd been in Edinburgh two weeks. Since the day of my arrival, Barbara Phanjoo, my landlady, had not seen or heard me. "I just wanted to be sure that you were well," she wrote. In the old days when gods wandered the earth pursuing nymphs or during more restful times granting wishes, the Rose begged Zeus for a gift. When Zeus asked her to be specific, the Rose demurred. She knew Zeus was imaginative and assumed that whatever he selected would be more magnificent that anything she might suggest. "You choose," she said. For a moment Zeus gazed thoughtfully through the distance, then he waved his hand over the Rose. Immediately thorns erupted from the Rose's stems, transforming shoots that had once been soft as shammy into saws.

"Oh, no," the Rose exclaimed and burst into tears, her blossoms wilting, petals weeping, pooling across the ground. She wept until dusk. Then a noise startled her. She looked up and saw an antelope approaching. "He will eat my buds," she thought, her canes trembling. When the antelope got within a pace of the Rose, however, it paused and bent its neck toward the ground the better to study her stems. The animal remained motionless for what in the life of a flower seemed a season. Then the antelope shook its head, turned, and trotted across a low rise. Just before it disappeared, though, it stopped in front of a patch of lilies. The lilies were blooming, and their blossoms were as sweet as camphor.

The antelope nuzzled the lilies for a moment, almost as if saying grace, then without more ado ate every blossom.

What a person gets often serves him better than what he thinks he wants. In Storrs people know me. They wave when I ride past on my bicycle. They stop me on the street to chat. They nod in the local café. They ask me about novels in the bookstore. Editors write and urge me to review books, and journals solicit my opinion. In silly moments this past fall I imagined that Edinburgh would broaden my literary horizons. I would write for the *Edinburgh Review* and perhaps a newspaper or two, the *Guardian* or the *Scotsman*. I'd meet people at the university and give guest lectures. Eventually strangers would greet me on the street, and we'd go into a pub and sandwich talks about books between bites of shepherd's pie. Of course none of that has happened or will happen. I am simply an aging stranger in a big city, a faceless gray shadow passing along the sidewalk, the invisible man whose animal spirits time has reduced to dregs. Even at the Institute for Advanced Studies I am bodiless. Almost all the other fellows are young. While my career grows weedy behind me, their futures stretch green and alluring before them. Busy with smoothing ways forward, they don't notice me except to nod. Not wishing to be snagged by a past that cannot serve them, they swivel out of sight when I enter a room.

For a few days I was lonely. I regretted leaving family and the appointments that defined me. But then I began to enjoy invisibility. I stood on street corners and listened to buskers playing bagpipes, and no one noticed me. I bought a baguette, and the clerk took my money without looking at me. In Tesco, the grocery store, crowds swirled around me, but no one spoke to me, not even the cashier. If I was unknown, I realized, then so was the Scotland surrounding me. Although people would never know I'd passed through Edinburgh, I decided to know the city. Indeed, because no one would interrupt my ramblings, seeing would be easier than at home.

Moreover, in roaming Storrs in December before I left, I saw things I'd seen for two decades, the sights coming to eye, as ideas came to the mind, matted and framed. Spears of ice pushed through dirt and leaves in the dirt road above the Ogushwitz Meadow, looking like striated spun glass, almost as if they were made out of sugar. From the stone seat near the gravel pit, the meadow appeared white and soft, as if someone had plucked down from the breast of a great goose and strewn it over the ground. In Edinburgh I roamed a different weather and landscape. Because I was invisible, no acquaintance interrupted my reveries, saying things I had heard before. The expected did not swirl into sight, limiting vision and thought to things I had long seen and pondered.

Even if a person lacks presence, physicality prevents him from remaining completely anonymous. Although people my age can slip unseen through society, they cannot escape the leash of body. While eating cereal at breakfast one morning, I broke a tooth on a hard raisin. The director of the institute suggested I visit a dentist near the university, and the next day I walked to his office. People in the waiting room appeared normal. A mother held a small child. A grim overweight man turned his arms into barrel rings and wrapped them around his middle in hopes of preventing his stomach from leaking through his shirt. A woman in a heavy coat glanced at her wristwatch and shook her head. I sat down and didn't speak until I noticed a poster on a bulletin board. Printed across the top of the poster was the question "So you think this helps?" At the bottom of the poster was the statement "Aggression toward staff will not be tolerated." "Have I come to the wrong dentist?" I thought and, standing up, walked into the hall and spoke to the receptionist. I described the poster, then asked, "Does my sort of person patronize this practice?" "Oh, yes," she answered. "Most people behave in a civilized fashion, but recently," she continued, shaking her head knowingly, "we have had cases."

I returned to the waiting room and studied the poster. Between the writing at the top and the bottom of the poster a man stared outward, head cranked back, a yell bursting from his mouth, his jaws so wide the bones seemed dislocated. The man's teeth, however, were perfect. They gleamed starched and ran across his jaw in pearly lines. He had no cavities, and his gums rose plump as pillows. "Why," I said to receptionist, "would that man visit a dentist? Clearly nothing has been done to his teeth?" "Wouldn't the poster be more effective," I asked the dentist later, "if a lance were jutting out of an abscess or a backhoe were thumping along the man's jaw ripping out wormy stumps? Then he would have a reason for screaming." "Do you want me to blacken a couple of the man's teeth or draw a pool of blood on his tongue?" I asked the dentist before I left. "No," he said, calculating his fee, "but thanks anyway."

Rarely can one escape habits of speech. Word leads to word, and no matter the place, words transport one to the familiar. While strolling back to the institute and rubbing my cheek, I visited Carthage. Harley

Bascomb was kneeling by his bed saying his prayers. I eavesdropped. "Thou knowest, Lord," Harley said, "that I own a house in Carthage and half a hotel in Red Boiling Springs. Preserve these the possessions of your humble servant from earthquake, flood, taxes, and bank failure. I have lots of fire insurance, so Lord you can toss your bolts of lightning every which-a-way, just so long as you keep them on the other side of the hill away from Junior Sims, my prize Hereford bull, or behemoth, as you winged folks in the clouds are wont to label big fellows in the ruminating tribe. Anyway, Lord, protect these my goods, and indeed your goods, for they are yours also, from thieves and housebreakers. Make my servants honest and my accountant flexible. And Lord, keep those consumptives alive and coming to Red Boiling Springs. Also, Lord, lock my sheep in your fold far from scabies and shelter my Guernseys from hoof and mouth disease. Nothing accompanies a slice of your manna bread better than their milk. Blight the smut before it lands on my corn and stomp on those potato beetles before they leave Colorado. This year Lord I'm dedicating the potatoes to you. And Lord, if for the sake of appearances, you reckon you ought to smite a member of my household, why don't you let your wrath fall upon Toodles, Mrs. Bascomb's goddamn cat. Lord, he is an unclean creature and does his business on the rug in the hall and behind the piano in the parlor something fierce. Besides he bedevils Old Thunder who, in your name Lord, treed many a devilish coon in his sallet days. That cat's yourn, Lord; brain him with a poker. Lastly, Lord, let the stock market rise in a flood and roll me, Lord, like old man Noah to that high ground where chickens roost in olive trees, where bread baked with wild oats tastes sweeter than molasses, and where the mules, even the three-legged ones, are always willing. Amen. Your dutiful servant. Harley R. Bascomb. Owner of Beulah Farm near Maggart and half owner of Healing Waters Hotel in Red Boiling Springs. Please address all correspondence to: Post Office Box 3. 18 Main Street. Carthage, Tennessee. United States of the America."

That afternoon I jogged. I put on seven-league running shoes, and my first step was a giant step, transporting me from Carthage back to Edinburgh. When I started to run, the clouds looked as if a knife had sliced through them, exposing yeasty slivers of yellow. "Here comes the sun," I thought. I was wrong. Suddenly the seams closed; the sky turned gunny blue; wind began to huff, and mists of sleet billowed swollen across the Meadows. Snow followed, smacking the ground in clumps that looked like tracks left by a small cat. By the time I finished running the sun had returned. The air had changed, however, and was alcoholic, simmering with the fragrance of burnt hops discharged from a distillery west of the Meadows. Later a drizzle began. Rain in January is weak, and the water seems to dribble out of small perforations in the clouds, holes that seal almost as quickly as they open. Rarely does rain hammer the ground, echoing hard and metallic. Unlike the cold in Storrs, which pounds into bones like nails, the cold in Edinburgh is damp and gathers over a person's shoulders like a wet shawl.

On my jogs I run through the Meadows and then south though a grid of streets around Marchmont Road: Whitehouse, Warrender Park, Kilgraston, Strathearn, Spottiswood, and Loan. Near the Meadows late-nineteenth-century buildings reach five stories and hang over roads like the sides of canyons cut by sharp streams. Because no one talks to me, I am free to ponder the weather and look at flowers. In Storrs the world is now white and black. Snow is thick on the ground, and branches break from the trunks of trees and shatter into veiny nets of twigs. Despite the cold and wind, flowers bloom in Edinburgh: periwinkle, witch hazel, snowdrops, rhododendron, and some roses and daisies. Pots of pansies squat on front stoops, and wisps of forsythia trail over iron railings, the bushes' ends split into yellow and looking like hair brushed forward from the back of a balding man's head toward the front in order to create the illusion of vigor. Common birds that would not interest residents thrill me: fieldfares, blackbirds, pied wagtails, magpies, and robins, this last not the big American bird scooting over the grass, head twitching, searching for earthworms, but the redbreast of nursery rhymes, small and vulnerable but plucky and quick to puff his chest into song.

Oddly, the more invisible, the less physically present I think myself, the more important food becomes, this despite consisting only of simple items suitable for eating alone: Scotch eggs; sultanas; clementines; sardines; pâté; Stilton and cheddar cheeses; breads, baguettes and multigrain, this last seedy between the teeth; and soups, cans of lentil, onion, mushroom, and broccoli. So that I can enjoy choosing, I stock three kinds of tea: English breakfast, Earl Grey, and Lapsang souchong. For breakfast I fill a blue bowl with Jordans Country Crisp containing "real raspberries." I slice a banana over the cereal and sprinkle a handful of sultanas over the banana, little actions that I did unconsciously in Storrs but which now give me extraordinary pleasure. Dark comes early in January, and when I walk home, streets are as busy as Christmas trees. Shop fronts are bright with lights. Students gabble along the sidewalk.

Buses snort, and cars pop and jerk. Curry seasons the air, and talk belches out of pubs. Although I drift down streets beyond the curb of things, sometimes I buy a table decoration, a raisin bun, or chocolate croissant.

After dinner I read at least a book a night. Like a ghostly substance freed from weighty intention, I meander through pages, during the past fortnight reading mysteries by Sue Grafton, Robert Barnard, and Ruth Rendell. I've read novels by Walter Mosley, Neil Gunn, Jim Dodge, Paula Fox, and Percival Everett. Occasionally I jot down a sentence. I copied the last paragraph from Iain Crichton Smith's *Goodbye, Mr. Dixon:* "Something about him told her that a crisis was past, that he had in some sense found himself, that he was ready to leave for another world, another place. That he was ready to be with her. There was about him the gaunt air of beginnings." I like the final phrase, "the gaunt air of beginnings." Someday I may stick it into an essay, then again I may not, the plans of the invisible lacking heft and likely to change quickly. From Max Beerbohm's *Seven Men,* I purloined the device of describing fictional characters as if one had known them. Under Beerbohm's influence I wrote an essay entitled "Obituary," recounting my relationship with Freddy Shotover. By the end of the piece Freddy had become part of my life in Edinburgh. I particularly enjoy reading at breakfast. I set my teapot and bowl of cereal on the pine table in the sitting room. I pull a chair out from under the table and turn it sideways so that the tea and cereal are on my right. I then lift a book from the table and read. I read slowly, so far only two books, *Duty* and *Self-Help,* both by Samuel Smiles. Yesterday I copied down a sentence from *Self-Help:* "Talkers may sow, but the silent reap." I liked the aphorism because I did not speak a word last Sunday, except to myself, and then I whispered.

Last week I explored Edinburgh. Since I am a stranger, no one accosted me, pressing me into conversation and identity. Early one morning I walked to St. Giles Cathedral, strolling up Meadow Walk and along Forrest and George IV Bridge to High Street, a section of the Royal or Tourist Mile running from Edinburgh Castle high over the west of town down to Holyrood Place low in the east under the brow of the Salisbury Crags. Rain began, and I hurried inside the cathedral. Although parts of the cathedral dated from the fourteenth and fifteenth centuries, time sweeps in great tides over huge churches, eroding and forcing people to shore them up, turning the buildings into conglomerates of repair and alteration.

Stone inside the church was gray and brown, splotched and seamed with veins like the skin of an old man. Instead of the weakness, however, the stones conveyed a hard, beautiful strength, cruel, seamed by tears and often stained cancerous by sackcloths of ashes, but beautiful nonetheless. Near the entrance stood a statue of John Knox, his expression righteous, stern, and ultimately discordant, in his left hand a Bible, his thumb atop the cover, his left index finger marking a page; his right hand crossing his body like a strap on a breastplate, the finger a shaft pointing at the Bible. Someone played an organ. The sound of sawing and of masons hammering scaffolding together shattered the melody, much, I thought, as the mailed fist of Christianity had so often crushed the soul-soothing dreams of the New Testament. In the alcove to my right was a marble sarcophagus, a memorial to the Marquess of Montrose, hanged in 1650. Carved on the lid of the sarcophagus was an effigy of the marquess. The effigy wore armor so that on Judgment Day the marquess could rise ready to battle for one of those causes that have separated man from man and men from virtue. On the other side of the nave was a memorial to the Marquis of Argyle, Montrose's enemy, beheaded in 1661, his effigy also armored, ready to clamor from the tomb and pass the Last Judgment, quartering undeserving souls in a final battle before ascending to heaven as one of the Lord's anointed.

On Montrose's tomb lay an artificial rose, its petals red linen and its stem plastic. "If we could only fabricate fealty and thus escape high matters so easily," I mused. At the east end of St. Giles a stained-glass window depicted the Crucifixion and Resurrection. Despite the window, the church was not a testimonial to the risen god, but to fallen man's inhumanity. Hanging like shields on the walls were scores of memorials to dead soldiers, almost all the tributes reflecting the old lies that transform horror and agony into honor. "His life was lovely and pleasant & He died in Glory," declared a tribute. "No," I muttered, "he died at the Hill of Gezer in Palestine." A brigadier won the Victoria Cross and died at Ypres in 1917. "A Gallant Soldier and Very Perfect Gentleman Beloved by All His Men," his memorial read. Mozart, Shakespeare, van Gogh, Martin Luther King, Abraham Lincoln, and St. Paul, none of these were gentlemen. A gentleman would not have chased the money changers from the temple. At their worst gentlemen sacrifice others for bad causes; at their best they sacrifice themselves also. What the world always needs is fewer gentlemen and more barbarians, people willing to risk the comfortable by opposing convention.

I wandered aisles, adding up names on memorials, the figures not putting me to sleep as counting sheep supposedly does but awakening me into a nightmare. In the Boer War, 90 members of the Royal Scots lost their lives, among them a drummer boy, J. Eagle. In the same war, 129 members of the Highland Light Infantry died, as did 127 members of the Second Battalion Royal Scots Fusiliers. Forty-one Scottish nurses perished in the First World War, the number small in comparison to deaths in the Royal Army Medical Corps, 743 officers and 6,130 noncommissioned officers and men. Near back of the cathedral a plaque commemorated the deaths of 669 people associated with the Seventy-eighth Highland Regiment "who died on the banks of the River Indus in Sinde, between the sixth day of September one thousand eight hundred and forty-four, and the fourth day of March one thousand eight hundred and forty-five"—2 officers, 21 sergeants, 27 corporals, 9 drummers, 439 privates, 47 women, and 124 children.

After reading the plaque, I fled St. Giles and, in hopes of pacing the faith of our fathers out of mind, strode rapidly downhill along Canongate. At Abbey Strand I turned around and hiked back up the Royal Mile. I wasn't always invisible. Three times during the day, I wandered into sight. I talked to a docent in St. Giles and gave him a scrap of paper on which I wrote "bookfinder4u," the most useful Web site I know for unearthing used books. For a pound I bought a bacon bun at a stall, and the owner of a shop specializing in prints told me his first wedding anniversary was only four days away. "What should I get my wife?" he asked. "The problem is that this is the second time we've been married. For five years we were apart. In the past I bought her lots of presents and have exhausted the possibilities."

I made no suggestion. Near the cathedral on High Street, I wandered into the Museum of Childhood. There I discovered toys that I coveted, toys that cheered and encouraged. Of course I did not want the actual toys but replicas that I could cart away in my head and store on a page and thus not clutter my flat. Guarding the end of a cabinet was a papier-mâché bulldog, made in France around 1910. The dog was two-thirds the length of my arm and tall as my forearm, measuring from elbow to wrist. He was bony, and his ribs flew up from his spine like wings, swelling his chest. Although the dog's ears and backside were black, most of his hide was bluish gray. Swelling like bruises, black circled his eyes. Thick wrinkles furrowed his forehead, and his lower jaw jutted forward like an old spade, his teeth the tip worn ragged from digging gravel. Circling his neck was a collar under which lay a saddle blanket of thick fur, this not woven from wool but looking as if it had been sliced from a cat, a Persian heavy with thick tresses.

Mounted on a wooden platform were two teams of draft horses. The platform rested on red wooden wheels wrapped in iron treads. Four hearts decorated each wheel, the tips touching in the hubs of the wheels, lobes swelling outward. The horses pulled a Kentish hop cart dating from 1820. The cart was yellow and open sided, twelve slats to a side. Piled in the cart were thirty-four bags of hops, each bag tied at the end and looking like a fat sausage. Together the horses and cart were four feet long. "A sideboard would make a fine stall for them. Except," I thought, "the owner would throw the hops away and fill the wagon with a bottle of wine, an expensive bottle, one a trifle more costly than the Australian wine Vicki and I drink in Connecticut." Not all exhibits were as intoxicating as silage, and after a glance, I reared and galloped out of the Doll Gallery. At the entrance to the gallery stood a curved exhibition case. Standing in the case, row above row, were bisque dolls, their glass eyes staring, their faces pale white, transforming them into zombies, not playthings from childhood but monsters from a movie like *The Day of the Dead*.

My favorite toy was a game manufactured in London by Myers & Company early in the nineteenth century, "Willys Walk to See Grandmamma." Printed on a square board were seven concentric circles. Together the circles resembled the shell of a chambered nautilus. At the center of the shell was Grandmamma's. Each of the circles was divided into rectangles, most white but some colored: blue, yellow, green, and brown, or so they seemed, the colors having faded out of clarity. Printed on the squares were statements that determined the course of Willy's progress, such things as "Gets a Ride" and "Spends a Penny." Players began at the lip of the shell or the outer circle and after choosing blocks with letters printed on the top spun a teetotum, on the sides of which were printed the numbers 1 through 6. If the teetotum settled with the number three up, the player moved his block three rectangles forward. The first player to reach seventy-nine, Grandmamma's house, won the game. The winner had to land on seventy-nine. If, for example, he was on seventy-eight and spun a five, he moved one rectangle forward then four backward, settling on seventy-five, where he had to wait until his turn for another spin came around again. Statements on the rectangles influenced a child's progress. If a player landed on sixty-two, "Lost His Glove," he had to return to fifty-two in order to search for it. On twenty-nine he discovered he had left a parcel on nineteen. On the other hand, at thirty-two he hitched a ride on a baker's cart and jumped ahead to forty. At twenty he fell down and was forced to miss two turns waiting "'til someone comes to pick him up." At thirty-five "something strange in a hedge" so distracted him that he again missed two turns. The oddest square was twenty-three, "Gives Away an Apple." Instead of being rewarded for giving an apple "to a poor child" and being allowed to leap ahead of his selfish friends, he was forced to miss a turn.

"What a game," I thought, walking home, regretting that my children were grown. The next morning I did my first load of laundry, the magical cloaks of invisibility not being immune to fragrance. Afterward I walked through town and along the Mound to the National Gallery. Most visitors to galleries hover on the edge of sight. Unlike paintings, which are permanent residents, visitors are transients. The murmur of stilled voices eddied through the gallery's exhibition rooms. Art galleries are not home, but to me they are part of the known world, and although I did not look at people in the rooms, I imagined them: thin men holding hands, adolescent lovers staring at each other, the woman with hair like porcupine quills, the pharmacist on holiday, students wearing sweatshirts and clutching notebooks, the man standing in front of a contemporary painting pursing his lips so that from the side his face looks like the head of a fish, the middle-aged couple bustling along a hall in a hurry to get to the tearoom downstairs and buy coffee and muffins, or maybe slices of cake, the woman in soft leather boots, a long skirt swirling about her momentarily turning her into a gypsy, her hair gray and swept back chromed, and finally the shy and the lonely, aching to meet people sensitive enough to see beneath homeliness or tatty clothes and spot Cinderella waiting open armed and responsible.

Of course most welcoming and reassuring are the canvases and their familiar sights: Hobbema's mills, Turner's circuses of color, Frederic Church's misty fountains of light, the Tasmania of John Glover, its trees coiling and writhing, Landseer's kennels, and the lumpy splatterware borders of Constable's countrysides. Before leaving a gallery, I always select a painting that I'd like to hang in the living room in Storrs. The paintings I choose are small and comparatively modest. They are usually landscapes, windows to the outside, not to the intellectual and the inside. At the National Gallery I chose a forest scene painted by Achille Etna Michallon, an artist of whom I had never heard and who painted during the first decades of the nineteenth century.

The painting was two feet high and fifteen inches wide. The canvas was a blend of green, white, and brown. In the center of the painting appeared the thick trunk of an old birch. The sun shone on sections of the trunk, turning them milky; other portions in the shade were green and chocolate. Filigrees of leaves hung down from branches, their shadows dappling the trunk. The leaves were newly green and reminded me of the fronds of southern maidenhair fern. The tree stood alone on a carpet of grass. A few yards behind the tree grew a blind of saplings.

I thought the tree a downy birch, but although I leaned close to the painting and studied the leaves, they were not distinct enough to label. In any case a man wearing a black vest broke my concentration. "Did you know," he said, approaching me from my left side, "that the muscles in the tongue of an angry woman move 1,619 times in a minute?" "No," I said, shifting slightly to my right, "that's hard to believe." "Well," he said, shifting in tandem with me, "maybe the number is 924." "How about 689?" I said. "That's possible, too," he said. My invisibility having worn off, I shut my notebook, said "take care," and walked away.

After leaving the gallery, I trekked back up the Mound. I paused for a moment at the corner of Bank and Lawnmarket. Across the street in front of St. Giles, four boys wearing kilts played bagpipes. I listened to them play "Amazing Grace." In its admission of folly and weakness, the hymn was warmly human. In 1985 a stained-glass window was placed above the front door to the cathedral. The window, engraving on a stone in the church explained, celebrated Robert Burns, "poet of humanity." St. Giles needed more such memorials, not necessarily to the poetic and the renowned but to ordinary folk, memorials on which inscriptions did not temper or elevate horror but that simply made readers smile and thus, perhaps, enjoy others and life more. Engraved on a tombstone in the mountain cemetery in Carthage is a couplet: "Here lies my wife, and Heaven knows / As much for mine as her repose." The couplet isn't original; still when I read it, I smiled. Carved beneath a weeping willow on another stone is a quatrain: "Where this bending willow weeps, / All alone, Myrilla sleeps. / Softly scatter nard and myrrh, / Lest you should awaken her." Of course, an awakened Myrilla would not be a sight to soothe sore eyes, I thought as I crossed High Street and walked toward South Bridge, the Doll Gallery suddenly coming to mind.

To change my mood, I scrolled through an old song, singing the words silently as I strolled along. "I won't marry an old girl, / I'll tell you the reason why. / Her hair's so long and stringy / I'm afraid she'd never die. / I won't marry a young girl. / I'll tell you the reason why. / She'd have so many children / They'd make the biscuits fly." At Peckham's delicatessen I bought a slice of lumpy-bumpy toffee cake, a sweet I had never heard of, much less eaten. As soon as I got back to my flat, I made tea. While the tea seeped, I thumbed an old notebook. Years ago I copied down the advice "Read books and men by all means but chiefly read thyself." I don't know where I found the sentence. But now I pondered it, deciding that it was impossible for a person who slipped beyond the margins of the familiar and became invisible to read himself.

I closed the book and laid it on a coffee table. The sky was black, and for a moment I was lonely. Once I was too young to travel by myself; now, maybe, I was too old. But then I poured a cup of tea, slid the lumpy-bumpy cake onto a yellow saucer, and set it on the table. The cake rose into a series of cream-filled mounds. Rails of chocolate trailed across the toffee icing. Contentment, Samuel Smiles wrote in *Duty*, was better than luxury or power, "and probably identity," I said aloud, thinking as I spoke that the three words were the twenty-fourth, twenty-fifth, and twenty-sixth words I'd said that day, adding them to the ten I said in the gallery and the thirteen I used in Peckham's to discover that I'd find my treat "lovely."

I decided to wait before tasting the cake. "To let the sweetness gather and ferment," I said, thinking, "now I am up to thirty-three words." I filled my teacup. Then I unzipped my backpack and took out *The Chateau*, a novel by William Maxwell. I opened the book and started the first chapter. "The big ocean liner, snow white, with two red and black slanting funnels, lay at anchor, attracting sea gulls. The sea was calm, the lens of the sky was set at infinity. The coastline—low green hills and the dim outline of stone houses lying in pockets of mist—was in three pale French colors, a brocade borrowed from some museum. The pink was daybreak. So beautiful, and no one to see it," I read. "No one but the invisible man," I said aloud, thinking, "that makes thirty-nine words. Boy, what a day!"

Obituary

FOR DINNER LAST TUESDAY I slathered Coleman's English mustard over a Scotch egg, toasted and buttered bread, brewed a pot of Earl Grey tea, and opened a can of Baxters Royal Game soup, this last containing, the label said, "Highland venison and pheasant in a rich stock." Later I brewed a cup of instant coffee, Nescafé's Blend 37. To sweeten the coffee, I ate two slices of Tesco's Sultana and Cherry Cake. "Just the sort of meal," I said to myself, "that Mole would serve his pal Ratty at Mole End in *The Wind in the Willows.*"

The next morning I received my first packet of mail from Vicki. Buried amid university notices was a letter from Harold Crumley. Although I hear from Harold occasionally, I have not seen him in decades. When I was a child, I spent summers on my grandfather's farm in Virginia. Harold lived six dirt roads away, and sometimes we played together. Harold wrote about another of my summertime playmates, Freddy Shotover. Freddy had died in Edinburgh, Harold recounted. "I heard that you were in Scotland, and although I know what I'm asking is inconvenient, I wonder if you could locate Freddy's grave and put flowers on it—for the sake of old times—maybe a lily and some bridal wreath." I have no idea how Harold learned I was abroad. Of course almost every day what people know and don't know amazes me.

In his letter Harold explained that Freddy's cousin Celeste had written, telling him that Freddy had visited the Tomb of Eagles on South Ronaldsay in the Orkneys. Harold read about the tomb in an encyclopedia. He said it was five thousand years old and made up of several chambers, "linked," he wrote, "folding into each other like the bellows of an accordion or concertina." Supposedly, Harold said, ancient inhabitants of the island lay their dead on wooden platforms outside the tomb so that eagles could strip the bodies. Once the skeletons were clean, they were buried in the cavern. In any case, Freddy, it seems, convinced the local farmers who served as caretakers of the cave to let him spend a night in the tomb. The cave was damp, and Freddy became chilled. The chill led to pneumonia, and Freddy died in Edinburgh shortly after returning from South Ronaldsay. "As you know, Freddy was never robust," Harold wrote.

The truth is I knew nothing about Freddy's health. The longer I live, the less it seems I know about anyone's life. Sometimes, I'm a mystery to myself. That aside, Freddy was an only child. He lived in Caroline County in a Georgian house his mother called Magnolia. A student of Christopher Wren designed the house, and it sat atop a mound at the end of a long drive, on both sides of which grew lanes of magnolia grandiflora. Each summer I spent three or four afternoons with Freddy at Magnolia. Oddly, Freddy never came to my grandfather's farm. When Mother fetched me from Magnolia, she always asked how I'd spent the day. Each time Freddy and I did the same thing. Freddy's mother served us lemonade, and we sat on the screened porch or in the yard under a big umbrella and listened while she read to us, first, as I recall, *The Wind in the Willows* and *The House at Pooh Corner*, then dog stories, *Bob, Son of Battle* being one. I remember the dog stories because Freddy had a fox terrier named Man, and when Freddy's mother served us butter cookies, she gave Man two sugar doughnuts, invariably two, not one or three.

I never met Mr. Shotover. He was always away, doing something with coal or the railways. In memory Freddy's mother smacks of Lear's Cordelia and seems slight and pale. Memories are usually fictions, and now if I saw a picture taken of her during one of the summers when I visited I wouldn't be surprised to discover she was pudgy. I do remember, though, that she called Freddy Frederick. For his part Freddy clings to recollection as a Christopher Robin figure. While I wore shorts and rough-and-ready striped T-shirts fit for country doings, Freddy always wore seersucker playsuits, covered with either blue and white or gray and white stripes. He had a small head and blond hair and turquoise eyes that shone like jewelry made by Indians in Arizona or New Mexico. His calves, however, were big as kegs and appeared out of character. Later he became ashamed of them.

On the back of the lobe of his left ear was a birthmark shaped like a coffin. Freddy's mother thought the mark an ill omen, and on noticing it, she broke into tears. Freddy was mischievous, and sometimes he began to play with his ear while she read, twisting the lobe back and forth, waving the mark in front of her. Eventually sobs punctuated her sentences. Freddy's mother collected Chinese perfume jars and silk camisoles. Mother liked hearing about the perfume jars, but my visits to Magnolia ended when Mother learned that Mrs. Shotover sometimes modeled the camisoles for Freddy and me. Not long afterward my grandfather sold his farm, and I stopped going to Virginia.

Rarely do friends disappear entirely from one's life. Like smoke from a distant chimney, a wisp of rumor or story suddenly trails through an hour. I discovered that Freddy attended Woodberry Forest School. My friend Bill Weaver also went to Woodberry Forest, and once I saw Freddy's picture in the yearbook. He didn't look like I imagined him. He was stooped shouldered, something that made him appear lanky and tall when in fact he was only about five feet eight inches tall. Instead of being round as a berry like the face of Christopher Robin, Freddy's face was angular and resembled a trowel, the top of the trowel a broad forehead, the bottom a sharp chin, a goatee clinging weakly to it like strands of periwinkle dangling from a ledge.

At Woodberry the phobia about his calves first appeared. Because fencers wore trousers, he tried to start a fencing team. The team failed to make, and he was forced to play basketball. He spent four years on the junior varsity. He refused to play on the varsity, though he could have done so his senior year, because he didn't want to appear in shorts in front a crowd. He also acted a little. In his last year he was part of the mob in *Julius Caesar*. His acting career did not last beyond opening night, however. He was the only member of the mob not swayed by Antony's rhetoric, and Bill told me that every time Antony said, "Brutus is an honourable man," Freddy yelled, "That's right. He is honorable, not an apostate like you!" Somebody, Harold probably, also told me that Freddy even called Antony "a no-good Yankee."

From Woodberry, Freddy went to Princeton. His career at Princeton was bookish but short lived. Perhaps drink had something to do with it. Who knows? In any case he spent days in Firestone Library, not reading textbooks but wandering the stacks hunting books published in the eighteenth century. When he found a book, he borrowed it. Sometime during his first year at Princeton, Freddy either discovered sheaves of old paper or learned how to cook paper so it appeared old. Freddy was a good, though unconventional, student. He manufactured ink, following a recipe he found in book published at the end of the seventeenth century. Similarly he mastered eighteenth-century handwriting and spelling. At night he composed letters sent from one minor eighteenth-century figure to another, a note, say, from Ambrose Philips the poet to his friend Daniel Pulteney, to whose daughters Philips wrote precious poems, earning him the nickname Namby-Pamby. After transcribing letters onto the paper, Freddy slit the bindings of the books he borrowed from Firestone. Beneath the binding of each book he slipped a letter. Afterward he sealed the bindings and the next morning returned the books to the library. To my mind this is Freddy's great achievement, in its anonymity smacking of both sweet and sour in a puckish, appealing, Winnie-the-Poohish way, something that makes him worthy of an obituary.

Freddy practically disappeared from my life after he left Princeton. His father died during his first year at Woodberry; his mother four years later at the beginning of his second and last year at Princeton. The sale of Magnolia and investments to which friends steered him brought him a modest independence, enough to keep him comfortably if he remained a bachelor. He did not marry. Perhaps his mother had been woman enough. Probably, though, he was content to live modestly. After Princeton there appear to have been no emotional highs and lows in his life. Instead a thin layer of sensible happiness seems to have spread across his days. No wife meant no children and few heartaches. As the tough old rhyme puts it, "As tall as your knee, they are pretty to see. / As tall as your head, they wish you were dead."

When I write that Freddy disappeared after college, I don't mean that he vanished completely. Occasionally he came to mind or, oddly, someone I knew remarked that he'd met Freddy and said that Freddy sent me his best, in the process almost always mentioning magnolias. Once Freddy gave me an actual magnolia, not one grown in Virginia, but an exquisite glass magnolia made in Bavaria. The magnolia arrived at just the right time, during one of those wintry moments when the trees are bare and the milky promises of spring have curdled. I was teaching at Dartmouth. One night I received a telephone call from a barmaid whom I knew. "Sam," she said, "Get down here now." A prominent member of the science faculty had locked himself and a male student in the men's lavatory at the Holstein, a local bar. Neither shouting nor pounding could persuade the faculty member to release the lock. "Get down here and get them out," were my orders. I hurried to the Holstein, but by the time I arrived, the couple had left both the lavatory and the building. In the frenzy of the moment, the faculty member had neglected to retrieve his back brace. "I found this behind the toilet," my friend said, pushing the brace into my chest. "Give it to him and tell him. . . ." My friend's language was strong. The next morning I went to the man's office and handed him the brace. I did not follow my friend's instructions. I said only, "You left this in the Holstein last night." After I returned the brace, I felt as if a cloud of soot had blown over me. Happily, that afternoon Freddy's flower arrived, and the day blossomed. On the card he had written, "Close your eyes and think of Caroline County. Freddy." Not only did I shut my eyes, but I leaned over the flower, and although it was glass, I smelled magnolia.

Through the years I received reports of Freddy. Someone told me that Freddy immigrated to Australia and was mining opals. I discounted the report as pushing Freddy too far out of character to be credible. Slightly more reliable was Estelle Brainard's account of seeing him playing tennis on Mykonos. Estelle was hardy and had graduated from Smith. "Freddy was wearing white trousers despite the heat," Estelle said. "What do calves matter to a grown man? Anyway he had a good lob and an adequate forehand and backhand, but his serve wasn't worth a damn. I wanted to shout *hello,* but he was in the middle of a rally so I wandered off to get a tankard of retsina. When I returned to the court, Freddy had gone—game, set, match over and done without a goodbye."

Once I thought I saw Freddy, but now I know I must have imagined seeing him. I was running though the Belgrade railway station, hurrying to catch a train to Budapest. As I leaped into my carriage, I looked behind me. On the opposite platform a train was pulling out, bound for Sofia. Waving at me from a window was Freddy. He wore a peppery gray suit, an orange necktie, and, incongruously, a sailor cap. I waved back. He yelled something, but the train was making too much noise, and I couldn't understand him.

The only dependable reports I received came from Anthea Opie, an old friend from my days in Cambridge then later in London. Anthea first ran across Freddy on the overnight train from Cairo to Luxor. They stayed up all night talking. "Quite a bit about you," Anthea said. Freddy told Anthea he was writing a long poem about the Sambatyon River that stopped flowing and rested on the Sabbath. Hedges of roses grew on the banks of the river, he said. The roses were tapestries of enameled color. Late in the day bright sheets of light bounced off the roses, making the horizon glow. "Forming the sunset," Freddy said. Two years later Anthea met Freddy at dawn atop Mt. Fiesole. Later they drank champagne together, and he told her he was writing a sonnet sequence celebrating mother love entitled "Rizpah."

Freddy probably never wrote a poem in his life. I suspect he described his poems to Anthea because he wanted to be thought poetic—so many people do. Perhaps he hoped that if he called himself a poet enough times he would become a poet. Or maybe publishing frightened him, and he worried that print would prove his ruminations commonplace. As the saying puts it, the higher the monkey climbs, the more he shows his tail. How much better to stay on the ground, stanzas safely out of sight, curling melodiously through dream. Who knows? What I do know is that Anthea was truth telling and good and solid. Of course I admired her too late. Many years ago after an indiscretion, she proposed to me, promising me not simply unlimited access to her person but the keys to an estate in Wales, land she would inherit from her father. "Marriage," she said, "would be our salvation." At that time I was unconscionably hardy and did not think myself in need of prayer, salvation, or property, so I turned her down. If Freddy had been present, I wonder what he would have advised me to do.

In any case I endeavored to follow Harold's wishes and discover Freddy's whereabouts, but I am afraid age has made me peculiar. Rarely do I answer the telephone nowadays. In fact I refuse to use the phone in my flat. I did, though, peruse the directory. To my relief a coroner was not listed. Before thumbing the yellow pages, I considered visiting funeral homes. Matters "morticious" filled five and three-quarters pages of the directory. "More businesses than an immortal could be expected to visit," I concluded. Next I studied the locations of cemeteries, thinking that if Freddy could be found in Edinburgh, he would be discovered in a graveyard. Cemeteries sprouted green and attractive across the city map. I decided to explore the graveyards, and I made a list, the names almost poetic: Grange, Newington, Dean, Eastern, Warrington, Portobello, and Piershill. I did not, incidentally, consider crematoria, as high temperatures made Freddy uncomfortable. Every summer at Magnolia he suffered dreadfully from prickly heat.

Unfortunately, just as I was plotting my peregrinations, I ripped a muscle jogging. To begin an odyssey in less than perfect health would have been foolhardy. Birth and death, indeed most of life itself, resulting from happenstance, not calculation, I decided to let chance guide me, if not to the plot in which Freddy actually lay at least to a patch in which, if he'd had his choice, he would have selected to while away eternity. A lifetime of casually knowing the man convinced me that I'd recognize the spot immediately.

And so it came to pass that as I strolled back to the university after spending a morning at the National Gallery of Scotland, I happened upon the statue of Bobby, a Skye terrier perched like a finial atop an iron post at the intersection of King George IV and Candlemaker Row. In 1858 Bobby's master died and was buried in Greyfriars Kirkyard. Appropriately enough, Bobby accompanied his master's remains to the graveyard and stood by quietly while his master was interred. Shortly afterward Bobby went mad and, as do many of the rabid, became the stuff of legend. Grief having deprived him of common canine sense, he refused to abandon his master's relics. For fourteen years he hung about the graveyard. Neighbors fed him and built a hutch for him. On Bobby's death, Dickens's friend Baroness Burdett Coutts, a philanthropist and heiress to a great banking fortune, commissioned a statue of the dog. In 1873 Bobby mounted the post, and there he has sat for over 130 years, never scratching or howling, no matter the weather or the barrows of fleas inhabiting Edinburgh.

All terriers are not the same, but when I saw Bobby I immediately thought of Freddy's Man. Behind Bobby a gate opened into Greyfriars Kirkyard, the oldest graveyard in Edinburgh. As soon as I entered the cemetery, I realized chance had directed my footsteps to a splendid last home for Freddy's spirit. Massive stone walls surrounded Greyfriars, turning it into the dark Petra of the North. Instead of being carved down the face of bluffs, monuments had been built into the walls, often rising hooded above them. Instead of rose red, this Petra was black and gray, and in places where moss flourished was feverishly green. Urns lay broken here and there, looking as if rage had hurled them to the ground. Roots lost their grip, and grass slid loosely over mud like skin slipping ripening flesh. Lime trees broke into burls and cankers, and twigs dropped from branches on walkways twisting like ribs wrung from spines. On monuments carvings eroded and, losing definition, became death's-heads of themselves.

Like the walls enclosing the churchyard, epitaphs were splotched with lesions and were black as lungs caked with coal dust. Instead of hosannas offering joyful consolation, the epitaphs were dirges begrudgingly acknowledging lives adequately lived. The spouse of the Reverend Thomas McCrie, Janet Dickson died in 1831 when she was forty-five years old. "Who," the carving on her memorial stated with peremptory affection, "discharged the duties of a wife and mother with the most affectionate and anxious assiduity and endeared herself to all who knew her by sweetness of temper and by the pious resignation with which she bore a lingering affliction." Elizabeth, the second daughter of William Henderson, was thirteen when she died in the second decade of the nineteenth century. "This Stone is erected," her epitaph read, "in affectionate Remembrance of a beloved child, by her parents, whose feelings of regret for her loss are heightened, by the Recollection of her amiable and endearing conduct during life." All that was said of John Alexander Longmore was that "He bequeathed the residue of his estate for the relief of persons suffering from incurable disease."

How Freddy would delight in enlivening Greyfriars, I thought, roiling through the dirt, humming and singing, talking about his poetry, describing magnolias, and tweaking the dour dead. He wrote me a letter once from Princeton, the week before he decamped, in fact. On the envelope he scribbled a stanza lifted from an old book in Firestone, or at least I assume he plucked the verse from a book, though, perhaps he wanted me to think he composed it. "Oh, the gladness of their gladness when they're glad, / And the sadness of their sadness when they're sad. / But the gladness of their gladness and the sadness of their sadness / Are as nothing to their badness when they're bad." In the same letter he said something I thought almost profound but that will probably upset longtime residents of Greyfriars. "Not only should my friends be religious but they should have good characters as well."

On a piece of white paper, 4 x 3 inches, I wrote, "Freddy Shotover. 1941–2005." Under Freddy's name and the dates of his life, I drew three lilies; among them I scattered four sprigs of baby's breath. Then bettering Harold's instructions, I drew a magnolia under the lilies, the petals spreading wide to catch beams of the Resurrection. I folded the paper in half. For some time I walked about, not sure where to put the paper, waiting for a sign. But then suddenly, and surprisingly, I heard a robin's wavering song. I walked over to the nearest wall, the Flodden Wall, erected after the battle of Flodden Field (1513) in the forlorn hope of slowing the English if they decided to sack Edinburgh. At the wall I inserted the piece of paper into a crack shoulder high and midway between monuments to James Baird and Alexander Stirling.

Outside the graveyard, I snapped my fingers as I turned up Forrest. I'd done right by Freddy. Because I spent most of the afternoon in Greyfriars, I decided not to return to the university. On Clerk I bought a baguette and two hundred grams of pâté, the sort of meal, I speculated, Badger might have pulled out of a cupboard after a hard day's digging in *The Wind in the Willows*. Once back at the flat I kicked off my shoes, brewed a pot of English breakfast tea, and stretching across the couch in the sitting room, ate the pâté and the baguette. I am afraid I was as messy as Badger, pinching hunks of the pâté with my fingers and flailing the bread about, scattering crumbs over the couch and across the floor.

Curio Shop

AT BREAKFAST EVERY MORNING I swallow four tablets: a small gel resembling a golden blimp fat with fish oil; a vitamin the color of red sandstone, the ingredients a gravel pit of mysterious, invigorating minerals, the print on the bottle too small for my eyes to sift into words; and, to keep my blood flowing no matter how long I sit cramped at a desk, an "adult low strength" aspirin, pink and about half the size of a currant. The fourth tablet I take is a capsule, blue at one end and white at the other. This turns me into a spillway and keeps liquids from backing up, preventing my blood pressure from bobbling and rising like a rowboat that has slipped its moorings.

I keep a week's supply of pills in a translucent plastic container six inches long. The container is divided into seven compartments, one little box for every day of the week, each box the size of the end of my thumb, measuring from the tip to the knuckle. Stamped on top of the compartments in gold are seven letters corresponding to the days of the week. Thus M appears above Monday's dose and W appears over Wednesday's. Lids to the compartments are the size of my thumbnail, and to get at the pills, I have to pry a lid back to the cuticle. Every Sunday morning, just after I have bolted the day's dose and after I've finished my cereal, I fill the container. Actually I look forward to filling the container, and I rush through breakfast. I like opening the little bottles and dumping tablets into my hand. I play a game, seeing if I can shake out seven without looking. When I shake exactly seven tablets into my hand, I usually nod and say "yes" as if I had won a literary prize. I also enjoy putting the tablets into the compartments appropriate to each day of the week. I move my hand slowly over the container, its lids gapping, and drop the tablets carefully, as if I am planting seeds in a furrow. Once I have put all twenty-eight pills in the container, I lean back and study the boxes. The pills fill the boxes, and here and there a tablet sticks up over the lid of a compartment, like, I enjoy thinking, a child peering over a fence—maybe, I imagine, a raggedy Huck Finn character watching bulldozers push aside hills of dirt and rock, digging a foundation hole.

Filling the container is one of the delights of my week. From small matters I derive great pleasure. Appreciating the small does not, as might first be thought, indicate diminished sensibility and capacity. Imagination often flourishes amid the small and the confined more easily than in the open. In malls I become claustrophobic, the harsh light dissecting and not illuminating, turning people into specimens paddling about inside beakers. In a little store, walls do not pinch like ribs broken by and to contemporary living. Instead they bow out, allowing one to breathe and dream.

The container reminds me of a row of shops, say, those near the university, a district frequented by students and office workers, these last headed home at dusk, harried by little responsibilities and pausing for a moment to pick up an item forgotten during a shopping trip to a mall. Amid the shops is a Chinese restaurant, named Lucky Star or, improbably, Miami Take-Out. Stacked outside a greengrocer's are flimsy wooden crates, sunny with clementines and marmalade oranges, grapes, tomatoes and apples, and then leeks, looking like green and white truncheons. Beside the boxes stand buckets bursting with tulips, the flowers not open and the buds finials of red, yellow, and purple.

Standing in the doorway of a cobbler's shop, I imagine smelling the grainy fragrance of leather. What I hear is the grinding of keys. Signs in the window of a health food store mention bioforce, body butter, and Keto-Slim high-protein shakes. A regimen of Chinese herbs will remedy all ailments and failings, a sign declares, from rheumatism to psoriasis and acne, from anxiety and impotence to bloating, water retention, and smoking. A butcher hawks duck eggs, potted meat, steak and kidney pie, and "haggis made on premises" as well as haunches of flesh, some silvery, others scarlet. Raisin buns, croissants, scones, and loaves of bread, a few crusty with seeds, the rest smooth mounds, fill the window of a bakery. From a basket below the window, baguettes stick up like a bundle of staves.

Outside a stationer's, broadsides proclaim the latest news, the print on the broadsides so bold it shouts. From the ceiling just inside the window hangs a birthday balloon shaped like a honeybee and striped yellow and black. Racks of cards, magazines, and candy lean against the walls of the shop. Here a person can pay the telephone bill, photocopy documents, and have pictures developed.

Because news always seems soiled, I hurry past the stationer's and cross the street to a new row and an eighth shop. A barber named Albert cuts the hair of an old man. Placards and postcards paper the walls of the shop, some of them so frayed they look like Albert clipped their side panels. Unlike fashionable hair cutters who dress in black shirts and blouses and wear sharp-edged dark trousers, Albert knows how to taper hair up the back of the neck. Earlier I broke my amble at the bakery to buy a Danish for lunch. I didn't waste time, though, because that morning I put fifty-nine pence, the price, into the right pocket of my trousers. Next to the barbershop is a used bookstore, shelves titling haphazardly, transforming the shop into a maze of cupboards.

I spend much time in bookstores. To foster collegiality the institute provides a buffet for the fellows every Tuesday at noon. Because I don't stop at a greengrocer's stall, on Tuesdays I graze on fruits and greens, so much so that I almost founder. Last week after sampling slivers of pizza, prawns in mayonnaise, and a wheel of cheeses, I heaped salad on my plate, both Waldorf and mixed green salads. I piled the lettuce so high that I buried my fork. Not until I sat down to eat did I notice that my fork was missing. Thinking that I had absentmindedly put it down beside a serving dish, I studied the table. When I didn't see the fork, I walked around the table. "A mystery," I concluded, taking another fork, "one of life's many puzzles." Only after I dug into the green salad did I find the fork. Although wine is served at lunch, until this past Tuesday I only drank orange juice. Solving the Case of the Missing Fork made the lunch special, however, and in commemoration I drank a glass of wine, the drinking of which, also being special, I marked by wolfing down two more glasses.

The wine made settling to the calm of pad and pencil difficult. Used bookstores are quiet places: the owners usually repressed; the customers, often mute, *um*s and *ah*s being the most demonstrative elements of their speech. Consequently, as a panacea for the elevating effect of the wine, I skipped along Meadow Lane to Pickering's Books on Buccleuch. "Do you have any books by Pickering?" I asked, bounding through the door. "By who?" a startled clerk replied. "Pickering," I repeated, "the great Pickering." "Who?" the clerk asked again. "Oh, nuts. Never mind," I said and left the shop. The day was sunny, and so I decided to wander Edinburgh, roaming always a catalyst suitable for solidifying heeltaps of drink. Purging books from mind is not as easily accomplished as purging wine from the blood, however. Ninety minutes later I entered Armchair Books on West Port.

Earlier in my stay I bought two volumes of Samuel Smiles's writings from Armchair Books, *Duty* and *Self-Help*. Every morning at breakfast I read thirty pages from the books, the reading bucking me up mentally, and maybe morally, much as the tablets shore me physically. Smiles's enthusiasm and rectitude appealed to me, so much so that I'd come to rely on him to start my days. On Sunday I finished *Self-Help*. On Monday I discovered at the university library that I could read Smiles's other books only in special collections, not a room in which I could slouch comfortably in pajamas while chewing cereal and tossing down pills.

A clerk pulled *Thrift* and *Character* from a shelf above the front door of the shop, climbing a rickety ladder that only the literary and the lethargic would dare to mount. Despite being two of Smiles's most popular works, the books had long been out of print, and the shop owner priced them at nine pounds apiece, an amount practically as high as the shelf on which they had lain. "I'll pay fifteen pounds," I said, slapping a twenty-pound note down on the clerk's desk. The sight of money moves people quicker than conversation. "Right," the clerk said, taking the bill in his left hand while pushing his right down the front of his trousers. From his crotch he extracted a codpiece of bills, off the top of which he peeled a five-pound note. I took the bill gingerly, using the thumb and forefinger of my right hand as tweezers. I did not slip the bill into my wallet immediately but instead fanned it for a moment in hopes not merely of disinfecting but also cooling it.

Published by John Murray in London at the turn of the nineteenth century as "popular editions," the books had initially cost three shillings and six pence apiece. Both were bound in red cardboard. Stamped on the front of each was a rectangle the size of a calling card. Instead of rising embossed, the embellishment was pressed into the cover. At the top of the rectangle appeared the name of the book in gold capital letters; at the bottom, the name SMILES. Between the words a design bloomed. Amid a lacy doily of leaves were eight clovers and two poppy blossoms, these last having sunken to seed and shapes vaguely suggesting the mouths of cannons. In the middle of the rectangle a literary poppy bloomed, implying that under the flower lay contents intoxicating yet salubrious.

Rarely do I talk to the young and glamorous. Their faces are almost as boring as their conversation. Instead I enjoy the company of the old, their minds and bodies ditched into interest, their thoughts twisting between pits and slag heaps, their expressions smoky as culm. Similarly I only buy used books, their pages marked by people and time. On February 25, 1898, Maggie and Andrew gave *Character* to their mother "With Best Wishes." The inscription was ornate, the last bit of each *W* rising into a curlicue resembling a cursive *e*. In April 1908, the Gateshead Education Committee for South Street Evening School "awarded" *Thrift* to J. Laws "for successful work during the Session," 1907–1908. The committee seems to have purchased inspirational prizes in bulk, for much of the writing on the bookplate was printed. For example, in the dates of the session only the *07* and *08* were handwritten, both *19*s being printed and followed by spaces in which years could be written on prize day. The rouged covers of the books had also aged, that of *Character* having faded into a bleached orange as if it had lain atop a table in the sunlight. On the other hand, grease speckled *Thrift* and, sinking into the cardboard, had bound the dye, preserving some of the red and liver-spotting the cover. "Breakfast reading," I said, anticipating beginning the book the next morning.

Last in the row of stores and my favorite, despite my penchant for buns and books, is the antique shop, a wooden sign running the length of the front, painted black and red or maybe green and gold and tilting over the sidewalk, not threatening to fall like the blade of a guillotine and sever passersby from their money but instead blowing quietly in the air, inviting strollers to slip the maddening rush and come in and browse. The name of the shop is comfortable, perhaps Then and Now or the Tolbooth, but more probably Whitehouse Antiques, Strathearn's, or Napier and Ettrick—the name of this last, of course, a fiction contrived by its owner, good Sally Brown with eyes not soft and dark but blue and sharp for things.

Owners of antique shops are often enthusiasts. Across the Meadows on Bruntsfield Place is Harlequin Antiques, a small, one-room shop twenty feet wide and maybe thirty-five long. Windows of the shop are so filled they resemble eyes cloudy with cataracts: cut glass, silver trays, figurines, blue willow and Worcester platters, cups and saucers, perfume bottles, snuffboxes, brass candlesticks, and plates light with blue and yellow flowers that I associate with good country eating, ham, cornbread, and tomatoes as big as softballs. Piled atop tables behind the window are boxes, one I coveted, a dispatch box dating from the Crimean War. In Storrs on a dowry chest sit other boxes, the oldest mother of pearl and bought in Damascus; another purchased thirty-five years ago in Leningrad, a firebird slashing red across the top; a third a gift, the giver forgotten but the box's use as a savings bank clear, slots for coins carved into the lid. Inside Harlequin Antiques tables stand atop ball-and-claw feet and straight federal legs. In a cabinet are coins minted during the reign of George III. "Americans like them," Mr. Harkness, the proprietor, told me.

I have visited Harlequin Antiques several times, not for the coins, the box, or a figurine I liked, a cheery small bulldog, probably whelped in the 1870s. My father was bookish, and forty-three years ago in London, I bought him a piece of eighteenth-century German porcelain, a bulldog studious with metal glasses low over his eyes. I don't remember what I paid for the figurine, but compared to pounds Mr. Harkness wanted for his dog, the price was pence. No, what lures me to Harlequin Antiques are clocks, so many the shop paradoxically seems timeless. On the walls hang clocks shaped like keyholes and fish boxes. Bell jars shelter clocks from dust, though there is little dust in the shop, for Mr. Harkness keeps his clocks ticking and polished. Steeple clocks stand on tables. Grandfather clocks rise in buttresses, their faces smiling, a robin on one, on another allegorical figures representing England, Ireland, Scotland, and Wales.

Brass school clocks, made obsolete by digital time, jut from the wall like periscopes. Janitors save them from dustbins and sell them to Mr. Harkness. Nowadays people buy them for kitchens. Mantle clocks squat low and to me unappealingly, clipping time's wings, bracketing hours to schedule and caging flights of fancy. A cabinet contains scores of pocket and wristwatches. A vineyard clock strikes the hour twice, repeating the time for the sake of workers. On a work table sits a clock manufactured in 1680, now owned by lawyer, its works being tuned. Imperial eagles spread their wings atop German wall clocks manufactured at the beginning of the twentieth century. During the First World War, owners of these clocks removed the eagles. Balls and steeples and carvings curling over each other in waves decorate the tops of other wall clocks.

My favorite clock is Austrian, a Viennese Regulator, tall and slender, its wood brown and black, decorations spooling dizzily over the box. I haven't read the price on the ticket pinned to the clock. Far better for me to confine my reading to inscriptions inside secondhand books. Thrift, Samuel Smiles said, was "the spirit of order in human life." Still, thinking like a spendthrift raises the spirits, especially when one covets the aesthetic, a clock as stylish and smooth as a Strauss waltz. Or so I thought until breakfast on Saturday. The savage, Smiles preached, was the "greatest of spendthrifts," giving no thought to tomorrow. Not only did prehistoric man ignore saving, but he lived "in caves, or in hollows of the ground covered with branches. He subsisted on shellfish which he picked up on the sea shore, or upon hips and haws which he gathered in the woods. He killed animals with stones. He lay in wait for them, or ran them down on foot." I am ponderous of foot; my shoulders are so arthritic that I cannot throw a rock, and the only gathering I'm capable of occurs in bakeries and groceries. According to Smiles, if I want to continue munching croissants and sleeping in a bed, I must live a regulated life and eschew all hankerings for the Regulator.

I will, however, return to Harlequin Antiques, not because I ache to own a clock or box, but because the shop smacks of my life. Let the young whose lives and dreams stretch vibrant and muscular before them frequent sporting goods stores. I have aged into appreciating the antique shop. Memories clutter days and crowd hours. Things my children dismiss as curios delight me. Who is in power and who shakes the world don't interest me. I'd rather stroke a Rockingham dog than read a political quarterly. Like the goods in Mr. Harkness's shop, my life is ordered, the arrangement obvious to me but perhaps not to youth or a casual acquaintance. Until my pendulum breaks, I will remain a collector, specializing in things I can display on the page.

Actually my mind is a curio shop. In Edinburgh an invisible cart accompanies me on my rambles. Into it I pack things that I see and hear. From the Robert Louis Stevenson collection in the Writers' Museum, I didn't filch a manuscript, the handling of which would have forced me to wear white gloves. Instead I lifted a pair of riding boots Stevenson wore in Samoa. The boots were black, and their laces wound in and out of seven eyes and around eight hooks. I coveted a tall cabinet, really a clothespress over a chest containing six drawers. Deacon Brodie made the cabinet in the eighteenth century. Brodie led multiple lives. By day he served Edinburgh as a member of the town council. By night he was a burglar, helping himself to the possessions of others. In 1788 he was hanged. When Stevenson lived on Heriot Row as a child, the cabinet was in his room. The wood on the doors of the press pools into two eyes, fright raising them into ovals, just the sort of sight to startle a boy into delicious nightmares. Behind the doors of the cabinet lurk *Kidnapped* and the house of Shaws with its square tower whose steps fell into "emptiness." "A fine furnishing for nights when I sit up late reading, body still as a corpse but imagination awake scribbling," I thought.

From the museum's holdings of Robert Burns, I took an enameled marble apple. Burns gave the apple to Jean Brackenridge when she married his brother Gilbert. Gray and small, the size of a child's fist, the apple was ugly—blighted enough for conversation. I also removed a china mug made in Sunderland in the 1890s. The mug was four and a half inches in diameter and five inches tall. Around the outside ran a frieze depicting Tam o' Shanter seated between two cronies, one clearly Souter Johnny, the other probably Tam's friend the miller. All three men clutched yellow boozing cans brimming with ale. While Tam's companions sat sideways listening to him, he lounged comfortably back in a chair, belly spilling through a red vest, legs akimbo, a staff between them, his right arm raised high, gesturing amid the clatter of exaggeration. Inside the well of the cup lurked a spotted green frog. Perhaps because the frog didn't appear in Burns's poem, it was trying to escape, its hind legs pushing it up the sides of the cup. The appearance of Tam's mare, Maggie, would have been more appropriate. Still, the interior of the cup probably would not have been corral enough for Maggie. Accordingly the potter should have baked Maggie's tail into the bottom of the cup, wrapped around and cinched in its hair the hand of Nannie, the witch who ripped it from Maggie's rump.

My fingers have been inky for thirty years, and as could be expected, as I wander aisles of weeks, literary matters attract me. In the Scottish National Portrait Gallery, I sought out paintings I'd seen in books, those of Stevenson, Thomas Carlyle, and George Williston's fleshly Boswell, Samuel Johnson's biographer. In the portrait Boswell was starting to run to cellulite. His fingers were fat as candy bars; his chin soft and meaty, and his stomach rumpled, forcing one of the lower buttons on his waistcoat open, exposing tissues of white shirt. Embroidered with gold thread, the waistcoat itself was scarlet and sybaritic. Over the waistcoat draped a dressing gown trimmed in fur, the mat running thick down the lapels and around the ends of the sleeves. In contrast to Boswell's full portrait was George Reid's head of Samuel Smiles, painted in 1891 when Smiles was almost eighty. Smiles's cheeks were ruddy, the sign of an active and lively man, and his skull was round and smooth, not complicated by knobs or ego, much like his thought. "Just the person with whom to share breakfast," I whispered when I saw the portrait.

I hurried through galleries hung with historical portraits, depicting people important in the early history of Scotland. About the boots of these people blood had gathered in lakes. My curio shop is peaceful, an insignificant place apart from the hard, great world, indeed like my books themselves. Occasionally I studied the portrait of someone who shook more dust from society than he did from the covers of books, for example, Andrew Morton's Henry Brougham, lord chancellor and supporter of the Reform Bill of 1832. Integrity shone from Brougham's face. Even here, though, the literary was partly responsible for my admiration. At the beginning of the nineteenth century, Brougham had helped found the University of London. In the 1970s I spent a year there, and two prints of University College hang in a hall of my house in Connecticut. In galleries as in antique stores, oddities lurk on the edge of observation, or at least off canvas. In the note below the portrait of David Scott, an artist who lived from 1806–1849, a curator wrote that although Scott's friends thought him a genius, "Twentieth-century opinion has been less adulatory, realizing that his art straddles uncomfortably the dividing line between inspiration and incompetence."

What a person sees in one place influences how he sees in another. After I left the gallery, Edinburgh itself seemed a mural, a great stone wall over which neighborhoods and people sprawled. I usually don't like murals. I associate them with graffiti. No matter their democratic intentions, if local artists began to paint the side of building on the street where I owned an antique shop, I'd give up my lease. Still, for a moment Edinburgh seemed glorious, a mural not so much on stone as of stone: Charlotte Square creamy in the sunlight, gorse yellow on the rocky south slope of Calton Hill, a great tit spinning on a twig, the black stripe running down his breast turning him into a dandy sporting an orange vest; on Saturday shoppers throbbing along Princes Street, clotting the corners of St. David, Hanover, Frederick, and Castle; packs of schoolchildren roaming Morningside Road at noon baying after fast food; and at the same time in the kitchen attached to the Edinburgh mosque, men serving lamb and chicken curry out of huge steaming pots, sitting in the tent raised next to the kitchen fifty more men eating and talking, only one an outsider, me, nervous that I will break my isolation by saying something inappropriate, like "Am I the only patriot here who works for the CIA?"

The person whose life is a curio shop transforms life into artifact. Moreover, he often sees through objects to his own life. Behind the shellac covering one or two portraits in the gallery lurked, I imagined, a portrait of me painted in 1943. My hair was blond. I wore a pink playsuit and in my left hand held an apple. The portrait hangs in the dining room at home. Last year Vicki tacked a handful of snakeskins around the frame. "Eden," I suddenly realized in the gallery, "snakes and the apple."

Literary matters have influenced my time in Edinburgh. At Princeton I wrote a dissertation on the *Edinburgh Review* and one of its founders, Sydney Smith, the essayist and divine. The *Review* was founded at the home of Francis Jeffrey in 1801. Jeffrey lived in George Square, almost directly behind the institute. One afternoon I went to Jeffrey's house. All traces of the *Review* were gone. The university had turned the building into a warren of academic offices, opening like rabbit holes off a concrete staircase. The door to the building slouched off a hinge, and the staircase was grimy, its yellow paint chipped and the steps sticky with pellets of trash. Still, books can furnish a life. A boy handed me a flyer when I stepped onto the sidewalk outside Jeffrey's house.

The flyer advertised the annual university boxing match between Cambridge and Edinburgh. In 1822 in the *New Monthly Magazine*, William Hazlitt described a match between Bill Neate and Thomas Hickman, the Gas-man, calling his essay "The Fight." Hazlitt's prose was muscular and powerful, his sentences, in boxing terms, grave diggers, banging like sledgehammers. Since "The Fight" strutted into the *New Monthly,* critics, referees of sorts, have judged it the finest piece of sportswriting in English. Many writers have turned out professional paragraphs, but none have produced an essay capable of standing verb to verb, noun to noun with "The Fight." I knew my prose could not enter the ring with that of Hazlitt. Nevertheless, as Hazlitt labeled Jim Belcher, one of his favorite fighters, the Game Chicken, so I plucked up nerve enough to test my literary mettle by throwing a few paragraphs onto the page.

Hazlitt traveled in the Bath mail coach to Newbury, where he spent a night at an inn, the Crown. The next morning he and devotees of what he called "The Fancy" rose early and tramped seven miles to Hunger-ford. He arrived at noon, an hour before the fight began. For my part I walked from Blacket Place, going north on Minto, staying on the road as it changed into Newington, then South Clerk, and Clerk. At Gifford I turned west. When Gifford ended a hundred paces farther on at Buccleuch Street, I turned right and walked north another ninety or so paces until I reached Meadow Lane, the small street running behind the institute, where I turned west again. Behind the institute I cut through a parking lot and, following a path between buildings, crossed Buccleuch Place, climbed steps leading to the library, and entered George Square, my journey taking twenty-six minutes. Like Hazlitt, I, too, arrived an hour before the fighting started.

After the fight, Hazlitt and his friend Jack Pigott hitched a ride in a post chaise traveling to Wolhampton, where they spent the night at an inn with an "old bow-windowed parlour." On arriving they drank tea and devoured "a quantity of toast and eggs." Afterward they discussed dinner, debating between "a roasted fowl and mutton chops with mashed potatoes." Before Hazlitt and Pigott settled on a meal, a crowd of interlopers, as he put it, "noisy pretenders, butchers from Tothill-fields, brokers from Whitechapel," simply "Goths and Vandals," burst into the parlor and interrupted their gastronomic deliberations, so much so that Hazlitt did not mention dinner again, leaving readers in culinary purgatory. In this section of the essay I, if I'm allowed to be both writer and referee, land more punches than Hazlitt and carry the round. Before setting off for the fights, I drank a pot of English breakfast tea and munched cheddar cheese and the rocky remnant of a four-day old baguette. After the fights, I walked back to Blacket Place. I met no Goths or Visigoths, Picts or even Celts. Much as the activity stirred the appetites of Hazlitt and Pigott, so the evening made me hungry. Once I was back in the flat I heated a small can of Heinz curried beans, poured a glass of orange juice, and grabbing a fist of Greek currants, flopped down on the couch in the sitting room in order to ponder the Fancy. Pigott took a pocket-sized copy of the *New Eloise* with him to the fight, which he read, Hazlitt reported, "in the intervals of our discourse." I do not like being outdone in literary things, especially by an amateur like Pigott even if Hazlitt dubbed him an ornament of life, so after I had mused for a while, I plucked Stevenson's *Kidnapped* off a side table and began reading, this, by the by, a Library of Classics edition, published by Collins sometime in the 1950s and, alas, devoid of inscription.

The fight between Neate and the Gas-man occurred in December, out of doors on a dazzling day "on a spot of virgin-green closed in and unprofaned by vulgar tread." The fights between Cambridge and Edinburgh took place on the fourth floor of the Teviot Debating Hall at eight o'clock on a drizzly January night. Indeed, the fights were staged in the hall itself, becoming an emblem of contemporary debate, an activity now more hormonal than verbal. A ring had been erected in the middle of the hall, one corner red for Cambridge, the opposite blue for Edinburgh, the remaining two corners neutral and white. One end of the hall ended in a stage. Before it sat a row of chairs for officials: judges, the two referees who alternated calling fights, an announcer, a timekeeper, a recorder, and a doctor. The doctor was not comfortable. During matches she frowned and sat back in her chair, to avoid, I assumed, blood gushing from a nose or mouth and, splashing over the ropes, landing on her clothes. I resembled the doctor, and the fighting often discomfited me. After watching the boxers endure tremendous batterings, Hazlitt exclaimed, "This is the high and heroic state of man!" For my part in the middle of rounds I often turned my head down and, looking into my lap, whispered, almost like a prayer, "Stop this. These children are going to hurt each other. Doesn't anyone know how fragile brightness and health are?" On seeing me taking notes, a member of the boxing club who had torn a ligament in his knee in a bout last year and who had been told not to fight for twelve months knelt beside my chair and asked, "Are you a big fan of boxing?" The boy was enthusiastic, and not wanting to undermine high spirits, I almost lied. Reading Smiles, though, had influenced me, and so instead of telling the comfortable lie, I told the truth. "No," I said, "I wouldn't let my sons box." After the boy described his injury, I said, "If you were my baby, I wouldn't let you fight again."

At the end of the hall opposite the stage and just beyond the door were rows of chairs, seventy chairs in all. The hall was longer than it was narrow, and along the narrow sides of the hall were some seventy other chairs, thirty-five to a side. Admission being ten pounds, I did not expect the hall to fill. I was wrong. Students crowded the stage, leaned against the walls, and sat on the floor. Almost as many girls attended as boys, something that startled me but led to no conclusion. The students were partisan and loud but always good natured. Throughout the fights they drank beer purchased at the union bar downstairs. Not once, though, did I hear an untoward shout. Friends pounded the backs of both winners and losers, and the evening was festive, the worry that plagued me and perhaps the doctor not concerning others.

Hazlitt reported that two hundred thousand pounds had been wagered on "The Fight," at the conclusion of which carrier pigeons were released to speed the result to London. No touts attended the matches in the debating hall. Scattered amid the room were clumps of adults, some devotees and others fans interested in all sports, but no nutters or swells, these last "parading in their white box-coats." The adults were predominantly large men. Most wore tweedy jackets gone ratty, but a few donned blazers, tarnished monograms of athletic or boys' clubs sewn on pockets. A very old man sat near the Cambridge fighters. He wore a double-breasted blazer, and I heard him ask a boxer what subject he was reading at the university. In attendance was a man who had played rugby for Scotland and the British Lions, winning some sixty caps during his career. I studied him. He smiled easily and seemed good natured. His hair was graying, but he walked quickly, rugby not having splintered his knees. Twice he was recognized, and twice he stood and waved. What must it be like, I wondered, to go through life being known and recognized for things accomplished when one was, if not a stripling, at least young? To be confined to youth and prevented from growing into a host of different people would be hellish.

Because I arrived early I sat at the end of the first row on the east side of the ring. Circling the hall was a balcony shaped like a staple, the end above the stage open. Walls were paneled, and the ceiling rose curved, molding the room into the shape of a loaf of bread baked in a high-sided pan. Hanging on the wall outside the hall were photographs of former presidents of the union, sixty-three photographs, a single space being vacant. Students in the pictures wore stiff collars and suits, many three-piece. They were solemn and looked older than their years, in contrast to contemporary students, who often dress below their ages rather than above. In great part Scotland is a tomb, monuments to war dead everywhere and inescapable. As I looked at the faces in the photographs, I wondered how many died in wars.

On the card were eleven fights, ten of them consisting of three two-minute rounds, the eleventh lasting four rounds. Between rounds a young woman, the girlfriend of a member of the club, climbed between the ropes and circled the ring, holding a sign above her head. Printed on the sign in black was 2 or 3, the number of the round coming up. The ring girl, as the announcer called her, had a sweet face and long blond hair. Indeed, hair covered more of her than clothes. She wore black high-heeled shoes and a black top like that of a skimpy bathing suit. A black skirt about as long and as loose as the fringe on a curtain circled her midriff. When she bent over to climb into the ring, she held the back of her skirt down with one hand, trying unsuccessfully to hide her black underwear. Although she smiled whenever she raised a placard, by the end of the evening she was tired of climbing in and out of the ring, longing, I thought and hoped, to vanish into jeans.

All the boxers, winners and losers, received medals. For ten pounds a member of the audience could become a sponsor and at the end of a bout climb into the ring and award a medal to a fighter. Tired of anonymity, I almost succumbed to ego. For half a round I considered sponsorship, not as dull Sam Pickering, however, but as that inspirational creation "Pickering's Essays." Eventually I decided to hold on to my money, not because of Smiles's warnings about becoming a spendthrift but, alas, the flesh being always liable to acquisitiveness, in order to save enough to purchase a curio from Mr. Harkness.

Boxers representing Cambridge wore silky red trousers and red sleeveless shirts. Boxers from Edinburgh wore similar dress, only the colors being different, blue and white instead of red. In three or so fights boxers represented clubs, rather than schools, and wore shirts with their club insignia on the chests. In shorts and shirts the fighters looked like schoolboys. The protective helmets, however, transformed them into alien creatures, swelling foreheads and cheeks, distancing the audience from the boxers' humanity, enabling the crowd to slip leashes of sensibility and concern, freeing them to bay, urging fighters to hound and tree. At the end of bouts, when boxers removed their helmets, I felt an odd sense of relief, as if the little space I occupied in the world had returned to normal. Indeed, after fights the boxers hugged each other enthusiastically, as if the heat of ordeal had forged friendships.

The announcer flew in from the Midlands for the fights, and he often supplied the local fighters with nicknames, Mad Dog and Raging Bull, for example. Neate was huge man, his knock-knees bending beneath his bulk, while Hickman was smaller, vigorous and elastic with a back that glistened in the sun "like a panther's hide." Hazlitt compared Neate to Ajax and Hickman to Diomedes. In doing so, he succumbed to the lure of words and elevated the brawl out of reason to the classical. Unknowingly, the announcer in Teviot got closer to the truth. At times the evening seemed mad. The floor of the ring thumped like a bellows as boxers raged back and forth, shouldering into each other and expelling air in great whooshes. For some participants this was a maiden match, while others had only fought once or twice. A handful of the boxers had fought several times. One had represented Scotland in international meets while two others, so far as I could make out, were regional amateur lightweight and featherweight champs. Another had won all sorts of collegiate matches while an undergraduate and had returned to fight as an emeritus. Opponents had pounded one boxer's face out of definition, his nose having sunken into three small lumps. I wondered why he continued to box, but then I realized that boxing, not physical appearance, furnished him with an identity.

The Edinburgh fighters mauled opponents, reacting in part to the throbbing crowd, swarming and throwing rocky overhead rights and looping lefts while leaving themselves vulnerable to uppercuts and short, direct right hands. Because the Cambridge boxers were generally inexperienced, only a couple withstood the wild charges of their opponents, and Edinburgh bulled through the night, five bouts to two, almost always getting bloodied and bloodying their opponents. The remaining fights were exhibitions, one because two light welterweights weighed in over the weight limit, the others because club fighters participated. Only a couple of boxers rose above the chaos and clung to memory once I left Teviot: a middleweight with a sleepy baby face who looked like he was dozing and would have been more comfortable in a different kind of crib, and a tall lightweight with a beaked nose and arms thinner than bones in birds' wings, a person who on first glance seemed to move awkwardly like a seabird stranded on sand but who was in fact a skilled boxer, fluttering about the ring, always keeping his shorter opponent a feather away from landing a punch.

People often see expectation rather than actuality. Certainly the only fight I recall fit a pattern, one almost literary in structure. A law student represented Edinburgh in the super heavyweight class. He had a short beard and a chest built out of two-by-fours. He was long armed and tall as barn door. His opponent was a club boxer. He was older and shorter. Scars crossed his cheeks and forehead in white seams, and his belly bulged up to his chest, giving him a convex appearance. Here and there flesh sagged off him like hunks of rock slipping a ledge. Before the fight he swung his arms madly and flapped his tongue incessantly. If I had walked into a pub and spotted him shouldering toward the bar, I'd have hustled back out the door. "There is no doubt who is going to win this fight," I said to the man sitting next to me. "The big fellow," the man said, gesturing toward the Edinburgh corner. "No," I said, "he doesn't stand a chance." The fight began as I expected, with the Edinburgh boxer moving around the ring, stinging his opponent with lefts and rights. At the end of the first round, the man next to me said, "You've got this one wrong." "No, I don't," I said, apprehensive because I knew the results. Like me, the law student, no matter his size, was suited more for chair and desk, for curios and legal curiosities, than for the ruinous knockdown of the ring. The referee stopped the fight in the second round. The club boxer suddenly butted through the jabs and with two blows that seemed to rise from the ground itself reduced the student to a bruised codicil.

The next morning after bolting my pills and reading a signature of Smiles, I drifted away from the literary and the athletic back to the comfortably small. I decided to hang plates along one wall of my shop. All the plates were manufactured in the nineteenth century. Circling the edges of the plates were maxims, statements such as "When the old dog barks, pay attention" and "The frog in the well can't tell you much about the ocean." In the bowl of each plate appeared a sketch enforcing the maxim baked onto the lip. Illustrating "If you look only at the clouds, you won't make the journey" was a man, head tilted back, looking up into a dark sky. Beside him dozed a dog, its muzzle resting on clothes spilling from a valise. I knew that I would have to bury some plates out of sight, much as people press untoward memories into closets in hopes of forgetting them. Although museums devoted to African American history pay high prices for the artifacts of slavery and discrimination, I won't display such items. Still, in the bowl of one of my plates appeared a racist cartoon, a black man on his knees, his eyes rolling, watermelons red about him, illustrating the statement, "The honest man does not pray in a melon patch."

After I hung the plates, except for the last, which I stuffed into the drawer of a federal sideboard, I polished a story. The story was insignificant, about the size of the bulldog for sale in Harlequin Antiques. After deciding to expand his nursery, Willie Chalmers realized he needed a partner. Consequently he advertised in the *Courier*, Carthage, Tennessee's weekly newspaper, the notice reading, "Wanted Partner for Nursery Business." Only one person answered the ad, Nannie Bird, who'd twice suffered heartbreak and who would soon molt out of breeding years. Nannie, of course, misunderstood the notice, not realizing that *nursery* referred to plants rather than children. My shop is warm, however, and when I see someone shivering outside the door, I invite him inside. Nannie had endured enough disappointment. In my figurine, love blossomed amid the compost of Nannie's misreading. She and Willie married, and both nursery businesses flourished. Soon they had two children, Mary and John, and a second store, this one in Cookeville. Mary inherited her father's green thumb, and when Willie and Nannie became old, she managed the nursery, opening a third shop and growing three children of her own, Iris, Gardenia, and a rough-and-tumble boy named Privet. John lacked Mary's entrepreneurial ability, but he also did well founding an umbrella lending company that succeeded, defying all odds except those determined by sentiment.

Later that morning I walked to Bruntsfield. After gazing at my Regulator, I looked around the shop. Antique shops distract people from themselves and transform melancholy's black dog into a pet, hardly noticeable in a bed beneath a keyhole desk. In a cabinet sat a red ceramic wheelbarrow. I wondered if the wheelbarrow was kin to Carthage wheelbarrows. Some of these were made in Scotland. Life was hard on immigrant wheelbarrows in Carthage. Mad dogs in particular were dangerous. If a wheelbarrow was bitten by a rabid dog, its owner roped it to the toolshed for three weeks. If at the end of that time the wheelbarrow had not exhibited signs of madness then the owner could untie it and use it safely. To employ a wheelbarrow without knowing whether it had been infected or not was foolhardy. Suddenly, on a path in the garden the wheelbarrow might lose its balance. The wheel might wobble, then crumple. Slats along the sides of the barrow would slip loose, and the cart would tilt, throwing its load to the side and into, say, a pool of water lilies, something that would be unpleasant, particularly if the load were fertilizer, the good natural sort, of course, the kind manufactured by cows and horses.

Tourist

"I'VE SEEN YOU A LOT. Are you a tourist?" the woman behind the container at Bonningtons delicatessen asked. "I am not sure," I said; "I live in the United States, but I'm in Scotland for four and a half months. Is that too long to be a tourist?" "I don't know," the woman answered. At noon I walk from the institute to Bonningtons and purchase either a raisin bun or a croissant, this last usually chocolate but occasionally almond. The woman now greets me by name, saying, "Good morning, Mr. Pickering, how are you?" At two or three other places people also recognize me and nod. I smile and wave. Sometimes I chat. No longer must I rely on a "streetfinder." I know my way around the city, and instead of leading me astray, a wrong turn only spins me back into a right turn.

I feel comfortable and at home; yet I suspect I'm a tourist. At the end of my family's second year in Australia, Eliza adamantly declared that we were not tourists, pointing out that we held "temporary resident" visas, adding she could not be a tourist in a country in which she'd spent an eighth of her life. "Maybe not in Perth," I said, "but when we went to Melbourne and Sydney, I bought guidebooks and maps, and we saw all the major tourist sights." "So what?" Eliza said. "We were traveling. Most people who live in Perth buy maps when they go to Melbourne unless friends take them around. We might not be Australians, but I guarantee that when folks from Perth vacation in Sydney they visit the same museums we visited."

In the 1940s and 1950s, Vicki's grandmother owned and ran an inn outside Yarmouth, Nova Scotia. In 1947 Vicki's parents were married in Yarmouth and bought "Four Winds," a farmhouse in Beaver River. Vicki first went to Nova Scotia in 1953, the year she was born. Since then she has spent practically every summer in Canada. For my part I have spent the better parts of fifteen summers in Beaver River. I think I could drive the twelve miles from Four Winds to Yarmouth blindfolded. We have donated items to the county museum. I recognize employees of shops, restaurants, and grocery stores, no matter their aging, something I cannot do in Willimantic, Connecticut, seven miles from Storrs. Yet every summer people ask if we are tourists. Often the questioners are themselves new to Yarmouth. Last July an American who had moved to Canada seven months earlier lectured us on southwest Nova Scotia. When I interrupted, saying that we knew the area well, she said, "No, you don't. Tourists only think they know a place."

Being asked if she is a tourist irks Vicki, and she replies that we are summer residents, an answer that satisfies her but not me. For a long time I've wondered how to define tourist. If a person visits a different part of his native country, is he a tourist? I grew up in Nashville, Tennessee. I knew only a sliver of the town, West Nashville, the other areas almost distant countries, their inhabitants foreigners. Occasionally I made excursions to South or North Nashville, but I never stayed long enough to learn street names or become familiar with the customs of the tribes who wandered the neighborhoods.

Of course people cannot escape being tourists. Time never ceases conducting us into new countries. People stride through childhood and explore youth. Almost before a person realizes it he has entered old age. Never are we allowed to escape the tour and pay a second visit to a favorite time. Perhaps *sojourner* is a better word than *tourist*. Of course people try to return to countries that sentiment convinces them that they enjoyed. The neglected husband recalls the first decade of marriage, a time when his wife actually cared for him, and he buys candy and flowers in hopes of massaging callused years away. Alumni return to universities. Some even don old college scarves and jackets. No matter how an alumnus tries, however, he does not belong. Soon he realizes that students think him ridiculous. After long absences people visit places where they were born in hopes of discovering reassuring traces of themselves. Inevitably they are disappointed. Instead of evoking memories quick with association, the shards people unearth make them aware of the passage of time, the years sextons burying the past in unmarked graves.

Three decades ago I lived a year in London by myself. I rented a two-room flat off the Finchley Road. I shopped nearby at a Sainsbury grocery, every morning buying bread, cheese, grapes, pâté, and for greens, parsley, of which I ate sheaves. I spent days in the British Library. That year, I thought, as I anticipated months in Scotland, would prepare me for Edinburgh. Despite my having aged, not much would be different. I would simply loop back through an eyelet of time and glimpse a forgotten me.

I grew up thinking much was expected of me. I'm not sure what fostered the expectations or even the nature of the expectations themselves. I was an only child, and perhaps only children create expectations for themselves. In any case I spent my evenings in London, and indeed the evenings of several summers following that year, attending opera, ballet, and theater. Six nights a week I walked from the British Museum to Covent Garden or the Royal Shakespeare. I was Henry James's American. I wanted to grow intellectually. I imagined that exposure to beauty and literacy would shape a more thoughtful and more capable me. Like the American, I tracked what I'd seen and where I had been, on note cards listing things I'd done. I wanted to stamp experience into memory so that over the years I would not slide unconsciously into the slipstream of ordinary prejudice and lodge in the narrows of cultural certitude.

Time eventually led me into another country. I married, and amid the budding of family hankerings for influence and concern for the self wilted. Habit, though, did not vanish. Instead like a toad beneath the dry pan of a desert, habit lay dormant, waiting for the familiar to soak through the ashy soil encasing it, bringing life, enabling it to push time aside and dig upward into the light. As soon as I settled in Edinburgh I unconsciously embraced theatergoing. This time I went not to shape a better me, but simply because in the past I'd haunted the theater when I was in Britain. One Wednesday at the Edinburgh Playhouse I watched *Sleeping Beauty* danced by the Chisinau National Ballet of Moldova. I attended a matinee, a performance for widows and children. Only a handful of men were in the audience, and they had white hair and tottered when they walked. Two rows in front of me a little girl sat beside her mother. Fish and chips had swelled the mother, and life had scraped her skin into sand. The girl was fresh as buttermilk, however, and wore a gold dress that swirled about her like furbelows wrapping a curtain.

Four rows behind me sat three tiny girls, two wearing glasses. All wore red coats, white socks, and shiny Mary Janes. When I saw the children, emotion, not memories of ballets past, swept over me, and I longed to hug a child.

When I was young, appreciation spread through me viscerally. The company danced wonderfully, and watching the ballet raised my spirits, almost transforming the granite winds that slung themselves through Edinburgh's dark closes into zephyrs, poetic and warm, not stingingly cold. Unfortunately, noticing gaps between what is and what ought to be comes more easily to the old than to the young. Impractically, I wanted the commerce that revolved around the ballet to disappear. In the lobby of the playhouse was a candy store, the sweets packaged in bright tutus, Nestlé Munchies red, Polo Clear Ice Blue Mints pale blue, and Rowntrees Fruit Pastilles rainbows of color. Two waterwheels churned ice, the ingredients of Slush Puppies, half the ice incandescently red, the other blue. A stall behind the first circle sold popcorn, "really sweet popcorn," the girl at the counter said. "Golly," I said. The only other time I muttered *golly* was at the beginning of the ballet. One of the hangers-on at the king's court wore saggy tights, the back a grocery sack hanging off the man's buttocks open and ready for filling with, I thought, remembering my last visit to Tesco, paper towels, Jordans Muesli, basmati rice, baked beans, a bar of Palmolive soap, and a cut of Stilton so bitter that after a nibble I tossed it into the garbage. "Did you see those saggy tights?" I said during intermission to the woman sitting beside me. "No," she said, "but I will be on the lookout." When the curtain rose for the next act, several male dancers posed bent over, tights taut, fingering their backsides like gloves. "No saggy tights there," the woman said, turning to me and adding, "though with all these children in the audience perhaps a touch of sagginess wouldn't be out of order."

Only at the conclusion of the ballet did the past float into consciousness. I remembered the last time I saw *Sleeping Beauty*. At the Royal Ballet, Rudolf Nureyev had appeared as the Prince and Margot Fonteyn as the Princess, both dancers now dead. Moreover, the ballet ended with the kiss that awakened the princess. At the playhouse the kiss led to a wedding celebration during which a host of fairy-tale characters thumped across the stage. Puss 'n Boots pursued Miss Puss; the Prince found Cinderella's slipper; the Two Bluebirds fluttered and cooed; and the Wolf chased Little Red Riding Hood, eventually seizing her and eating her. Of course, recollection might have failed. Maybe I simply wanted the ballet to end with the euphoria of a first kiss, that innocent time when love itself is enough and doesn't need the stimulus of entertainment.

The next night I saw *The Gondoliers,* staged by the university's Savoy Opera Group. I timed the walk from my flat to the Church Hill Theatre. The stroll took thirty-eight minutes. After turning west off Minto, I walked almost in a straight line to the theater, along Salisbury, Grange, Beaufort, and Strathearn Road and Place to Greenhill Gardens, then Church Hill to Morningside. Piled above sidewalks were houses thick as rock quarries, their fronts dark, soot and traffic fumes having seeped into the stones. The night was cold, and as I walked I looked into windows, trying to glimpse embers of warmth. Here and there a desk lamp flickered and a shadow staggered, but I saw little else.

While the playhouse had once been a movie palace, the theater had been a church. Refurbishing had transformed the playhouse practically into a seraglio, with red seats, a red and black carpet, and red velvety wallpaper. In front of the stage hung a red curtain, two strips of yellow and three whisks of fringe at the bottom. Red so dominated the theater that it spilled over the gilding adorning the walls and the ceiling, turning the gold feverish. In contrast the Church Hill Theatre was spare and Presbyterian. Although seats in the theater were red, they appeared soiled and seemed drains sucking brightness away. Likewise the walls and ceiling of the old nave were gray and white, ribs spanning them like stays, confining the flesh.

In the past my experience of Gilbert and Sullivan was partly fleshly, for I fell in love with Vicki at a performance of *Iolanthe.* Inexplicably, as she walked across the lobby at intermission, she suddenly changed from a friend and the daughter of one of my old professors into someone with whom I wanted to spend my life. At Church Hill despite a magical performance nothing extraordinary happened. I did not speak to anyone during the evening, though I chatted to myself as I ambled back to the flat, mostly about the comfortable pleasures of Gilbert and Sullivan. The following night I went out again, this time to the Kings Theatre and the Royal Scottish Academy of Music and Drama's production of Verdi's *Falstaff.* Once more I walked. Before I left my flat, the sky collapsed into a damp cave, from the ceiling of which water seeped in metallic drops. I folded my trousers and jacket, wrapped my good shoes in plastic bags, and stuffed everything into my backpack. At the institute I changed clothes and set out for the theater. I sat on the second row. For a while I studied decorations, wondering what the putti were playing on their horns. I counted the boxes, three tiers of three each, all occupied by lights. Before going to the theater I was sure I'd seen *Falstaff* in Vienna in 1963. Memory proved false. To prevent myself from thinking that the past, or at least the past I recollected, was fiction, I scrolled back through the years, eventually convincing myself that I had seen *Aida* and *Don Giovanni* in Vienna. Again I did not talk to anyone in the theater. During intermission when I mentioned one or two things to the man sitting on my left, he nodded. Never, however, did he address a remark to me or stretch his response from a fragment into a sentence.

The three outings purged the old pattern from my system. No more would I board the present in hopes of sailing into the past. I hurried home after *Falstaff* and ate a can of sardines. In Edinburgh I am both tourist and sojourner. I eat tourist meals, skimpy because I am simultaneously going somewhere and nowhere. I paid a pound for lunch on Saturday, buying a bacon roll from a stand on Rose Street. For dinner two nights ago I ate a can of Tesco's black-eyed beans, two pakoras, an end of brown bread, and seventy grams of cambozola, a soft German cheese, the last three items bought at Peckham's delicatessen. I drank a pot of Assam tea and for dessert gobbled a handful of sultanas. Tonight I will dump a can of baked beans atop instant rice, this last a serving for two. In the five weeks I have been in Edinburgh, I have not eaten fresh vegetables.

Home appoints identity. Away from home a person loses his individuality and, becoming a tourist, assumes a platitudinous identity, one that enables others to classify him and thus deal with him mechanically. Although the phrase "another tourist" labels a person, it also frees him from the burden of introduction and camaraderie. The tourist meets other people, but as he is soon forgotten so he forgets them. Almost all his relationships are fleeting. Most are commercial and clean, based upon money, not emotion or some bruisingly vague commitment. Friendships are impossible, being raised, as Cicero put it, on a "community of views on all matters human and divine, together with good will and affection."

"A man may usually be known by the books he reads, as well as by the company he keeps," Samuel Smiles wrote in *Character,* "for there is a companionship of books as well as of men; and one should always live in the best company, whether it be of books or of men." For the tourist keeping company with books is easier than with men. When I first arrived in Edinburgh, most of my bookish associates were disreputable, and I prowled mornings in the company of detectives and roustabouts. Consequently I determined to better my literary acquaintance, and I spent several evenings reading a selection of Cicero's essays and two volumes of sermons by Isaac Barrow, the seventeenth-century Anglican divine. Unfortunately keeping high literary company is difficult, perhaps impossible, amid letter and electronic mail. No matter the rigor of my efforts to shake the shackles of home, home ran me to ground. Readers of my books wrote me. In their letters they described doings of my characters, invariably low antics that I had overlooked.

For three weeks, aside from a note or two from Vicki, I received little mail in Edinburgh. In the fourth week correspondence filled my box at the institute. "I'll wager you are lonely over there," a man wrote from Georgia, "so I thought you'd like to hear about Proverbs Goforth's cousin Buckie Tallowick." Buckie lived near Steeple Bell, a small town in the hills above Carthage. The diet of people in Steeple Bell was so poor that everybody suffered from goiters. One day when Buckie was sitting on the porch shelling peas with his mother, Slota, a salesman hawking Bibles walked up the road. The man lived in Nashville and did not have a goiter. "Mammy, look," Buckie said, pointing at the salesman, "that man ain't got no goiter." "Hush, son," Slota whispered. "I thought I'd raised you to be polite. Well-bred folks don't call attention to deformities. People will think you are laughing at them, and that's hurtful. Tonight when you say your prayers, just thank the Lord for giving you all your body parts."

A second correspondent related that one morning when Hoben Donkin was lounging on a bench near the courthouse sunning himself a talking pigeon landed on the ground near his feet. The pigeon was polite, and after saying good morning, he and Hoben spent fifteen minutes chatting, discussing roosts, rat snakes, the price of eggs, and "even literary matters, particularly the phrase 'a feather in one's cap.'" Conversation ran so easily that Hoben invited the pigeon to his house for lunch. The pigeon accepted, and Hoben hurried home and asked his wife, Darlene, to "whip up a crumb sandwich." "Talking pigeon!" Darlene exclaimed, scowling and muttering, "Drunk again before noon." Still, she made two sandwiches, using leftovers she had saved for bread pudding. Unhappily for Hoben, though, by three o'clock the pigeon had not appeared, so angering Darlene that she stormed out the house, saying she had enough of Hoben's antics and was going to Maggart to visit her mother. Shortly after Darlene left, the pigeon pecked the front doorbell. "Sorry I'm late," he said when Hoben opened the door, "but the weather was so lovely I walked."

In a sermon entitled "Against Foolish Talking and Jesting," Barrow called "true festivity" salt, saying it gave "a smart but savoury relish to discourse." Such festivity did not initiate disgust or create sores but instead excited appetite and occasionally cleansed. On the other hand, Barrow declared that jesting that gave "a haut-gout to putrid and poisonous stuff, gratifying distempered palates and corrupt stomachs," was "indeed odious and despicable folly." In his remarks Barrow was preaching more against destructive scoffing than against the smutty or the untoward. Alas, I think the smutty medicinal, a tonic good for unknitting brows or loosening muscles cramped from traipsing about. Readers know my pharmaceutical tastes. "Poor Celestial Tolliver was not bright," a woman wrote. Rarely did she talk, even when her mother invited eligible bachelors for meals. Her mother worried that Celestial would not marry, and one Sunday when she invited a farmer from Maggart to lunch and Celestial was silent, her mother kicked her on the ankle. Immediately, Celestial turned to the young man and asked, "Where do you come from?" The question pleased the man, and he smiled and said, "Over to Horseshoe Bend. I got a milking herd of a fifty Jerseys." For twenty minutes conversation lagged then Celestial's mother whacked her on the ankle again. Again Celestial sat straight and spoke, asking, "Did you see that big pile of shit in the garden?" "Yes, yes, I did," the man replied, swallowing a mound of sweetbreads. "Lord-a mercy, it was big." Celestial was now in a conversational mood, and ten minutes later, just as the man bit into a slab of pecan pie, she spoke without being prompted. "I'm might glad you seen it," she said, "because I done it all by myself."

The tourist is not free to wander. Guidebooks determine the course of his days. Friends expect him to visit celebrated sites. On his return home, they will quiz him. If he has neglected a major attraction, they will shake their heads or, pausing and glancing about knowingly, will make him feel guilty or inadequate. Until my fourth week in Edinburgh, I was more sojourner than tourist. I hadn't gone to the city's most famous places, Edinburgh Castle and the Palace of Holyroodhouse. I was saving them for March or April in hopes that either Vicki or Eliza would visit. Alas, Eliza met Travis, whose company she preferred to mine, and in answer to my invitation, Vicki wrote back declining, saying that hell could freeze and heaven could burn before she wore herself out flying to Scotland for a week.

In a sermon on contentment, Barrow wrote "that we should curb our desires, and confine them in the narrowest bounds we can." Every man's castle is ultimately the grave. Most graves are narrow, and few occupants spend eternity fretting about being tourists, their traveling days, as Celestial Tolliver might put it, "shot all to shit." For me graveyards are calming, happy places, and I decided to begin my exploration of Edinburgh's attractions in Calton Burial Ground. Grass in the burial ground was thick as peat and soft as carpet slippers, just the surface on which to rest one's feet before trudging roads bumpy with setts. On a rise in the burial ground stood a memorial to Scots killed in the American Civil War, fighting as soldiers in, among others, the First Michigan Calvary, the Sixty-fifth Regiment of the Illinois Volunteer Infantry, the Second Illinois Regiment of Artillery, the Fifth Regiment of Maine Infantry Volunteers, and the Fifty-seventh Regiment of New York Infantry Volunteers. Atop the memorial on a marble pedestal towered Abraham Lincoln, in his right hand the Emancipation Proclamation, his left behind his back pressing into his spine, holding him firm and upright. At his feet crouched a slave, his eyes gazing upward at Lincoln, his right hand raised in supplication, the palm open and imploring. Carved into the marble were four words, one word to a side: *Suffrage, Emancipation, Education,* and *Union.* The memorial was unveiled in 1893 and was, I read later, the first statue erected in Lincoln's honor outside the United States.

I spent most of an afternoon in the burial ground, so much time that necessity forced me to freshen the soil inside a mausoleum erected in 1823 to house the remains of Alexander Henderson of Warriston. The roof of the mausoleum had collapsed and vanished, and great masses of ivy hung over the wall, thick and dark as witch's broom. Outside the tomb a dandelion bloomed in a crack, its purchase fragile and delicate, the only flower I saw in the graveyard. Soot had gnawed into tombstones, and inscriptions were bleak, not looking forward to "the light" but back to days wracked by darkness. In 1866 a group of citizens re-erected the stone above the grave of "Mr. Woods," a friend of Robert Burns who from 1772 until 1806 "was the favourite and leading actor, on the Edinburgh stage." Carved into the stone are Shakespeare's famous lines "Life's but a walking shadow—a poor player / That struts and frets his hour upon the stage, / And then is heard no more."

Some few people walked through the graveyard, but I did not speak to them. A single man is suspect, and I did not want anyone to assume I was trolling for affection when, if I had spoken, all I wanted to hook was an interesting remark. Graveyards are dumping grounds not simply for rancid flesh but also for the skeletal remains of Christmas trees and "dead soldiers," not the kind who fought in wars but bottles once brimming with cheap wine, among alcoholics the two most popular brands being Buckfast Tonic Wine and Lambrini Slightly Sparkling Perry, this last in big bottles containing 750 milliliters. I jot down such small things because they constitute not simply the texture of place but also of life itself. How nice of Plutarch, whom I had read in accordance with Smiles's urging, to relate that the first Artaxerxes, the Persian king, was familiarly known as long handed because his right hand was longer than his left or that the skin of Alexander the Great was so fragrant that it perfumed his undergarments.

After leaving the cemetery I wandered Calton. Eventually, though, I turned back toward the university and climbed High Street. I stopped at St. Giles Cathedral. I told a docent that the burial ground was cold. "I hope I don't come down with a chill," I said. "That could lead to a coffin fit." "Oh," he said, then told me that John Knox was buried behind the church. "He is under a parking lot now. Guidebooks say that he lies beneath space 44, but recently the lot has been repainted, and he is under 23. On most days a BMW parks above him." When I left the church, I walked to the parking lot. The space above Knox was empty. I have since returned to the parking lot twice, both times finding the space vacant.

I was in a happy underground mood. The next morning at ten I walked back to High Street and toured Mary King's Close, an alley off of which opened a series of houses and shops, all having been buried during the building of the City Chambers, the last shop closing at the beginning of the twentieth century. Nobody else signed up for the tour, so I spent an hour wandering a neighborhood that eventually sank into a forgotten basement, some of the dwellings and the tales attached to them dating from the sixteenth century. Although crowds had milled through the centuries, leaving behind beams, fireplaces, windows, stairs, and stenciling, the underground was empty. A guide tried to populate the dwellings with ghost stories and wraithlike history, but I prefer basements cluttered with the concrete detritus of living: chairs stacked like kindling, rugs rolled into firewood, toy dump trucks rusting under a sofa, the fragrance of dead mice, and disappearing through a hole in the foundation, the tail of a snake. Moreover, the very presence of the guide inhibited mental wandering. Instead of reacting to place, I reacted to him and was unable to escape the conventions of conversation.

Earlier in the week I received a letter from a librarian in Kentucky. The man is a rummager. For six years he has sent me poems spaded out of forgotten periodicals. "Thought you might like this one," he wrote. "It's entitled 'On a Roman Nose.'" In the Cowshed I drifted away from Mary King's Close and began to repeat the poem silently, leaving my body behind as corporeal ghost, something solid to reassure the guide that I had not slipped his lead. The poem began weakly with a reference to taking snuff. "Knows he, who never took a pinch, / Nosey! The pleasures thence which flows? / Knows he the titillating joys / Which my nose knows?" The second stanza was stronger, indeed more poetic. "Oh, Nose! I am as proud of thee; / As any mountain of its snows; / I gaze on thee, and feel that joy— / A Roman Knows!" Alas, mind over or apart from body is but a philosophic conceit. In the middle of the guide's account of the Plague House, I snorted, then cackled with laughter.

The next morning I walked to Edinburgh Castle. The Royal Mile resembles a spiny torso, closes and roads curving down from it in ribs. At the west end of the mile, Castle Rock swells like the upper body of a man lying on his side, his head lopped off. Atop the rock is the castle, from a distance looking like a socket from which an arm has been wrung, ligaments and hunks of bone jutting up twisted and foreboding. Although the castle sinks deep into the rock, in the mind it teeters over Edinburgh, its presence a reminder of the fragility of beauty and decency. The castle is a modern-day visual Sermon on the Mount, an emblem of the night that festers in all humans. To live under its shadow is not simply to live beyond innocence in historical awareness but also to live within sight of man's demonic glorification of his own fallen nature.

One's perspective changes as one walks through the gatehouse. Suddenly the rock becomes a jaw prognathous without a palate above it. Buildings and walls are transformed into teeth, caps rising, cavities sinking into doorways, root canals winding out of sight, forewalls amalgams. Cannons appear dark and unflossed, the half-moon battery rolling like a tongue, plaque green and yellow between overbites of stone, gold dabbed here and there, and for tourists, false teeth newly buckled into place. Overcast days stain the stones brown and gray. In the sun colors appear, blues and reds, hints of yellow and pink, and imagination seduces one into awe and uncritical appreciation. Families stand behind walls and, staring out over Edinburgh, point to landmarks. At one o'clock a gun is fired, after which people laugh nervously and talk loudly.

My favorite building on the rock was St. Margaret's Chapel, constructed in the twelfth century. The chapel was small and from below in the Middle Ward looked like a shoe box, one that once contained a child's dancing slippers. The chapel was plain and modestly decorated and offers respite from the braggadocio strident across the rest of the rock. At the castle I roamed the National War Museum of Scotland. Initially I behaved as I usually did and noticed small things: an apron belonging to a sergeant-major who belonged to the Independent Order of Rechabites at the end of the nineteenth century. The Rechabites abstained from drink. Stamped on the bottom of the apron was the phrase "Peace and Plenty the Reward of Temperance." Above the words stood two female figures: on the left Peace, an angel; on the right Plenty. Between the figures rose a small pyramid-like structure. Atop it sat a beehive; to the left of the hive stood a rick of grain; to the right, a sheaf of wheat. In front of the pyramid appeared a crock, maybe a butter crock. On the lid of crock rested a lamb. Decorating the front of the crock was an eye, vaguely Masonic in appearance. A larger version of the eye appeared above the beehive. I studied the eye carefully, concluding that the eyebrow curving above it was brown. In a nearby case sat Bob, a dog. Bob died 145 years ago. He was small and appeared to have a touch of beagle in him. He had been the pet of the First Battalion, Scots Fusilier Guards, and during the Crimean War distinguished himself by chasing cannonballs. Scots sentimentalize death and dogs. Midway between the Middle Ward and Upper Ward, near the Lang Stairs, was a dog cemetery. Twenty-three stones stood upright, other stones lying flat between them, primroses blooming yellow around them.

The museum was beautifully appointed. Fans of muskets spread like peacock's feathers, their bayonets so silver they manufactured light. Dirks gleamed like commemorative spikes. Swords curved and shone like the nail edges of sunsets. Constellations of medals glimmered, ribbons hanging beneath them like the tails of comets. Silver cups and tea services sat untarnished. Uniforms stood at attention, pressed into review. Like medallions hung around the necks of whiskey bottles, shoulder plates glittered intoxicatingly. Buckles gleamed. Sporrans bristled full furred. Bagpipes played stirring martial music, and feathers burst exuberantly from bonnets and caps. Pistols were spotless and looked like toys as harmless as the engines that pulled Lionel trains in the 1950s. Stern but wise and kindly men stared from portraits. In Robert Gibb's painting, the "Thin Red Line" stopped the Russian cavalry at Balaclava. The truth was that riflemen halted the Russians. Still, the painting was bright and inspirational. Uniforms were red and green. Smoke rose from the battlefield in pastel puffs, belying the resolution on the faces of the Scottish soldiers. Of course, the museum so distorted war that it was itself a lie. "What's missing," I told an official, "is truth: cases of bones, shelves of skulls, broken hearts and families, agony, and weeping." "If childhood experience shapes adults," I said, "children should not be allowed to come here. The museum glorifies war, making it so colorful and appealing that kids will grow up wanting to fight, and die." "Well," Vicki responded when I described my remarks, "you've done it now. You've thrown a paragraph against the castle. The whole edifice will probably collapse. After the castle, who knows? Maybe society itself."

I wasn't behaving like a good tourist. Tourists are usually in such a hurry that they stride mechanically through attractions, moving too quickly to ponder and often being too tired to disbelieve, glitter and presentation satisfying them. Still, I am not sure why I reacted critically to the museum. Perhaps the swell of thoughtless patriotism that plagues the United States affected me. I winced when I read newspaper accounts describing the deaths of young soldiers in Iraq. Invariably the reports praise the dead, calling them heroes, no matter that the soldiers did not control their fates but had been unlucky, riding in the wrong trucks at the wrong time. Perhaps, though, the spit and polish of the museum repelled me. My favorite poet is William Wordsworth, the English romantic who wrote that we half-create the world about us. The museum was so well shaped that it stifled imagination. I was more comfortable and happier alone amid the silent ruins of the Abbey Church at Holyrood. There I could winkle through the tracery of the East Window and imagine stars flashing golden across the heavens, not shells exploding into shrapnel; the air not choking with chlorine but wheaty like a meadow; daffodils, not bayonets, sprouting beside a hedgerow.

I tried to shake the mood that dogged me though the castle, but no matter my steps, melancholy rose into buboes. I wondered how many prisoners had died in the castle's cold vaults. I marveled at the hammer-beam roof in the Great Hall, the beams sliding through each other like fingers of hands clasped in prayer. The trappings on the walls of the hall, alas, were not ecclesiastical but military, smacking of the Old Testament and not the New, spear beside spear, suits of armor, long and short swords, and beside the door, looking like a clock, a wheel of pistols, imprisoning people in brutal time. From the hall I walked to the Scottish National War Memorial, opened in 1927 to commemorate Scots who died in the First World War. I almost skipped the memorial. Decades ago I read the famous poetry and prose of the war: among a battalion of others, works by David Jones, Wilfred Owen, Siegfried Sassoon, Robert Graves, and Edmund Blunden. War memorials are reverent and almost always genuflect before horror. Like the ancient Egyptians binding mummies and hiding the ravages of decay, memorials wrap high words around the unspeakable—words like *duty, honor, sacrifice, holy, god and country, courage,* words that create fogs as thick as glaucoma.

The memorial itself seemed Teutonic, cut sharp into pillars and angles. On stone platforms beneath the names of regiments sat folios bound in red leather, their pages gluttonous with the names of the dead. Visitors shuffled and whispered. I longed to hear someone moan or shout "No" or "Dear God," anything to startle realization. Carved around the names of regiments were places in which they fought: Marne, Somme, Ypres, Aras, Delville Wood, Cambrai, and Palestine, Mesopotamia, Gallipoli, Flanders, Loos, Beaumont Hamel, and the Hindenburg Line. Although I didn't want the names to scan and thus slip hypnotically into mind, the places read like poetry. I hurried from the Hall of Honour into the shrine. On a dais sat a steel casket containing a roll listing the names of all the Scots who died in the war. Hanging from the ceiling above the dais was a statue of Michael the avenging archangel. Would not a statue of Jesus have been better—Jesus on his knees, not praying for those who died but begging forgiveness for those who sent the dead to their deaths, Jesus weeping and saying, "Forgive them, Lord, for they knew not what they did"? Wrapping the walls around the dais were bronze friezes depicting a death march of people butchered in the war: sailors in slickers, nurses, airmen, infantrymen in sundry dress, in shorts, in snowshoes, or wearing gas masks. Soldiers played bagpipes and swung swagger sticks. They carried bombs, binoculars, revolvers, coils of rope, pickaxes, shovels, and wrenches. In one part of the frieze appeared the front of a biplane; in another part a horse and the nose of a camel; in another a mule. Just the thing, I thought, to appeal to children used to hunting animals hidden in cartoons: here a rabbit; upside down in the lower right corner a fox; a butterfly near the left margin; a dog, his tail raised after sniffing the air; hiding from him behind brambles of lines a tabby cat. "No," I said aloud and left the memorial and the castle.

Isaac Barrow got things wrong when he urged readers to keep their minds intent upon higher callings. At least he was wrong if by higher callings he meant matters like duty and courage, as defined by the lords of this world. Far healthier for the self and one's neighbors to live in Celestial Tolliver's garden, in which the fertilizer is human rather than abstract and ultimately inhumane. After I left the castle, I walked back to my flat. A letter awaited me. "The enclosed is a bawdy old tale, loose around the hem but alive and inviting," a friend wrote. "Trips abroad can dislocate, and I send the story as contraceptive in hopes of preventing high seriousness from infecting you. Never forget that buttermilk smells like butter."

An older brother, so the tale goes, arranged a marriage for his younger sibling. The boy was remarkably innocent. He knew nothing about fleshly cavortings, and after marriage, he treated his wife as if she were his sister. The wife was full blooded and, not surprisingly, felt deprived and complained to the older brother. "I will instruct your husband," the brother said. Unfortunately the instruction didn't take, the boy becoming horrified and saying he could not do such a thing to his bride, particularly after she cooked and washed and took "such good care of me and the house." Once more the wife complained to her husband's brother. "Tomorrow morning," he told her, "don't get up. Don't clean or cook. Stay in bed and pretend to be dying." The wife did as she was told, saying she had the flu, tossing and moaning, warning her husband that if she did not feel better by the next day he had better start her coffin. Immediately the husband ran to his brother and asked if he knew how to cure the flu. "There's only one medicine and only one way to give it to your wife if you want her to live," the brother said before repeating his earlier instructions. "If you love your bride, go home immediately and set about curing her." The younger brother raced away and followed the instructions so well that by noon his wife felt good enough to eat lunch. That afternoon she even got out of bed and, putting on her housedress, began cleaning the kitchen, singing all the while. The next day the older brother asked his sibling if the cure had worked. "Oh, that medicine was just wonderful, a real miracle drug," the boy exclaimed. "But why," he continued, thought furrowing his brow, "but why didn't you tell me about it when pappy was ill? If you had, I could have cured him, too."

The story was a cure-all, purging the castle from mind. I brewed a pot of tea, opened a can of Tesco's butter beans, snapped the end off a baguette, chopped the nose off a slab of cheddar, and stretching out in the sitting room, began reading *Nicholas Nickleby*, this for the fifth time. The next morning I woke up refreshed and after breakfast set off for Holyroodhouse, glad to be alive, spring in my steps. Holyroodhouse lay sunken at the east end of the Royal Mile, resembling not so much a foot loose at the base of a long body but a stool, the top not crushed under heel but rising puffed, covered with needlepoint. Included in the admission was an "audio," a small tape recorder that one held, earplugs connected to it by a black wire. "Are the plugs clean?" I asked when a guide handed me the tape. "Ear lice are worse than chiggers. A friend of mind suffered so badly from an infestation that he poured petrol down his ears, reducing his auricles to ash and even singeing his Adam's apple." "Oh, yes," a warder replied, pulling two aerosol cans, one yellow, the other green, from under the counter, "we spray the plugs with disinfectant as soon as we receive them back."

A part of Holyrood dated from the sixteenth century, and although turmoil stalked Scotland until the aftermath of Culloden in the middle of the eighteenth century, even blooding Holyrood itself, I didn't react to the palace as I did the castle, imagining the First World War a mill, grinding humans to chaff. The palace did not lour darkly. The central entrance didn't push one into a narrow vault but instead opened into the great Quadrangle. Built in the seventeenth century, the Quadrangle seemed an emblem illustrating that not only could order and beauty endure chaos but also that they could stay confusion. Brooks of silver light flowed from the buildings, eddying and pooling as I turned my head. I stood a long time in the Quadrangle. I didn't want to leave. I counted window panes, eighteen to a window. I studied the decorative columns, Ionic, Doric, and Corinthian, carved into the walls, halfheartedly trying to decide which I liked best.

Despite iconic portraits that invited readings and the "informative" chatter of the audio, I drifted from history to appreciation then into covetousness, this last a healthier, kinder, and more neighborly passion than patriotism. Above the Great Stair flowers blossomed across the ceiling in lush, creamy circles, making me long to seed my own barren ceilings, if only with weeds. Across the Royal Dining Room stretched a mahogany five-pedestal table probably dating from the Regency. At home in our dining room in Storrs sits a similar table, resting on two pedestals, however, not five. In the fireplace sat a cast-iron and steel fire grate. "What a present that would make for me," I thought. Later I paced the Great Gallery thinking how I'd enjoy eating dinner there. "Of course," I whispered to myself, "I didn't bring fancy dress to Scotland." "I didn't know I would be dining out so often and so well," I said, then stopped and laughed so loudly that the guard looked at me and smiled. I hurried away from the castle. In contrast I lingered outside Holyrood. I wanted to cart something bright away with me and in the gift shop looked at bone china. Prices were high, and so I decided to put off buying, in case, I thought, I had to purchase formal dinner dress. I wondered if I could dine at the palace in a kilt, the McClarin plaid, my great-grandmother being a McClarin from Ulster.

After leaving Holyrood, I meandered up the Royal Mile. On St. Mary's near High Street was a knickknack shop. I'd seen my tourist sight for the day, so I entered the shop and looked around, examining two or three plates that were almost Worcester. "Are you in town for the match with Ireland?" the proprietor asked, referring to a rugby international. "No," I said, "I'm just a tourist, rather a former tourist." "What do you mean by former tourist?" the proprietor asked. "That's hard to explain," I said. "Maybe a story will clear things up." The story, I said, took place at the Tabernacle of Love, a church in Carthage, Tennessee, owned by the Reverend Slubey Garts. Early one Sunday morning before church began, a countryman knocked on Slubey's door. He was visiting Carthage from Steeple Bell, Tennessee, and although he was illiterate, he wanted to sing in the choir that morning. "That's mighty fine," Slubey said, "but before I let you join the choir, even as a visitor, I've got to hear you sing." "O sheep of god which taketh away the sins of the world," the man began. "Wait, you've got that wrong," Slubey interrupted. "The word is *lamb*, not *sheep*." "About this time last year I attended church and heard the choir singing about that lamb of god," the man said, looking exasperated. "Now, Reverend, I don't know where you come from but up in the hills where I was raised unless a lamb gets cooked or stole it generally turns into a sheep after a year." "What?" the shop owner said. "I've got to move along. I'm hungry and need to buy something for lunch," I said, stepping toward the door, "maybe a raisin bun or a chocolate croissant, one of the two."

Anchorite

"HAVE YOU BECOME AN ANCHORITE?" my friend Josh wrote after I said
I didn't plan to leave Edinburgh. Anchorites were Christian hermits. In
the fourth century they settled in the deserts of Egypt and Syria. By retir-
ing from society they hoped to mortify the devil and control temptations
of flesh and the world. Anchorites usually lived in caves dug into ridges.
For my part I live in a basement flat under a blocky stone house. The
front windows in the sitting room are at ground level. Because the windows are just beneath the ceiling, I have to lean back and look up in
order to see through them. A hedge of bars rises immediately in front of
them. Nevertheless, on cheery mornings the windows seem skylights. To
reach the flat, I walk to the right of the house and unlock an iron gate,
eight feet tall and topped by a stone arch. Once through the gate I step
down nine stairs. On my right is a tall, dark wall. Unlike other windows
in the flat, my kitchen window faces the wall, providing an austere view,
a sight that might appeal to someone wrestling a fleshly imagination.

At the bottom of the steps I take four paces forward then swivel to the
left and unlock my door. I push the door open, step up, and enter the flat.
The flat is shaped like the letter T and is furnished well beyond the needs
of an anchorite. The door opens at the base of the T. Ahead stretches the
vertical leg of the letter, a narrow hall seven paces long. Oriental rugs
cover the floor, making the hall slightly eastern. Two-thirds of the way
down the hall on the left stands a spidery Victorian coatrack, its arms
curving upward in hooks, an obstacle I lean to the right to avoid. On the

right side of the hall are two doors, one opening into a small bathroom, the other into a tiled shower. To reach the shower I climb two steps and enter a cabinet, the walls of the room forming two sides of the cabinet, glass panes the other two. The cabinet is small, and if I drop my soap while bathing I cannot lean over to retrieve it. Instead I squat down, bending at the knees.

The vertical leg runs into the horizontal crosspiece, another hall eight paces long. At the right end of the hall is my bedroom, a large room five by seven paces. On the right side of the room are two tall windows, a shutter of iron bars separating the room from a garden behind the house. On the left side of the bedroom is an open room the size of a pantry. Closets line two walls; on the third is a sink, a mirror above and a tiled top cradling it. Here I keep toothbrush and paste, hairbrush, razor, and shaving cream. Because the lavatory is thirteen steps away, the sink is useful in the middle of the night. At the end opposite from my bedroom, the hall opens into a small washing room that contains buckets, mops, brooms, and the meter for the electricity. The meter takes pound coins. I don't use much electricity and insert a coin every two or so days. To the left at the end of the hall is the kitchen, well appointed with pots, pans, plates, refrigerator, a microwave that I am afraid to use, stove, and washer and dryer. On the right at the end of the hall is my sitting room, broad and comfortable with three tables, pine chairs, bookcases, built-in shelves, a leather chair shaped like the palm of a hand and in which I haven't sat, lights, a couch on which I lounge to read and think, and across the room a small television.

Although a burrow, my cell is luxurious and in the mind of an anchorite would probably stir longings for society. On the other hand, I live simply. I have two pairs of walking shoes, one German and reddish looking like bowling shoes, the other made by Dexter and bought at an outlet in Ellsworth, Maine, nine years ago. I alternate the shoes, wearing the red ones one day, the Dexters the next. For trousers I don corduroys and permanent-press khakis from Sears. I wear long-sleeved cotton shirts and thick gray athletic socks with green stripes around the tops. Once every eleven days, I toss socks, shirts, and the permanent-press trousers into the washing machine. I keep the temperature low so the shirts don't shrink. Although cleaning wrinkles them, I don't iron them. I simply wear them under a sweater. I wash my underwear in the shower, and as suds run off my body I knead the underpants with my feet. At the end of the shower I grapple the underpants up with my toes, saving me from squatting. I wring the water out of the underpants then hang them on the radiator in my bedroom to dry, something that takes less than an hour. In fact I often hang socks and shirts on the radiator as the dryer never quite spins damp away. When I walk to the institute I wear a summer-weight jacket atop a sweater and shirt, no matter how chilly or blustery the day. Vicki packed a heavy coat for me. I don't wear it often because cold keeps me alert and makes me hop along. The thick coat keeps me too warm. I become dozy and, walking unconsciously, don't notice my surroundings.

I enjoy preparing food, watching butter sink into a slice of whole wheat toast pebbly with sunflower and pumpkins seeds or peeling a mandarin, removing the peel without breaking it into pieces so that if I set it on sheet of paper it looks like a bud spreading into bloom. Insofar as food itself is concerned, I am bit anchoritish, last night dining on sardines, stale bread, Morbier cheese, and four green olives stuffed with pimentos. Sometimes the edible seduces me into intemperance, however. Last Wednesday at Tesco I paid £1.38 for a Genoa cake, a bar of fruit cake thick with sultanas, cherries, and "mixed peels." With every meal I drink tea, though sometimes I start with orange juice. Never do I have wine or beer. So far I haven't entered a pub. In hopes of escaping the reciprocity of conversation, I eschew conviviality. Like a teetotaler, I have pledged myself to avoid questions I've answered scores of times. Of course I have to answer some questions.

Two days ago an intern at a quarterly sent me a questionnaire. The intern was young, and she asked questions interesting only to children not weaned from school. I filled in the questionnaire, at least where possible. Although being a hermit may make one brutish, it also teaches patience. Among other things, the girl wanted to know my nickname, my hobbies, my favorite authors, and if I retreated to a sanctuary "in order to create." Under the category of favorite foods I listed the meal I ate the night before: red beans, brown bread, cheddar cheese, two stuffed olives, and a pot of tea, Assam, not my usual English breakfast. The concept of a young anchorite is, by the by, a philosophic oxymoron. Life spreads so broadly before the young that life in a cave seems unnatural. In contrast, time ultimately transforms even the liveliest people into anchorites, forcing them to restrict and focus. In Edinburgh I generally talk only to people of a certain age, adults in whose presence conversation flows as leisurely as memory instead of tumbling idiosyncratically along a stream of consciousness. Indeed, before chatting with a man, I look for a hearing aid, generally a sign not only that conversation will amble sensibly but also that the man has lived.

As crooks on the lam hole up in out-of-the-way places, so, shut away at nights in my flat, I think myself larcenous, stealing time for my pleasure. Paring back frees me to wax curious. As a result I have learned a little about many things. Last week a man asked me if I were an horologist. The question was a compliment, declarative in intention if not in structure. Alone, I enjoy the silence of my company. The man standing on a bare hill can laugh as long and as loudly as he pleases, and so I chuckle oblivious to others. In my cave I shed the fetters of opinion, indeed the expectation of having opinions.

I roam the university library. I check out books only because I notice them. Stacked on my bedside table are books by John Buchan, Tobias Wolff, Russell Hoban, and Patrick White. Instead of matters urged upon me by newspapers or acquaintances, I ponder what comes to mind. Thirty years ago I read a biography of Kenneth Grahame, author of *The Wind in the Willows*. To the woman he eventually married, Grahame wrote letters in baby talk. Grahame's biographer speculated that courtships raised on baby talk probably did not lead to unions strong enough to endure the abrasive domesticity of married life. "Why not?" I thought twelve days ago at three in the morning. "Almost anything can be a good or a bad basis for marriage." "I suppose," I said, opening the refrigerator and taking out a mandarin, "the biographer thinks sexual congress a solid foundation for marriage."

I ate the mandarin and slept two more hours. At breakfast I pondered the cuneiform of the past, trying to decipher something that occurred fifty-five years ago. I was eight years old and spending the summer on my grandfather's farm. One afternoon my friend Johnny discovered a snake under a cattle trough in the side pasture. Johnny said the snake was a copperhead, and so he, his brother Donald, and I grabbed sticks and poked it. When the snake tried to dig deeper beneath the trough, the poking turned vicious. Eventually we killed the snake, discovering that it wasn't a copperhead but a hog-nosed snake. For years I have regretted the killing. Like all people, I have misbehaved. Thankfully, though, I don't remember the past clearly, and what I do remember often seems more fictional than true. Yet killing the snake remains vivid, and rarely does a month pass without my thinking about that day in the pasture.

Hermits are free to sit at the mouths of their caves, drawing circles in the sand, be the sand real or imaginary. Supposedly Theon the Anchorite left his cell at night and as a type of St. Francis supplied animals with water. In the morning the tracks of antelopes, gazelles, and wild asses formed arabesques in front of his cave. I roam during the day, not drinking or eating much but seeing sights that refresh me. I always walk, some days for six or eight hours. Not since arriving have I ridden in a vehicle. Often I beat steps into a path, returning to places I have been before, an impossibility were I not alone. With a family a person maps days in which landmarks follow one after another in a distinct series. Last week I returned to the National Portrait Gallery. I looked only at a few portraits then hurried away. If I'd had companions, they would have thought me selfish. I stood by myself and studied Legros's Thomas Carlyle, the old man sinking into a chair, a greatcoat shrinking over him, pressing him down like age. Richmond's Andrew Lang slung himself over a chair, an arm over the back, looking intellectually and seductively bohemian. James Hogg was sixty when Gordon painted him. Yet despite a cane slumping between his legs and a blanket over his left shoulder, Hogg looked like a comparatively youthful rambler. I visited the gallery, however, to look at Henry Raeburn's portrait of James Hutton, known as the founder of modern geology. Hutton sat in a straight-backed chair, legs crossed and hands together, fingers interlaced, his left arm latched around the top spool of the chair, locking him in place like riprap. His clothes were of a piece, trousers, vest, and jacket all earthy brown. Stacked atop a table to his left were manuscripts and an assortment of fossils, among them a single scallop shell. His face was extraordinary, his forehead broad, chin tapering into a spade. His nose was long and straight and so sharp it smacked of an awl.

Life is a tangled skein. Paradoxically only the anchorite who has disengaged himself from much of life has the leisure to toy with knots and enjoy their unraveling. The person responsible for others must simply snip knots, patch holes, and stitch rapidly on. One morning I drifted into the City Art Centre on Market Street. Canvases on the first floor looked like wooden pallets, colored rectangles piled atop them, turning the gallery into a warehouse of broken boxes. On the third floor were cases exhibiting crafts. To the midvein of a leaf of opaque black glass shaped like a hosta clung a pool of milk glass. "I hope that's supposed to be dew," I muttered. "It isn't," a woman said. "Oh, dear," I said and retreated to the fourth level. At one end of a long room three televisions sat on the floor, each with a twenty-four-inch screen. The sets were on. They showed a man wearing a gray T-shirt sitting behind a table in a studio. Although long-distance shots occasionally appeared on the set on the right, the man's head was rarely visible, the other two screens cutting off his face at the bridge of his nose.

I studied the portion of his face that did appear. On the left side of the man's neck about an inch from the ridge of his Adam's apple was a dark mole. The man's ears were streamlined and lacked lobes. His nose twisted to his left, and his upper lip was thin and turned downward. Throughout the film the man remained solemn, never changing his expression and on two of the screens not opening his mouth. The film was entitled *Unnatural Acts*. On the set at the right the film showed the man lighting a pack of cigarettes one by one, eventually holding seventeen in one hand and three in the other. The other sets showed the man performing unnatural acts, the films almost collages slipping back and forth between scenes. When the man pulled a string dangling from a party popper and the popper banged, shooting ribbons into the air, I sat on the floor and watched the film. Next the man peeled a banana. Later he crushed the banana and rolled it into a mushy ball. He unraveled a ball of twine and pulled film from a cassette containing the movie *It's a Wonderful Life*. Next he shredded a plaid cap. "He has taste," I thought, as an ugly blue mesh covered the cap. Carefully he removed the end from a loaf of bread, after which he dug out all the bread. Then he stood the loaf upright and pushed the bread back inside, placing the end back on the loaf like a lid.

He read a newspaper, after which he tore it into long, thin strips. He destroyed a yellow retractable measuring tape by bending and twisting it. He took pictures with a hand camera, sometimes focusing on himself, other times just swivelling the camera back and forth, the light flashing as he snapped pictures. He emptied an aerosol can of shaving cream into his left hand, the cream eventually sliding lumpy over his palm and onto the table, looking like the base of a stalagmite. At the end of the film he punched eyeholes in small brown bag, after which he put the bag over his head, pulling it down like a stocking cap. When I first looked at the television, I was puzzled, but then when the man began spraying the shaving cream into his hand, I laughed. "Yes, it's a wonderful life," I thought and watched the film twice, rocking with laughter. "You enjoyed that; did you, sir?" said a warder when I got up to leave. "Damn right," I said, adding, "that was funny as hell. Do you like it?" "Not really, sir," the warder replied. "Well," I said, "the film is about as artistic as my ass. Still, I liked it." The warder said, "Thank you for that, sir."

Anchorites who in the clear desert light saw the unnatural courses of men's lives would have approved the film. For the anchorite truth was otherworldly, and he would have admired unnatural acts that undermined the seductive order of social life. I enjoyed the film because like an anchorite I think much of the world's doings absurd, a belief I do not express except when I'm alone. When I am by myself, I enjoy Dada and surrealism, paintings by Dali, Tanguy, Picasso, and Max Ernst, canvases like *Bird, Never Again, Nude Woman Lying in the Sun on the Beach,* and *Max Ernst Showing a Young Girl the Head of His Father.* No man behaves consistently, however. Never would I hang Dada or surrealism on the wall of my cave. Although such paintings are often witty, they are toxic. They undermine resolve and enervate, at their most destructive making decent behavior seem silly. For the true anchorite with thoughts only for the otherworldly, my concern would itself, of course, be beside the point, a sign of being too fleshly.

Actually much life outside family is unconventional. In Edinburgh I explore antique stores, staying longer than I would if Vicki were with me. I say things I wouldn't say if she accompanied me. On Saturday while I was in gallery, a large man stormed through the front door and, standing before a painting, said in a blustery empty voice, "I am glad the judge hasn't bought this painting yet." A landscape, the painting was as garish as a can of fruit cocktail. "If the judge buys that canvas," I said to the woman manning the gallery, "he should be disbarred. A man who cannot distinguish good art from bad isn't capable of separating guilt from innocence." "Oh," the woman replied, "the judge won't buy that painting and neither will the man who was just here." "I must shut the gallery for a few minutes and take Polly for a walk," she continued, Polly being an aged Yorkshire terrier. "I am going to Queen's Gardens. Robert Louis Stevenson played there when he was a child. The garden is locked, and strangers cannot get inside. Come with me, and I will show you Treasure Island." I accompanied her, holding Polly's leash. "There's Treasure Island," the woman said once we were through the gate, pointing to a small pool, a lid of land floating in the center. "There it is. What a thrill," I said. "Isn't it wonderful?" she said. "Astonishing," I said, adding that if I could unearth a dead man's chest I'd buy a painting from the gallery.

My remark was too worldly for an anchorite. The real anchorite doesn't need money. He studies the desert and like Hutton sees curiosities lurking under the ground. In Edinburgh curiosities hide behind walls. At the back of Surgeons' Hall off Hill Square and up a switchback of stairs is the Sir Jules Thorn Exhibition, a small museum focusing on the history of surgery in Edinburgh. Around the room cases glitter like reliquaries, their contents bright but peculiar, many the sorts of bony things with which an anchorite might furnish a cell to remind himself of mortality.

At the entrance of the museum sat a volunteer, a retired surgeon reading Jane Austen's novel *Mansfield Park*. In fact the museum was almost literary, reminding me of Mr. Venus's shop in Dickens's *Our Mutual Friend*. In a leather case rested a stone cut from the bladder of one Thomas Murray in 1876. Three inches in diameter, its surface nicotine yellow and cracked into plates, the stone looked like the shell of a small turtle. Anatomical displays of a hand and foot stood upright in another case, both chopped from the right side of a cadaver, the flesh boiled away, leaving only bones and blood vessels, the former stale caramel in color, the latter writhing like tendrils of ivy. In another case stood an "infant" twenty-two inches tall and "injected and varnished." Dark gray, the corpse leaned forward, pushing its arms backward and thrusting its chest out, the cavity splayed open. The neck curved backward and to the left at such an angle that it seemed to have been levered into position. The top of the skull had been lopped off halfway up the forehead, making it resemble a dark goblet—a porous one, as all liquids were certain to seep out through the eye sockets and the nose cavity.

War furnished many cases: a dozen musket balls removed from soldiers wounded at Waterloo, some of the balls flattened; three Russian bullets extracted from British soldiers at the siege of Sebastopol in 1855; the cranium of a French cavalryman killed at Waterloo, nine saber cuts visible, some slicing deep and straight down, others glancing to the side and shearing off hunks of bone; the upper end of the femur of a soldier wounded at Waterloo, the ball nestled comfortably in a cave just below the ball joint; the lower end of a femur of a soldier wounded in the Crimea, the ball just above the ankle looking like a raccoon dozing in the trunk of a broken tree; the scapula of a soldier who died from wounds after the battle of Corunna in 1809, the ball resting against the bone, cracks radiating from it; and the skull of a Highlander shot and killed at Culloden, a hole visible in the upper left portion of his head where the ball entered his skull, its exit hole in the lower right just above the neck.

Displayed in a separate case along with historical matter describing William Burke's malevolent doings was a pocketbook, the cover of which had been fashioned from Burke's skin. "Skin from his forearms," a volunteer told me. Burke lived in a lodging house owned by William Hare in Tanner's Close in Edinburgh. In 1827 when a laborer died owing him money, Hare decided to sell the body for dissection. He and Burke carted the corpse to the anatomy rooms in Edinburgh. A student met them and told them to take it Robert Knox at 10 Surgeons' Square. In need of bodies for dissection and instruction, Knox bought the body and thus set in motion the ruination of his career and over the next year the deaths of sixteen other men. Burke and Hare plied their victims with drink then suffocated them, suffocation not leaving bruises on the bodies. Eventually the two were caught. In January 1829 Burke was hanged. Afterward his body was dissected, some of the skin being cured and becoming the cover of the pocketbook. In Edinburgh Burke's skin has the status of a relic, demonic but still a relic worthy of display. The front room of the Lothian and Borders Police station on the Royal Mile is a small museum. Amid collections of truncheons, handcuffs, skeleton keys, and counterfeit coins is small leather case used for carrying business cards. The leather came from skin peeled from Burke's left hand. For his part Hare enjoys no such status. He gave evidence against his accomplice and was freed, probably making his way to another life in Australia.

Next to the exhibition was the Menzies Campbell Dental Museum, one room, a sort of priest cavity, I thought. Living like a hermit concentrates the attention. Oddly, instead of narrowing an individual, focus makes a person see more and indirectly broadens, thus making the anchorite appear wise and knowledgeable. For many years, I read, corpses at Waterloo continued to serve their fellow men, providing dentists with a rich source of false teeth, as did, incidentally, the battlefields of the American Civil War. On a shelf stood apple scoops four inches long and carved from bone. People who could not bite into apples because they had lost their teeth used the scoops to dig out pulping-sized hunks. In cabinets sat nineteenth-century tongue scrapers with ivory handles; false teeth fashioned out of hippopotamus bone; and willow toothbrush sticks, the tips of one end of the sticks frayed into brushes, tips at the opposite end sharpened into picks. In the eighteenth and nineteenth centuries a person could buy instruments for scraping and filling his own teeth. Sets cost four, six, or ten guineas, sets at this last price including cement for fillings. In 1905 Claudius Ash, Sons, and Company sold children's skulls "showing First and Second Dentition, mounted or unmounted, supplied to order." On the mounted skulls, adult teeth pushed down on baby teeth while veins and nerves ran around the jaw and into teeth like cords connecting electric lights into sockets.

In coming to Edinburgh and living in a basement, I escaped the advertisements that fill my mailbox in Connecticut, every day turning it into a loft heavy with papery bales. Occasionally absence makes the absent interesting. In the museum advertising tokens appealed to me. Stamped on one side of a copper token the size of a nickel was "Harrison Hair Dresser No. 64 Long Acre West Smithfield." Circling the rim of the other side of the token was "Bleeding & Tooth Drawing." In the middle of the token two figures faced each other, both with long hair. Under them appeared the date 1797. Basil Burchell, one side of another copper token proclaimed, was "Sole Proprietor of the Famous Sugar Plums for Worms." Burchell, the reverse side stated, was also "Sole Proprietor of the Anodyne Necklace for Children Cutting Teeth." On the upper left side of the token appeared a small hole, making it easy to string the piece on a necklace. Despite coveting coin of the corporate realm, my favorite advertisement was a Doulton plate eight inches in diameter. A garland of flowers shaped like a horseshoe decorated the lip of the plate. Below the last flower fluttered a yellow butterfly, its wings trimmed in brown. Although a morning glory bloomed amid the garland, most of the flowers were bells, predominantly yellow but blue or red at the tips. Adorning the middle of the plate was a porcelain container shaped like a spool. Printed above the container was "Jewsbury & Brown's"; below "Oriental Tooth Paste." I leaned close to the cabinet and read the printing on the lid of the container: "Oriental Tooth Paste for Cleaning Beautifying and Preserving the teeth and gums prepared by Jewsbury & Brown chemists 113 Market Street Manchester." I coveted not just the single plate but a set of eight, thinking how much I'd like to serve a dangerously sweet dessert on them at the end of a dinner party.

No one else visited the museums in Surgeons' Hall while I was there. The appointments of my days were spare, and unlike people bound to workaday lives, I was free to meander. Anchorites are wintry people. They enjoy wandering spare landscapes alone. Last Saturday I walked to the Royal Botanic Garden in North Edinburgh just beyond New Town. I wanted to visit the garden before spring made the grounds too rich for eye or mind. Although sleet slipped from the sky, many plants were blooming: among countless others, gorse; grape holly; daffodils; snowdrops; cornelian cherry; quince; daphne bholua, its pink buds spilling perfume; miniature iris; sophora, the blossoms yellow bell clappers tumbling over shingles of green leaves; and then evergreens, not blooming but so bright they seemed flowers themselves—Scotch pine, their twigs sparklers, and Alaskan cedar, its twigs looking like they had been dipped in cream.

In great part I went to the garden to see trees before flowers and leaves so distracted me that I did not notice bark. Tracks of bark stretched across the trunk of Spanish chestnut, sand filling ditches between the rails. Limbs of southern beech burst into twigs that dangled, their ends becoming the thin fingers of ancient ballerinas, arthritic but still turning up at the tips. Far above the ground European black pine broke into a whirl of limbs. Below, the bark looked like chain mail, the links once quartered in paint, flecks of orange, black, red, and white visible against the gray. While bark unraveled in orange strips from small white birches looking like crème brûlée, a large Himalayan white birch glowed so white that it drifted ghostlike out of vision. The trunk of a Formosan alder resembled a bundle of ligaments tied together in a tight faggot. A curtain of catkins almost hid the trunk of a European filbert. Wild pear was dark and messy while larch fell to the ground in filigrees of buds and cones. I pressed my fingers into the damp bark of a sequoia, and atop the hill in front of Inverleith House, I strode around three great beeches that leaned toward the city. The roots of the beeches pushed out from the trunks ridged and looking like the horny feet of big birds. Circling one of the trees took nine steps. Of course some trees were green, holly and evergreen oak and monkey puzzle, its limbs saws bundled together.

Eventually I became chilled and went into the greenhouses. In retreating to the desert anchorites tried to break associations that linked them to place and people, memory and regret. In the first greenhouse I stepped into an Australia thick with memory, immediately noticing drumsticks, tree ferns, bottlebrush, an acacia yellow with blossoms, hill banksias, she-oak, and jacaranda. Nearby, mats of water plants filled aquariums. Schools of tropical fish swam amid the plants. I'd raised tropical fish when I was a boy, and I recognized mollies, zebras, neon tetras, loaches, angelfish, catfish that vacuumed the bottoms of tanks, suckers that scraped algae off glass, and guppies, to my mind the most satisfactory of all fish, the tails of the males signal flags of yellow, blue, black, and orange.

The greenhouses invigorated instead of relaxing me, and I raced along walkways, orchids blooming high above, ferns spilling in green falls, and rhododendrons rumpling into bushes. Pitcher plants looked like beakers filched from a science laboratory, and giant philodendron leaves resembled the backs of armchairs, their lobes rising over the shoulders. Sometimes I paused before plants, giant horsetails or bush allamanda. In the cactus house I studied an East African tree cactus, *Euphorbia obovalifolia*. In Ethiopia latex from the cactus was an ingredient of a herbal remedy used to kill ticks on cattle. Rudderlike protrusions sprouted from the trunk of the cactus while its leaves were wrinkled and shaggy, smaller leaves waving from their margins.

Eventually I longed for my basement, and I fled the glasshouses. I stopped outside for a moment and breathed deeply. At my feet an orange cat slept atop a metal cover under which lay controls for steam pipes. I hurried back toward Leith Row. "Did you enjoy the garden?" a caretaker asked me near the entrance. "I loved it," I said. "I'll be back." "Just like MacArthur," the man replied. And I will return, but not until April. This morning Eliza e-mailed, saying she'd decided to spend spring vacation with me. In April, color will flow across the garden like oil. The weather will be just right for my girl, before whom I want life to stretch like a garden, border after bushy border, open woodland after open woodland. Together we'll sow memories. Later, after I have retired to my last cell and become a real anchorite, memories will bud, and Eliza will remember the bright days she spent with her daddy in Edinburgh.

A Traveler in Little Things

AT THE BEGINNING OF THE twentieth century the English writer W. H. Hudson spent a night in a commercial hotel in Bristol. The next morning he ate in the hotel's coffee shop. A manufacturer's representative joined him, assuming Hudson was also a commercial traveler. The man was successful. He wore fine linen and gold-rimmed glasses. His clothes were stitched from the "blackest broadcloth," and from a heavy gold watch chain seals waved like flags atop a circus tent. Hudson and the man chatted. While the conversation ranged over politics and trade, Hudson said little. Only after the man brought up agriculture, saying things that were incorrect, did Hudson speak. "I perceive you know a great deal more about the matter than I do," the man said, "and I will now tell you why you know more. You are a traveler in little things—in something very small—which takes you into the villages and hamlets, where you meet and converse with small farmers, inn keepers, labourers and their wives, with other persons who live on the land."

I have long been a traveler in little things. The biblical tale of loaves and fishes is not about feeding a multitude. Instead the story celebrates making do with small things, a fist of bread and a hunk of fish. The little appointments of ordinary life are about all most of us have, but they are also the best we have. Alas, glittering seals sometimes lead people astray, and they neglect the ordinary. This morning as I strolled up Newington toward the institute, I heard someone whistling. The melody was gay and bouncy and was the first whistling I'd heard in Scotland.

Parked by the curb on East Preston was a hearse, the lid to the trunk raised. Along the windows in the back of the hearse, an undertaker was arranging flowers, whistling as if he were in a garden. The man wore a black suit. Clearly he enjoyed life because he'd gained weight since purchasing the suit and his stomach spilled over his belt, pushing a white shirt out of his trousers into loose and lively furrows. "Good morning," I said. "Good morning to you," he answered, standing up and smiling. The door to the funeral home was open, and I looked inside. Atop a table sat four diminutive coffins. "For ashes," the man said. "Aren't they something?" "Really something," I said, thinking how much I'd like to have one for my desk at the institute. I'd bury all matter of things in it, pens, tape, rubber bands, and braces of paper clips. "Oh, well," I thought, crossing the street to Bonningtons to buy an almond croissant, all the while blowing air between my teeth, unconsciously piping "Dixie." When people ramble about content to savor moments, they discover that things they once ignored as scraps—fish and bread—are wonderfully satisfying. Scraps nourish the spirit, and suddenly one hears whistling and realizes life is a gift. "Crossing a bare common, in snow puddles, at twilight, under a clouded sky, without having in my thoughts any occurrence of special good fortune, I have enjoyed a perfect exhilaration," Ralph Waldo Emerson reported in "Nature."

I travel widely in books, practically every day roaming the byways of the university library, perusing volumes that have so slipped from popularity that they have been consigned to stacks dusty with "the rarely borrowed." I enjoy the society of books more than that of people. I can take my leave at a whim. Ritual does not matter. I can return at a moment's notice, as I do at night, reading in bed until I fall asleep, then waking later and reading once more until I slip into sleep again. When books are my company, I do not fret about dress. Food matters little. A Scotch egg, a pot of tea, and a book furnish a banquet. I can escape the yoke of manners. I do not have to be sympathetic. I talk only to myself and do not feel obligated to shape my conversation to the needs of others. Ceremony does not compel me to genuflect before people's superstitions, be they religious or social. I can be ornery and contemplate the unacceptable. I have given up believing man can be improved. Instead of sitting beneath candelabra and telling sad stories of the deaths of kings, I can lean back from a kitchen table and laugh about the funerals of friends. The ambitious might think me misanthropic, but as J. B. Priestley put it in *Delight,* "One of the delights of age and beyond the grasp of youth is that of *Not Going.*"

I rarely ponder the important, about which opinions are inevitably machine made. Snippets attract me: in *Small Talk,* for example, Harold Nicolson's advice to cultural aspirants, "Be careful not to say that you prefer the original version of the Sonnets from the Portuguese," or in *Talking of Books,* Oliver Edwards's dedication, "For Her Who Has Kept Them, and Me, Dusted." As I stroll through hamlets of thought, I have leisure enough for the rhythms of words, for example, the entry for caravans in Logan Pearsall Smith's *Trivia:* "Always over the horizon of the Sahara move those soundless caravans of camels, swaying with their padded feet across the desert, till in the remoteness of my mind they fade away, and vanish." In passing, I should note that I rarely read newspapers, their contents appealing more to commercial travelers than to amblers like me. Still, occasionally I read a paragraph. Last week a fellow of the institute sliced a sentence out of an obituary and put it into my mailbox. "Then his marriage broke up, his parents died in a road accident and an irreversible eye disease destroyed his sight."

Truth never attends ceremonious dinners. Truth rankles, souring even the sweetest confections. Only alone can one mull disquieting truths without making others bilious, in, for example, *More,* Max Beerbohm's observation that "in England, the poor want to live like the rich. When they shall want the rich to share their poverty, then there may be some possible danger of a Millennium," or in *Post-Prandial Philosophy* Grant Allen's attack on education, saying it had become "a vast vested interest in the hands of men who have nothing to teach us." "Forced to admit the utter uselessness of the pretended knowledge they impart, they fall back upon the plea of its supposed occult value as in intellectual discipline. They say in effect:—'This saw dust we offer you contains no food, we know: but then see how it strengthens your jaws to chew it!'"

Mentioning religion during a meal gives even pagans heartburn. Thoughts about religion go best with bed socks; a couch, between the pillows of which lurk raisins; and mismatched pajamas, the top claret, the trousers blue, both halves stained by an assortment of sweets— Turkish delight, truffles, nougats, and dark country caramels. "In the gardens of Haroun-al-Raschid," Humbert Wolfe recounted in *Circular Saws,* "just past the corner where one pale rose watches her tranquil shadow in the ice-blue water of a marbled pond, grew a black tree that could not wait for the Arabian spring." In a single night, the tree blossomed, a shawl of red flowers rather than leaves covering its "graceful shoulders." The next morning sight of the tree startled the caliph's gardeners. "Oh miracle," the first gardener said, "red snow has fallen in the night." "Oh marvel," exclaimed the second gardener, "a swarm of red butterflies." "Oh wonder," cried the third, "a little lanthorn in each lighted twig."

"You must be blind," the first gardener said. "Or a numbskull," said the second. "Or mad," cried the third. "And thereupon, as was only to be expected," Wolfe wrote, "the three fell to fighting furiously one with another." "What are those men doing?" the terrified blossoms whispered to the tree. "We are afraid." "Hush! blossoms," the tree murmured, "they think we are a divine manifestation." "What is that?" the blossoms asked. "The appearance of the God they worship upon earth," the tree responded. "And how do you know that they think so?" cried the blossoms. "Because," the tree said, as the last gardener fell heavily to the ground, "they are killing one another."

As I ramble through books, I pick up lines and paragraphs, litter often ignored by travelers "in something very large"—maxims, for example, statements like "half-wits recognize each other"; "the dirty hand keeps the house clean"; "only the old can tell their fortunes"; and "sometimes people say more after death than before." This last statement is especially true if people attract biographers, all of whom manipulate their subjects' words. Lurking in the seventh edition of Hilaire Belloc's *On Everything* between pages 242 and 243 of an essay entitled "On Fantastic Books" was a clipping sliced from the *Times*. Age had turned the paper brown. Printed on the clipping was a poem mailed to the paper on February 16, 1933. "Sir," I. T. wrote, "Taking tea this afternoon at the City Women's Club in Wine Office Court, I discovered an old slip of paper with the following verse upon it. Two initials which appear to me to be 'O. G.' are very faintly discernible at the foot." Modeled on Oliver Goldsmith's "The Deserted Village," the poem consisted of nineteen couplets and described England's defeating Australia in cricket and winning the Ashes in Brisbane. "Sweet Brisbane!" the poem began, "loveliest village of the tour, / Where Paynter hit the winning English score, / A mighty six, that left the fielders still / and very nearly topp'd the neighbouring hill."

A reader annotated Van Wyck Brooks's *Scenes and Portraits: Memories of Childhood and Youth*. Most of the notes were inanities foisted off as wit, statements such as "Only a surgeon could get into this man's head" or "she wouldn't notice a brace of kittens hanging in a butcher shop." At the end of a chapter describing his long friendship with Maxwell Perkins, the famous editor, Brooks recounted a remark an aged general made to Perkins's mother. In the afternoon the old man often walked downtown to chat with a bookman. On one of these excursions, he saw Mrs. Perkins licking a stamp. "Mrs. Perkins," he exclaimed, "that is something I never expected to see a lady do in public." In the margin beside the anecdote, the commentator wrote in red pencil, "RIDICULOUS!!" I erased the word. I have never licked a stamp in public. When obliged to moisten glue on a stamp, I retire from sight, usually into a lavatory but sometimes stepping outside the post office and ducking behind a tree. Indeed, I think stamps with adhesive attached to their backs a genuine refinement, the only recent invention that I know that contributes to rather than undermines civility.

The commercial traveler carries a briefcase. I carry a backpack. While the commercial traveler's case is black or mahogany, my pack is green. Vicki bought it in the Buckland Mall two days before I flew to Edinburgh. On the pack are five zippers, all opening pockets, three of the pockets large and two small, one of these containing, however, an inner pocket, its lips sealed by Velcro. I fill the pack every day. Into the smallest pocket behind my neck I put my wallet and reading glasses. In the second smallest pocket I place keys to my flat and my office. In the other three pockets I cram snacks, Collins's *Edinburgh Streetfinder,* and library books and notebooks, at least three of the former. When I shop at Tesco, I "bag" purchases in the backpack, usually big or heavy items like milk and cereal. On a shelf and a hook behind my door at the institute I keep old clothes. I jog around the Meadows late in the afternoon. I undress and dress in my office. Because there isn't a shower at the institute, I put on old clothes after running and wear them back to the flat. The clean clothes that I put on that morning I push into the backpack. As soon I return to the flat, I slip these clothes onto hangers so that I can wear them a second day. The pack sticks out so much that I am top heavy, and I imagine that strangers avoid me, worrying that I might topple over and knock them to the ground. Sometimes I suspect they think me afflicted or, if not that, a street person, clearly someone to steer clear of on the sidewalk.

On rambles I leave the pack in my office, and talking to people is easier. Yesterday in Canongate Graveyard I chatted with a girl tossing an orange ball to a springer spaniel. The dog was only seven months old, and to retrieve the ball the girl pinned him against tombstones. On Grassmarket a boy advised me to eschew farmed salmon. He'd worked on a fish farm and said that owners ignored regulations and killed sea lice by dumping pesticides into the water. Beneath fish farms the sea was dead, the boy said. "An atomic bomb could not strip the ocean floor cleaner." In an antique shop a woman described her children. One was in Toronto, another in Holland, and a third in London. "My oldest boy was lovely," she said. When I heard *was,* I knew what lurked in the next sentence. The boy had been killed in a car wreck two days before his twenty-eighth birthday. Three days ago on Blacket Place I talked to a mason rebuilding a chimney. He was rubbing the small of his back. "Some days the pain is terrible," he said, adding that the pain clattered down his legs. I advised him to buy a brace and directed him to a medical supply house. "I don't know anything about braces," he said, shaking his head. "I don't have much time left anyway."

I usually start the few conversations I have. People approach me infrequently, and those who do rarely resemble Hudson's successful traveler. Last week a man yelled as I jogged around the Meadows. I couldn't understand him, and thinking he might be asking directions, I ran to him. He was drunk, and when I asked him to repeat his remark, he said, "You're the slowest runner I've ever seen. You should walk." In truth I clip along at a good pace except when I daydream. When the man shouted, I was thinking about Murdo McKay. Murdo died last week. A doctor explained to Beatrice, Murdo's relict, that although Murdo's legs were stiffer than fenceposts and his lungs were thick with clabber, a petrified bowel killed him.

Murdo's left eye was glass. Buried in the eye was a blinking red light. When Beatrice pulled Murdo's eyelid down, the light remained visible, not a matter that concerned Beatrice until her distant cousin Martha Washington viewed the body. Martha did not know Murdo had a false eye, much less one that blinked. "Save me sweet Jesus! It's alive and winking at me," she screamed when she leaned forward to study the corpse. "Uh," she moaned, flopping over into the casket. While Martha's head slammed into Murdo's chest, the powder on her face exploding in a cloud, one that would have made Murdo sneeze had he been breathing, her lipstick streaked his shirt, forcing Beatrice to haul the corpse back into the kitchen and change "its" shirt. While Murdo lay on the kitchen table, Beatrice wedged the eye out with her thumb and clicked the switch behind the retina from *on* to *off*.

I suspect Beatrice was relieved to hand Murdo over to the Lord. For two years Murdo had been a trial. He had become deaf, not something, however, that stopped him from listening to and repeating gossip, getting details wildly wrong, causing scandals, saying, for example, that a man who was taking the nerve cure and a woman suffering from a touch of rinderpest had become Methodists. Beatrice had Murdo cremated. Aside from baking an ashy green patina into it, the firing did not affect Murdo's bowel. Because she was sentimental, Beatrice didn't toss the bowel onto the nearest rock pile as most folks would have done. Instead she paid a stone mason to carve the bowel into a pair of dachshunds, which she put on the mantle in the living room, both dogs lying down, curled into semicircles, the tail of one dog twisting to the right, that of the other twisting to the left.

Of course, I might have been daydreaming about Murdo's cousin Mulberry McKay. Actually the man's Christian name may have been Teigncombe. In any case Mulberry's or Teigncombe's family immigrated to Pennsylvania when he was a boy. Teigncombe did well, attending college and seminary, eventually becoming the Episcopal bishop of Pittsburgh. He never married, and his closest companion was Mr. Green, a parrot. Last week Mr. Green died, and Teigncombe wrote in his dairy, "My beautiful Mr. Green died at ten-thirty last night. At six he was healthy and ate a full dinner of dried pineapples, banana chips, monkey and macadamia nuts, white sunflower seeds, and a crunchy vegetable stick. When he finished the stick, he said 'amen,' something he had neglected to do recently." That night Teigncombe removed the American flag from its pole in the Sunday school auditorium and from the upper left corner snipped off the blue section containing the stars. After wrapping the cloth around Mr. Green, he laid him in a humidor, tacking the lid down to prevent Mr. Green from kicking the top up when rigor mortis set in. The next morning he buried Mr. Green under the birdbath behind his residence. To allay his grief Teigncombe opened a bottle of brandy, forgetting that at noon he was scheduled to preside at a baptizing. Just before noon Teigncombe's curate appeared and after reminding him about the baptizing steered the bishop toward the church. Unfortunately, Teigncombe was fuddled, and he had trouble finding the baptismal ceremony in the prayer book. "Jesus H. Christ," parishioners heard him say as he flipped through the Prayer Book, "this is a goddamn difficult child to baptize."

The McKays inhabit one of those out-of-the-way villages known only to travelers in little things. In some ways I am a commercial traveler. Every ten days I make rounds. I begin at an antique shop, last week Bow Well on West Bow. Fifteen cabinets in the shop contained china. I coveted two Whieldon tortoiseshell plates. The plates were ten inches in diameter and dappled with brown, the result of being sponged with manganese oxide. For the traveler in small things, time is never money. Indeed, such travelers routinely ignore time. On a shelf above the plates was a figurine, manufactured by Thomas Rathbone at Portobello around 1830 or '40. A hunter stood on a green mound. He wore a red and white checked kilt. On his head perched a black cap from the front of which sprouted a yellow decoration resembling a rack of horns. In his right hand he held a bugle. In his left he grasped a rifle, the butt resting on the ground between his legs. Near his right foot lay a dark bird, probably a greyhen or female black grouse. Slung across his back were brambles, roses blooming on them, making them, I thought, uncomfortable camouflage. On the man's left stood a spaniel, its head turned to the right and looking up at his master, ready to race after a downed bird. "Beyond my purse," I thought. "The only way I can own this figurine is to put it on a page." "I will see what Father can do for you on the price," Alasdair, the owner's son, said. "Pop in next week."

Ten days later I dropped by the shop. The price had dropped 20 percent to £1,500. "At the most I've got five years to live," I said. "Accordingly, for each year of my life," I continued, bringing my actuarial skills to bear, "the figurine would cost me £300. Moreover, once I purchased it, I'd stick it on a shelf and not notice it more than ten times a year, the price working out to £30 or $57 a glance." When Alasdair was silent, I refined my mathematical wizardry. "If I studied the figurine for ten seconds every time I glanced at it, the cost would amount to $5.70 a second, a glaze too pricy for my wallet."

I look at nice things, but I never buy them, and occasionally I worry that I have aged into miserliness. Still, I am not as penurious as Amos Jackson. Amos lived with his mother on a farm near Horseshoe Bend, just outside Carthage. Amos appeared to be a confirmed bachelor, but one summer after his mother died while cooking beet greens, he proposed to Olive Niddrie. Olive accepted him, stipulating only that they be married at Slubey Garts's Tabernacle of Love. At the ceremony Slubey gave the couple a box of chocolates as a wedding present. As they were driving back to Horseshoe Bend, Olive asked Amos if she could open the box and eat a chocolate. Amos nodded. On the outskirts of Carthage, when Olive ate another piece, Amos looked thoughtful and stared down the road. However, when Olive reached for a third piece, Amos said, "Hold on there," and taking his right hand off the steering wheel, closed the box. "You are eating too much," he said, shaking his head. "At the rate you're going there won't be any left for the children."

My next stop was the National Gallery. I looked at one painting, Corot's *The Goatherd,* painted in 1872. The painting wasn't big, probably sixteen inches wide and twenty-two tall. In the left front of the canvas a goat stood on a rock; above him on a dark slab in the middle of the painting the goat herder leaned on his staff, a red cap on his head. Above the goat herder and to his left trees spread smudged across the sky, giving the painting a soiled look, almost as if Corot had rubbed the canvas in dirt. "Wouldn't you like to own that? I wonder what it is worth," a woman said. "A bundle," I said, then left the gallery. The time had come to escape monetary concerns, something impossible for travelers in things large to accomplish.

I crossed Princes and walked north for my second visit to the Botanic Garden. Cross-leaved heath was pink, and cyclamen daffodils were blooming, rocketing toward the ground, petals flaming behind them. I brushed my hand across a mound of Pyrenean hedgehog, the needles thatched through each other yet sharp. A chaffinch crouched in the hip of a boulder, and a pair of blue tits foraged through a hairnet of bamboo. Leaves of leatherleaf viburnum gleamed, the upper surfaces wrinkled and beaded. The limy-orange limbs of Pacific madrona were smooth and effervescent under the fingers. On the way out of the park I noticed *Helleborus cyclophyllus,* its green blossoms melting like fat. The last stop of the day was the Kings Theatre, where I watched *The Yeoman of the Guard.* I sat in the second row and studied people in the stalls. Two girls accompanied their grandmother. A couple in their midthirties sat in the twelfth row. Everyone else resembled me, travelers whom age had confined to small villages. Aside from the couple and the grandchildren everybody in the stalls was at least fifty, the great majority being over sixty-five, people who in wandering their years knew the McKays.

I think *The Yeoman of Guard* the most melancholy of Gilbert and Sullivan's operettas, and the next morning I didn't bound from bed, having, as did Elsie Maynard and Jack Point, "a song to sing, O." Still, once

I began my rounds, my spirits rose. Because stature rarely concerns them, travelers in little things are free to risk rejection. Recently friends invited me to dinner at their house, this after earlier entertaining me at an expensive restaurant. Because the couple did not drink, I could not give them wine. I knew they liked chocolate, so I walked to Thorntons, a candy store on Princes. Marked down from forty to thirty pounds was a box containing 1,500 grams of candy. "I can't spend thirty pounds for a present," I said to the manager. "I'll give you twenty-five," I continued, stepping up to the counter and handing the manager my charge card. "We don't. . . ," the manager began, after which she paused and looked at my card, turning it over in her right hand. "All right," she said. "Twenty-five pounds it is." "People can't bargain in candy stores, certainly not in Thorntons," an acquaintance said later. "I did," I said.

From the candy store I walked to the Royal Society of Edinburgh at the corner of George and Hanover. The society had been founded during rich cultural times at the end of the eighteenth century. On hearing that I liked buildings, an employee volunteered to escort me through the society's rooms. Seven portraits hung in the lobby, six of them depicting, in Hudson's words, "intensely respectable-looking old" gentlemen. The seventh portrait was of George III. The king lounged across a chair, his red coat the blouse of a circus clown and his oval face moronic, looking like a loaf of bread from which the crust had been peeled. A stairway led upstairs. From the banisters burst iron flowers, one bloom the seedbed of another. Above the staircase rose a cupola, resembling a pool turned upside down and pushed skyward, the moldings around its edges tile steps shimmering underwater. Trustees and officers of the society met in the Scott Room upstairs, sitting in chairs on the backs of which their titles appeared in gold lettering: *Vice-President, Treasurer,* and *Curator,* among others. The building was a warren of rooms, the floors broken into boxes like knowledge itself, the specialization of which no society could ameliorate, no matter the number of doors opening into a room.

On leaving the society I walked back to Old Town, stopping at Iain Mellis, a cheese shop on Victoria. The shop was small, resembling the mouth of a musky cave. Stacked in threes along shelves to the left of the door were thirty-six round cheeses slightly smaller than curling stones. To the right and again farther down the store on the left were cheeses wrapped in cloth, some as big as small barrels and weighing twenty-six kilos. Molds splotched the cloth, their colors yellow, white, blue, gray, and brown. Along the left wall stood a marble-topped table four and a half feet tall. On the table an assortment of cheeses rose in towers, four storied, at the bottom a round, above half a round, atop the half a quarter-round, then finally an eighth or slivers sharp as battlements. The names of the cheeses read like poetry—Caerphilly, Grimbister, Orkney, Berkswell, Lincolnshire Poacher, Montgomery cheddar, and Mimolette, this last not mincing but garishly orange. The first time I went to the shop I bought Tomme de Savoie, a pale French cheese, its fragrance grassy. Unfortunately the cheese smelled stronger than it tasted. To strengthen the taste I ate the rind along with the cheese itself. The next time I was in the shop I bought Mrs. Appleby's Cheshire and Lincolnshire Poacher, two glorious cheeses that scraped plaque and enamel from my teeth. I also bought Isle of Mull, a sharp cheddar smacking of sweat clothes, and Bonnet, a "naturally rinded" goat's milk cheese.

Routine is the staff of age and business, even that of traveling in small things. I walked back to my flat. I put the teakettle on the stove then changed into pajamas. Afterward I broke a baguette in half that I had stored in the refrigerator. Next I sliced hunks off the Bonnet and Isle of Mull and poured hot water into my teapot. I carried the "treats" into the sitting room and set them on the table in front of the couch. From the floor rose a small stack of books: William Davenport Adams's *Rambles in Book-Land, Genius Loci* by H. W. Garrod, Cecil Torr's *Small Talk at Wreyland*, George Saintsbury's *A Scrapbook*, Vernon Lee's *The Handling of Words*, and *Horae Subsecivae* by John Brown. I poured a cup of tea, turning it caramel with milk. I took a long sip, then I reached down and picked up *The Handling of Words*. I opened the book and read the dedication, "To the Many Writers I Have Read and the Few Readers Who Have Read Me." "Yes," I thought, "I'm on the road again."

Exploring

In "Little Gidding," T. S. Eliot got things wrong when he wrote, "the end of all our exploring will be to arrive where we started and know the place for the first time." Exploring does not weave experience into a carpet that enables a person to fly back through years into diapers and knowledge. From exploration comes awareness of disjunction. One thing may lead to another, but the only connection between the two is mind forged and weak as memory. Events happen discretely. Eleven days ago I wandered the collections of Dada and surrealism in the Dean Gallery. Sprawling across an upstairs room was "The Lamp of Sacrifice," cardboard replicas of the 286 "places of worship" in Edinburgh. The replicas were big, some steeples almost as high as my waist. I didn't stay in the room long. The aroma of cardboard was nauseating, and I fled downstairs to the tearoom and bolted a double cappuccino. Afterward I walked back to my flat on Blacket. By the time I reached Brougham snow had begun to fall.

That night I awoke at two o'clock. Although I'd pulled the curtains by my bedroom window together before going to sleep, a seam had opened. A futon of snow covered the garden. Lights from the city bounced up from the snow, turning the sky yellow as old slipware. I spread the curtain and looked into the garden. Two foxes hunted along the walk, digging and brushing their noses through the snow. Occasionally they lost their concentration, and they gamboled like children escaping a stuffy classroom. They came within a foot of the window.

Then the bigger darted up a flight of iron steps while the smaller ran a circle around a rhododendron, disappearing on one side then reappearing on the other, almost teasing, barking, "Now you see me. Now you don't."

Four days later I walked across town to a dinner party in an apartment off Colinton Road. Snow was falling heavily, and I walked slowly and gingerly, the trek taking fifty-two minutes. I wore boots and carried my dress shoes in a cloth bag given to me six years ago by the University of Tennessee Press. When I reached my destination, I took off the boots and put on my shoes, sitting in the hall outside the apartment. Because a new carpet had recently been laid, my host didn't want me to leave the wet boots in the hall, thinking they might stain the rug. Instead he took them into the apartment and placed them in the bathtub, the toes pointing toward the drain. "Dada," I thought when I saw them in the bathroom, "influenced by Marcel Duchamp's urinal."

By the next afternoon the snow had melted. I went to the library. On the third floor I rummaged through neglected books. Opposite a shelf sagging under the works of Graham Greene, I met a retired member of the English department. We chatted for a time, and I asked about a man I had not seen in three decades. "He died last year," the man said. "He had a heart attack." "Here today," the man said. Later I stood in the courtyard of the institute. A magpie gnarled through the afternoon. "Here today," I repeated, listening to the bird.

People are curators more than explorers. Life itself resembles a museum more than it does a journey. Experiences furnish rooms, the doors to and the contents of which are always changing. Time strips walls and empties cases. Often rooms remain shut so long they vanish from memory. New rooms appear, some cluttered, others almost bare. Ultimately items jumble together, here a collection of seashells, there enamels, along the hall a toy train, on a shelf a fox stuffed for conversation—the whole a gallery of moments that once seemed poignant but now are insignificant.

My explorations repeatedly lead to museums. For me museums are comfortable places. Time has educated my eye, that is, so blinkered my sight that my vision rarely strays from the familiar. On Saturday I walked down the Royal Mile to the Canongate Tolbooth, now a museum called the People's Story. Exhibits depicted the lives of ordinary folk living in Edinburgh from the eighteenth century almost to the present. More often that not, history records stupidity and brutality, its pages belying optimism and illustrated by the artifacts of injustice. In a corner stood a Lochaber ax, a tall, heavy pole once used against demonstrators, the powers behind the axes invariably labeling the demonstrators rioters. From the end of the pole sprouted a hook; from the side a blade spread sharp and curved like the wing of a kite.

Before the Reform Bill of 1832, only the thirty-three members of Edinburgh's town council were allowed to vote for the city's member of Parliament. After the Reform Bill, the franchise rose to an eighth of the city's male inhabitants. In 1867 the fraction increased to a third; in 1884 to two-thirds. In 1918 the franchise was extended to all men over twenty-one and all women over thirty. Ten years later the voting age for women was reduced to twenty-one. Bloodletting often preceded extending the franchise, particularly the early expansions. On the walls of the museum hung banners waved by demonstrators. In November 1866 Edinburgh's Tin-Plate Workers carried a square banner the size of a hall rug. The banner was blue, and tassels dangled from the corners and sides. Printed in gold on the banner was "Manhood SUFFRAGE & the BALLOT." A smaller banner appeared in Queen's Park in July 1884. Except for red rope binding the edges, the banner was unadorned. Against a white background appeared "Since the House of Lords has thrown out this Bill, / And refused to bend to the People's Will, / These proud dictators soon shall know / That the death knell's rung for their overthrow." I talked to Bob, a warder. Bob was born in western Scotland. He had left decades ago, lamenting that he hadn't seen a skylark in twenty years. "Tom Paine," he declared, "was the greatest Englishman ever born," a statement with which I almost agreed. When I mentioned that the Anglican Church had fallen upon a Lochaber ax and was eviscerating itself, not because of a controversial war or man's inhumanity to man but over the insignificant matter of an American bishop's homosexuality, he said, "That's what happens when a church has no religious convictions."

Every splinter of history draws blood, causing anxiety, so I turned away from Bob's robust trenchancy and the miasma of political doings to the lighter appointments of rooms and individual lives. Hanging from a wall was a three by two-and-a-half-inch card, blue and red bells nodding around the edges. Stretching across the middle of the card was a medallion that looked like a belt buckle. On November 23, 1893, in South Queensferry, Gideon Fairlie joined the Band of Hope, pledging "to abstain from all intoxicating Liquors as beverages and to discountenance all the causes and practices of Intemperance." Nearby a brown coal scuttle stood beside a fireplace. Shaped like an urn, the scuttle dated from the end of the nineteenth or the beginning of the twentieth century. Sitting cross-legged and wearing a straw hat, a small Chinaman perched atop the scuttle, metallic Chinoiserie for the middle class. On each side of the scuttle were wrought-iron handles shaped like ears. Adorning the bucket of the scuttle were floral decorations depicting clappers of grapes falling from flowers shaped like cornucopias, these last straight forward, all twist and complication wrung out of them.

Across the street from the Tolbooth is Huntly House, a sixteenth-century building with seventeenth-century additions, restored and converted into the Museum of Edinburgh. Although the museum's holdings are arranged historically, they are appealingly eclectic, consisting in part, for example, of collections of shop signs, Edinburgh glass, and Scottish pottery. Instead of eliciting judgment, the collections invite appreciation and provoke rumination. Like action, thought is habitual. Often my wanderings bring childhood to mind, a time, in contradistinction to Eliot's poem, often evoked and well remembered. Against a wall lay a bundle of wooden pipes hollowed out of elm and used until 1790 to convey water from Swanston to Edinburgh. I could fit my head into one pipe, but not the rest of me, I thought, suddenly remembering having crawled through culverts under roads in Nashville. Dirt and gravel so filled some pipes that I had to lie on my back and inch forward, pushing myself along with my heels. What has vanished from memory are the reasons I explored culverts and the pleasures I received from doing so.

In any case I have always liked snug places. In museums the appointments of rooms appeal to me. Once I glanced at the house's Hepplewhite chairs with their legs ordered and straight and their harmonious violin-like backs, the shrieks of crowds clamoring for the right to vote vanished from mind. In two rooms silver glittered in glass cases. Serving spoons wobbled when I walked past a case, flickering like fireflies. Shelves were set with urns, ladles, cream boats, sugar vases, egg frames, platters—bouquets of silver flowers clinging to their edges—saltcellars, rolltop dishes, and communion cups. For a while I studied a Monteith made near the end of the seventeenth century, this a punch bowl with a rim notched into leaves. Eight notches decorated the bowl; into them wine glasses could be inserted to rinse or to cool, their bases facing up, looking like lenses pried from the frames of eyeglasses. An eighteenth-century wirework breadbasket looked like a spiderweb, its sides spun by an orb weaver. Only in heated moments do I long for the flashy. Amid the veins of silver, I coveted only a nugget, a mustard pot made in 1800 by Francis Howden. The pot looked like a diminutive cap, one worn by a cardinal, rising at the peak into a round ball. The pot was small enough to hold in the palm of my hand. Except for an *L* engraved on one side, the pot was unadorned, the silver running still and smooth over the surface.

The truth is that the furnishings of my life smack more of the coal scuttle and Chinaman, his junk blown far off course by the typhoon of fashion, than they do silver services. Only on holidays does my family eat in the dining room, and then our place mats are plastic and our utensils stainless steel. In the attic or basement are boxes of silver—where, I don't know, or care. In any case, despite my admiration of silver, I enjoy pottery more. Story clings well to chipped glaze. In some sense the expense and beauty of fine silver isolates it from the pasty human world of teapots and mantles tacky with figurines. The profile of George IV rose lumpy from the bowl of a plate baked in 1822 to commemorate a royal visit. The head was not appetizing. Flesh dripped from the king's chin like lard, and his eye was beady. Woven through his hair and sweeping forward over his head were vine leaves that looked spiked, giving the old boy a punk appearance. On a teapot made for the same visit, George's legs were meaty little drumsticks, plucked, say, from guinea fowl. The curve of the pot hid the legs, however, as good dress often hides flaws in appearance, and anyone standing above the pot or pouring the tea would not have noticed the king's lack of knees, calves, and ankles. Among the teapots in the museum was a pot made from soft paste porcelain baked by William Littler of West Pans in the eighteenth century for the third Duke of Rutland. Despite its provenance, the teapot was down-to-earth. When fired in the kiln, the blue glaze covering the pot had run, creating the effect of a sky, white clouds slipping sideways into the blue like light sifting through a crack in a doorway. On the side of the pot hung a white medallion, its decoration the stuff of country life, a red rose blooming to the left, a pink to the right, above them a tangle of green leaves.

Of course one cannot take even a Dopp kit when he boards the Midnight Express bound for the great suburb in the clouds, not, alas, even weightless paragraphs describing possessions he didn't possess. After leaving the museum, I walked across the street to Canongate Church, built in the seventeenth century. I didn't enter the church. Instead I explored the graveyard wrapping the building like a horseshoe.

Eliot might say that I went into the graveyard to purge this world from my mind. He would be wrong. On foot, I cannot pass a graveyard without at least a cursory glance. Never am I more relaxed, perhaps happier, than when I am amid tombs. The most important corpse in the graveyard was that of Adam Smith, who died in 1790. Smith wrote *The Wealth of Nations* and *The Theory of Moral Sentiments*. Forty-five years ago in college I admired Smith's books, so I searched for his grave, finding it immediately, just where I expected to, firm against a wall, the marker well kept. Afterward I rambled, wrens chattering around me like a relief circling a teapot. In the graveyard I met a man. After determining that neither of us was prowling for affection, we talked. The man was a tourist, and we discussed tombstones. I described an interesting epitaph, and he pointed to a marker, suggesting I look at it. I asked what he did for a living. "I'm a stonemason," he said, "and when I go on holiday I visit cemeteries." "Wonderful," I thought. The tombstone he directed me toward was that of Robert Boog, a cutler who died in 1766. The stone resembled a fireplace, the mantle above bare, but scrolling down both sides were carvings instead of tiles. Through the middle of both sides hung a chain attached to a ring. Carved below the ring on each side were an arrow and a scythe, the arrow running from upper left to lower right, arrowhead at the lower right, the scythe right to left, the blade beginning at the lower left and curving back toward the center of the carving. The arrow and the scythe crossed in the middle of the carving, forming an X over the chain. Below this X appeared a second X, this formed by two long bones, probably leg bones. Carved below the bones on each side was a skull, the skulls staring at each other.

I showed the man a stone, at the top of which was engraved "The Burying Ground of John Brown," followed by Brown's temporary address, "Spring Gardens Abbey Hill." Carved into the base of the stone was "Ground 9 Feet by 8 Feet." Neither of us had ever before seen the size of a plot carved on a stone. Listed on the stone were a dozen Browns. "Unless they were midgets or the undertakers were magical slicers and dicers," I said, "twelve people could not be wedged into this plot. When the skeletons rise on Judgment Day, there will be a clattering of bones and a helluva hullabaloo." Flat stones paved the plot of the Macdowalls. Atop the pavement lay four other stones, three large and one small, all life sized and shaped like coffins. Carved atop the coffin farthest from the wall at the head of the plot was "L. D. Macdowall Aet. 2," followed by the date 1814. Louisa Dorothea was the granddaughter of Mary and John Macdowall and the daughter of their only son, William. Mary's coffin stone lay at the foot of that of her grandchild. Mary died in 1833 when she was eighty-three years old. She was nine years younger than her husband, John, and lived thirty-two years after his death in 1801. John lay on Mary's left. He was sixty-one years old and had served as captain in the Inniskillen Regiment of Dragoons. On Mary's right lay her son William, who died at sixty-seven in 1837. William's wife, Louise Helen Dunbar, outlived him and was buried elsewhere. Engraved on the family stone was a tribute to William, in its warmth a rarity in Edinburgh's old graveyards and perhaps a rarity in domestic life itself. "This stone is placed here by the mourning widow and family of a kind indulgent and justly beloved husband and father in testimony of their sincere affection esteem and respect."

Exploring graveyards does not separate me from the world but instead immerses me in the needs of the flesh, making me hungry. I climbed High Street. On South Bridge I bought a chicken club sandwich for £1.75 at Greggs, the shop part of a chain. I crossed the street to Hunter Square and, sitting on a marble bench, ate lunch. Attached to the back of the bench was a brass plaque. Printed on it were two lines from James Hogg's popular poem "Kilmeny." At the beginning of the poem, Kilmeny, a maiden, wandered off to a spring, not to meet a rosy monk or Duneira's men. "It was only to hear the yorlin' sing, / and pu' the cress-flower round the spring, / The scarlet hypp and the hindberrye, / And the nut that hung frae the hazel tree," Hogg wrote, the yorlin' being a yellowhammer and the hindberrye berries from brambles, probably raspberries. On the top of platforms on either side of the bench sat brass wicker baskets, cornucopias overflowing with nuts, berries, rose hips, bramble leaves, and pears as round as backsides.

Hogg's poem resembled a ballad and was lyrical and gentle. Kilmeny vanished, only to reappear seven years later. In the green wood she had strolled into high, damp grass and, pushing into a furze bush, had disappeared into fairyland. "A land where sin had never been," Hogg wrote, "A land of love and a land of light, / Withouten sun, or moon, or night; / Where the river swa'd a living stream, / And the light a pure celestial beam; / The land of vision, it would seem, / A still, an everlasting dream." On Kilmeny's reappearance the world momentarily smacked of Eden. Bison knelt; cattle crooned; and hinds tripped blithely over the dew. Blackbirds flew alongside eagles, and wolves and kids rambled abroad together. The blessed dead inhabited the paradise Kilmeny left, and she returned to her village to tell maidens "That all whose minds unmeled remain / Shall bloom in beauty when time is gane," *unmeled* meaning unblemished. After a month and a day had come and gone, Kilmeny returned to the wood and the furze bush. She lay on its green leaves and "on earth was never mair seen."

Almost no place could have been farther from fairyland than Hunter Square. Only brass berries could have thrived amid the grime. On my right was the Hotel Ibis, home to flocks of tourists and pigeons, these last not the birds of the pharaohs or for that matter yellowhammers. Spittle and chewing gun speckled the paving stones at my feet. Below to my left was a pub, the Tron, its exterior black trimmed with yellow. Around the corner from the entrance to the pub, the sidewalk was awash with vomit. To the left of the Tron was a recessed doorway. Humped beside the doorway were nine plastic garbage bags, three purple, three white, and three black. Beyond the bags was a tourist store, the Scotland Shop. In the window of the shop a company of kilted metal figures played bagpipes. Below them lounged teddy bears dressed in plaid. Nearby sat Nessie, the Loch Ness Monster, wearing a red-checkered cap and bow tie. Nessie swam through the loch in different sizes, all green and friendly with swollen black eyes. For £99 one could buy a six-piece "kilt outfit," consisting of kilt, belt, buckle, leather sporran, socks, and a choice of shirts. "To clear" swords had been marked down to £30 and £50.

Directly in front of me, Blair Street stumbled downhill to a construction site across Cowgate. Behind a fence built out of advertising billboards lay a warren of smashed walls, the ground between them trenched and broken with bottles, wood, bricks, plastic sacks blowing about like froth, and paper, this last sliding slowly over concrete into the maws of cellars. Six doorframes stood in a line. Gone were the doors themselves and everything on either side except brambles festooned with trash. Beyond the site loomed a scabrous red wall, slabs painted black, its windows patches of bricks. Hunter Square was a place to leave, not one at which to arrive or start, as Eliot put it. When I finished my sandwich, I stuffed the bag and napkin into a trash barrel and strode westward.

I walked along High Street, then Johnson and Castle terraces to Lothian and Sandwick, ending on Melville Crescent facing St. Mary's Episcopal Cathedral. Schisms in churches are as common as crosses. Still, I was in an afternoon mood. The sky was gray, and gas fumes oozed up from roads heavy as flannel, turning breaths into coughs and making my sinuses ache. I walked around the church and entered it from Palmerston. St. Mary's was built in the last quarter of the nineteenth century in the Gothic revival style. Vaults soared ribbed over the nave, lifting sight upward toward the high altar. Unfortunately my vision didn't rise very high. Instead I saw a version of Blair Street sinking toward Cowgate, stone glowering over aisles. "A building in church's clothing," I thought. Although St. Mary's was clean, dust metaphorically overpowered the nave and sifted into my thoughts. If a decent person's sexual inclination could fracture the Anglican Communion, then Anglicanism was moribund.

A little learning is distracting. Before I settled into indulgent melancholy, I remembered that *nave* was derived from the Latin word *navis,* or ship. For some people *nave* brings Noah's Ark to mind. What Anglicanism needed was another Big Rain, as a wag once dubbed the Flood. That would distract divines from the doings of people's privates. A wedding was taking place, so I stood in the rear of the nave near a book stand. A box of buttonholes lay atop a table, each a small bouquet, a chaplet of buds of rose of Sharon surrounding a red rose. I picked up a buttonhole and sniffed a rose; it was not fragrant. Nevertheless, I unzipped my jacket and pinned the flower on the pocket of my shirt. I hoped the little bouquet would raise my spirits, if not making me optimistic at least harrowing gloom, making me receptive and able to appreciate the church. During the reading of St. Paul's letter to the Ephesians, I thumbed a guide to the church. History, alas, hardened me. To the left of the nave near the front was the King Charles Chapel, dedicated to the monarch, the guide explained, because in 1633 he had created the Diocese of Edinburgh.

Why, I thought, would clergymen dedicate a chapel to Charles I, particularly in the nineteenth century? Charles's rule led to the loss of his head in 1649 and a hundred years of blood. Charles believed in the divine right of kings. He was stiff necked and knew himself not above the law but the law. How could any man who undressed think that he was God's anointed? The originator of my line of Pickerings settled in Salem, Massachusetts, in 1630. If "we" had lived in Britain during the Civil War, or wars, I suspect, indeed hope, we would have marched with Oliver Cromwell. The time had come for the Episcopal Church to separate itself from dusty Anglicanism. "Can you believe," I said to a chauffeur standing nearby, "that a chapel in this church is dedicated to Charles I?" "Who is Charles I?" the man said.

A minister who was a friend of the bride and her family addressed the congregation, throughout his talk referring to the bride and groom by their first names, Adelaide and Ronald, fourteen times during the first half of the talk. After fourteen I stopped counting. Three kinds of talks occur at weddings. The most elegant is silence, no palaver, just the ceremony itself. Second best is that delivered by a stranger, usually a minister new to the parish. Because the stranger doesn't know the bride and groom well, he does not talk long. He does not surf swelling personal feeling into embarrassing reflection and interminable anecdote. Instead he confines himself to the dignity of biblical quotation. Friends make the worst talks. At this wedding the speaker rambled through dull stories and good wishes inelegantly expressed. A stranger would have whetted words into style. A stranger would not have relaxed and carelessly allowed intimate feeling to become insensitivity. Neither the bride nor the groom were young, something the speaker commented on, saying that because someone as nice as Adelaide had remained unmarried for so many years, he had long thought that something was wrong with modern man. Ronald, he continued, has changed "all that." I studied the bride as she left the church. True, she had aged beyond playing forward on her secondary school's field hockey team, but she had not been on the sideline long enough to gather dust, as the speaker implied.

Standing beside me at the bookstall was a boy dressed in full Scottish drag, bagpipe and all. The boy had been hired to play "Highland Cathedral" at the end of the ceremony. As the speaker waffled on and the clock rolled passed two thirty, the boy fidgeted. "I was told the wedding would be over at two, and I am supposed to be playing in a football game," he said to me, taking out a cell phone and stepping outside the church to make a call. Eventually the speaker ran aground and broke down, and the wedding couple swept down the nave, blessings pushing them out of the church. Before, however, the couple reached the West Door, a woman addressed the congregation. "Ladies and gentlemen," she said, speaking into a microphone, "take your papers with you if you can. We have another wedding coming." Sure enough, almost before Adelaide's train was off the front stoop, throws of people burst into the church, many of the males in full plaid, adorned more for a costume ball than a marriage in a church that frowned upon freedoms of choice, be those freedoms sexual or sartorial.

Outside rain was falling. The day had blackened, and by the time I reached the Meadows, clouds were spitting sleet. Back in my flat I brewed a pot of tea. I ripped an end off a loaf of Italian bread, and after spreading pâté across some bits and cambozola across others, I stretched out on the couch in the sitting room and ate dinner. The bread lasted a long time because I read as I ate. I read *A Writer's Notes on His Trade,* a collection of essays by C. E. Montague published posthumously in 1930. I had not heard of Montague and had found the book, as I find most of my reading, in the section of the university library housing unpopular volumes. Dust mice had bred atop the book, and when I removed it from the shelf I blew the dust into the air, much like a boy blowing seeds from a dandelion.

After reading a few pages, I realized I'd stumbled into Kilmeny's green wood. Montague quoted well, Swinburne's song, not that of the yellow hammer, but still musical. "From too much love of living, / From hope and fear set free, / We thank with brief thanksgiving / Whatever gods may be / That no life lives for ever; / That dead men rise up never; / That even the weariest river / Winds somewhere safe to sea." By evening's end, the world of Blair Street and St. Mary's had vanished, and instead of dozing in a basement flat I was lying on the green leaves of a furze bush. In an essay in which he took the cult of clarity to task, Montague wrote, "Ours is a free country; anyone may take his mental ease if he likes. Only, if you are going to stand out for clearness at any price, then you are going to shut yourself out from a good many things. For a good many things cannot be put so clearly except by being put falsely. If everything in every shadowy corner of a Rembrandt interior were painted so that you could tell just what it was, what would become of the picture, its beauty and truth? Where would be the song that ends *Twelfth Night* if its inconsequence were gone and its unreason put to rights? It gaily defies any meagre and captious rationalism that it may meet in a reader's mind; it flaunts in his face a divine clearness of its own, a clearness that passes understanding; with unsurpassable distinctness it calls up precisely the mood that its author desires, however incoherent the terms of the summons may seem."

Early the next morning I set off for the institute. A crust of ice covered sidewalks, and commuters looked grim. Ahead of me, though, walked a girl. She was a university student, not a schoolgirl. She was short and wore a beret. Instead of trudging toward class, she danced, every so often shimming her feet to the side, first left, then right, then back to the left again. Sometimes she skipped and slid. I never saw her face, but I knew she smiled as she walked. Certainly she made me smile, so much so I slowed down and bought a raisin bun at Bonningtons. I ate the bun as I walked along Clerk. Despite clouds louring over Edinburgh, the day seem bright, and so instead of settling at my desk in the institute, I turned off Nicolson at College and strolled over to Chambers.

I hadn't been to either the Royal or the Museum of Scotland, two large museums that stretched along Chambers linked like two heads joined at the frontal bones. The museum's collections were vast, and I wasn't in a foraging mood. Instead I raced along, glancing at things that interested me. Occasionally something sprang at me from an exhibition case, from amid stuffed birds in the Royal a kakapo. The kakapo lives in New Zealand and feeds upon plants. The bird crams plants into its crop. The crop is divided into sections and is muscular, its lining hard and horny. In the crop plants disintegrate and ferment, the bird forcing them from one section to another. For decades I've fabricated stories about the derivations of words and expressions. "Ah, ha," I thought, "I've discovered the origin of the phrase Kickapoo Joy Juice. Instead of visiting Dogpatch and chatting with Lonesome Polecat and Hairless Joe at their still, Al Capp traveled to New Zealand and talked to a couple of kakapos." "Isn't that right?" I said aloud. The bird did not respond, and losing interest, I strode off to look at Staffordshire.

I stopped before a teapot, a piece of salt-glazed stoneware dating from the middle of the eighteenth century. A lamb slept on the lid. Wrapping the pot itself was a molded relief painted in enamel colors. In the middle of the relief sat a three-story Georgian house with a blue roof, chimneys sticking up at each end. Orange mortar divided the stories. While six windows opened off each of the upper two stories, only four windows opened on the ground floor, two on each side of the door. The lawn in front of the house was green. On the left side of the lawn sheep grazed, on the right red cattle, none polled. While the sheep milled under the shade of four trees, the cattle stood in the sun, there being only one spindly tree on their side of the yard. "I'll fill this with English breakfast, the George IV pot with Assam, and the Duke of Rutland's rose garden with Earl Grey," I thought.

When the pots were not steaming, I planned to put them on the mantle, bracketing them on either side with Staffordshire figurines, on the left the Two Babes in the Wood, both dressed in pink, the little girl exhausted, her brother cradling her head in his lap, on a limb above her a robin staring down, its expression pitying and motherly. On the other side I placed Uncle Tom and Little Eva. Tom sat on a reddish stump wearing a white sailor suit. In his right hand he held a tablet, in his left a pen. Tom was trying to write his "poor old woman" and his "little children," the base of the figurine explained. He was not succeeding. Eva stood beside Tom on the stump and, looking over his left shoulder, said, "O Uncle Tom what funny things you are marking there."

Much as I left Huntly House after studying pottery and walked to Canongate Graveyard, so I now went to the Museum of Scotland and looked at mourning jewelry. Manufactured in Yorkshire in the nineteenth century, the jewelry was jet. My favorite piece was an ornamental comb worn far back on a widow's head. Above nine sharp tines curved a black tiara. Decorating the tiara were four black balls, each as full bodied as a purple grape. Between the balls glittered three multi-pointed black stars, in the center of each star a small ball. Next to the jewelry lay an iron mortsafe, *Airth* and *1831* cast on the lid. The mortsafe deterred body snatchers. Before burial a casket could be locked inside the mortsafe, which itself resembled a huge black coffin. After some time underground, bodies lost their marketability. Then the grave could be dug up and the mortsafe removed. "Would you like to stretch out in that thing?" I said to Evelyn the warder. Evelyn was more conventional than Bob at the People's Museum. "No," she said, wincing. "Think about it," I said, "cheese, bread, a tumbler of wine, away from people and all their palaver. Wouldn't that be splendid?" "No," she said again, swiveling her head, searching desperately for other warders. "It's hard," the old saying states, "to awaken the person who is not asleep."

The time had come to know a place other than a museum or, if not that, try a new tea. In fact I have just the pot, from the eighteenth century a piece of glazed earthenware Staffordshire molded into the shape of a cauliflower, the top of the pot the head rumply and white, the rest of the pot, including spout and handle, leaves, those at the base of the pot splaying up like hands, the fingers broad midveins. Or if I am not in a vegetable mood, I could use another piece of Staffordshire from the eighteenth century, this marbled molded earthenware, the spout opening into a yellow bill and lounging atop the lid a lion, marbled blue and white. Actually the marbling shatters into shards of color: shades of blue and purple, white, and hints of red and yellow. At first glance the side of the pot appears rough; in fact, however, the side bulges out, ribbed in the shape of a scallop shell. The pot is small and holds only enough tea for one person, and I cannot use it if I invite someone to the flat. That is all right, though; I am sure to pick up more and bigger pots.

If I am really lucky, I will stumble upon pearlware tea canisters, figures baked bright around them. I store my Assam in a canister that resembles a flask about five inches tall, two deep, and three wide. Summer dances across the front of the canister wearing a white dress spotted with blue. In her arms she holds a yellow shawl, her left arm pushing the shawl out from her body, her right pulling it toward her chest, forming a basket. Heaped in the basket are green marrows. Just last week I saw a canister for English breakfast tea, a drink to which I am almost addicted. Staggering across the front of the canister was a toper, in his right hand a flask, a black pot-shaped hat pushed back from his brow, his shirt unbuttoned, his blue trousers loose at the knees, a long orange coat swaying behind him, and his right leg in the air, his foot searching for the ground—the man illustrating the dangers of straying from the seeped and the milky. Alas, once a person starts collecting, only the grave can stop him, and then only if he is locked a mortsafe, beyond the reach of resurrectionists.

Mind Ajar

In *The Right Place* (1924), C. E. Montague described "knowing a road." To know a road entailed more than "seeing it all once or twice from a seat in a car." On the other hand, a person did not have to "learn it by heart, to the last house and tree." "There is a mean," Montague explained, "to know it as people soon come to know the daily way home from a new place of work. Of that you make no set study; you do not cram it up; rather you leave your mind merely ajar, to let in such ideas of it as may come."

When confronted by the unfamiliar or the disturbing, some people treat their minds like doors, shutting them, slamming bolts home and hunkering by the lock, mallet in hand, ready to bludgeon unwelcome ideas that might seep through the keyhole. Other people remove minds from hinges and, becoming social anemones, let thought wash over them, waving this way or that, wafting with the fashionable. Montague's suggestion to seek a mean and keep a mind ajar is good advice. In Edinburgh small things slip past the sweep attached to my mind, awakening and entertaining me. As I am unimportant, so they are insignificant. Still, they form the landscape of my days. They are the roadside attractions I see and ponder as I amble through weeks, mind ajar.

Last Wednesday I explored the Grange Cemetery off Beaufort Road. Epitaphs in the graveyards I've wandered in Edinburgh had been almost to a stone grim or resigned. Because many graves in the Grange Cemetery were comparatively fresh, dating from the nineteenth century,

I hoped to find inscriptions that were, if not joyous or playful, at least refined and polished, finished, this last not just stamping "The End" on a life but being balanced and conversational. Alas, the only engravings I read that were conversational smacked of commerce and gossip. Carved into the stone marking the grave of a merchant was "Also Mary Stoddart His Wife Second Daughter of Admiral Stoddart." After granting that Mary was a second wife as well as second daughter, not the mate of the merchant's early amorous years, surely she must have been more than a pedigree. In 1873 John Ferguson died. On his gravestone he was more occupation and advertisement than person. Ferguson died at thirty-five "after sixteen years," his epitaph stated, "as a commercial traveller with Mr. William Dickinson Merchant Edinburgh."

"Words, words, words," I muttered, quoting *Hamlet*. Nearby a stone palm sprouted from a marble planter at the base of a tombstone, flourishing despite the snow on the ground. The palm was seven feet tall, nine leaves erupting from the top in cowlicks, wrapping three bundles of dates like grocer's paper. Suddenly I noticed stones themselves. Obelisks rose above graves in the hundreds like scouring rush at the damp end of a meadow. Scrolls unraveled. Families of angels gazed skyward. Celtic crosses flourished in battalions. Turrets defended keeps, and doves perched on the upper right sides of stones. The doves always leaned forward, heads low, tails raised, dividing the stones, the tops of the stones bald, the birds themselves parts run wildly astray, their feathers clumps of unruly hair. Urns sat atop many markers—236, in fact, 129 of the urns shrouded, from behind appearing hunched, looking like owls. Of course my numbers might be a little off. While I counted, a pair of tree creepers distracted me, darting about the cemetery with a flock of tits. The sight of a white cat sunning itself on mat outside a caretaker's house also broke my concentration. Moreover, thoughts themselves occasionally disrupted my enumeration. At the end of a long alley of stones near the loggia of a Greek temple I pondered setting Loppie Groat up in an essay as "a chicken merchant." Later I considered getting a tattoo, the only tattoos suitable for people my age being those of a walker or a wheelchair. The next day near the institute I approached two strangers and solicited their advice, asking where on my hide such a tattoo should be placed. Neither person replied.

The two must have been natives of Edinburgh. If they had been from Glasgow, they would have responded. Folks from Glasgow are comparatively lively. On Monday I bought groceries at Tesco. When I handed my charge card to the clerk at the checkout, she looked at it for a moment then said, "Pickering—that's a distinguished name." "What?" I said. "Pickering," she said; "there is a very famous author by that name." "What?" I repeated. "Yes," she continued, "he's in Edinburgh right now." The woman was from Glasgow. Six weeks earlier she had waited on me at the checkout. At the time she asked what I was doing in Scotland, and I told her I was trying to write a book. How she remembered me is a mystery.

I don't know anyone in Edinburgh well. Occasionally someone sticks his head in my door, rustles papers on my desk, then withdraws, not before becoming part of the landscape along my road, however. On Tuesday I crossed the Meadows on Jawbone Walk. Clotheslines of trash hung on the fence around the tennis courts, soiling sight. Ahead of me walked a student. Suddenly she darted to her left and scooped up a plastic bag that had just blown across the path. The girl carried the bag across the Meadows and stuffed it into a trash barrel. The girl's name was Charlotte. She was from Glasgow and was in her second year studying medicine. "I really like medicine," she said. "You'll be a fine doctor," I said, thinking what a good, bright companion she must be.

For many people trash is treasure, albeit not plastic bags. On the way back to my flat that afternoon I stopped at an antique shop. The shop looked like a large closet in which clothes had shaken loose from their hangers, falling to the floor, forming great mounds. I took my backpack off outside the shop and laid it on a stuffed chair that was missing half a leg. I worried that the hump on the pack might knock something off a table when I entered the shop. I shouldn't have been nervous. Moving beyond the front counter was impossible. A pack of twenty-six ceramic dogs lounged atop a table, none registered with a pottery, all mongrels, having been whelped since 1970. On a shelf stood a Staffordshire figurine. Two jovial men wearing green caps posed beside a deer. The deer had a long, elegant neck; unfortunately the deer had been decapitated, and the neck swam upward into nothing. "A bit like one of my essays," I thought.

I didn't think long. Cricket balls bubbled up from a pail in a brown distraction. Vines bright with impossible flowers twisted around vases. Beside the counter sat a box, seams sprung by brass faucets, sides bowing out like the stomachs of middle-aged men, indeed like that of Donald the owner. Donald wore jeans; dirt, however, had sunk deep into the fabric and forced the threads so far apart that the trousers looked tweedy.

Instead of a belt Donald wore suspenders, once red but now brown. Like a gray sack, a sweater hung over a shirt of indeterminate color. Donald himself was a bachelor. He was forty or forty-five years old and lived at home with his parents. Aside from decorating his room with an item or two, he was not allowed to bring things home. Instead he stored his possessions in garages. "I like nothing better," he told me, "than opening a lot of boxes that I have just bought. Who knows what I might find?" Donald and I talked a long time. He told me that only Americans bought teapots, Scots having "gone over to bags." Behind the door stood a thicket of golf clubs, all with wooden shafts. A man used to buy every wooden club Donald found, but the man died and, like an ancient Egyptian, took the market with him into the tomb. All things military, Donald said, sold, adding, "But I don't like handling them." Donald showed me a pair of candlesticks. "I used to sell brass candlesticks as soon as I displayed them," he said, shaking his head and looking miserable, "but I can't sell these." I looked at the candlesticks. Concentric circles twisted up from the base. "The reason they won't sell," I said, "is that they look plumber's tools."

I liked Donald, and that night I imagined accompanying him on a house-clearing expedition. "I'll have to buy old clothes," I thought, "probably from Donald. He must own a furniture store of armoires stuffed with appropriate dress." Suddenly my road had slumped into potholes. On my travels I avoid potholes. I worry scrambling out will be difficult. The next day I changed direction and, walking to New Town, spent the morning roaming its neoclassical squares, crescents, and circuses. In the light the hard houses shone like silver, untarnished, not like Donald's shop, reminding me of candelabra atop the Federal sideboard in Mother's dining room in Nashville.

Early in the afternoon I visited the "Georgian House" on Charlotte Square, owned by the National Trust for Scotland. Furnishings in the house were generally eighteenth or early nineteenth century. The rooms reminded me of childhood in Tennessee: chairs, their back legs curving forward then bending back in bows; pier glasses; a bookcase with astragals or wooden glazing bars dividing the doors; and a chest of drawers, its serpentine front rippling in a wave, yellow and red shining through the grain of the wood. When I first roamed the house, I was still under the influence of Donald's shop, and I noticed the incongruous. In an opening in the middle of a dressing table sat a Sunderland pink luster chamber pot. Although its provenance was respectable, the chamber pot was a low conversation piece and as such detracted from the curried elegance of the rooms. Printed on the side of the pot in black beneath the word *Marriage* was a naughty poem, smacking of postcards from the 1950s depicting fat men on the beach at Brighton, hands searching frantically for their privates. "This Pot it is A Present Sent. / Some mirth to make is only Meant. / We hope the same you'll not Refuse / But keep it safe and, oft in Use. / When in it, you want to P-ss, / Remember them who sent you this."

As usual, covetousness restored good cheer. In my mind I rearranged my furniture in Connecticut in order to accommodate a pair of demilune pier tables. At their broadest the tables were four feet wide, too big for my house, and so after moving everything back to its accustomed spot, I selected a smaller item, a toasted cheese dish made from Sheffield plate. From the middle of the dish rose a circular handle, the lower part of the handle shaped like the rack of a deer. Stamped on the lid in front of the rack was a swan. The rest of the dish flowed smooth and glossy, pressed and so neat that looking at it made me almost believe that even if life itself was not orderly I could lead an orderly life.

Before leaving the house I went downstairs to the kitchen. Impaled on a rack were three orange plaster chickens. "Just the thing," I thought, "for Loppie Groat to hang in the window of his Fowl Emporium." Sitting amid wicker baskets, wooden bowls, silver serving dishes, and stacks of blue and white Wedgewood china was a salt bucket, called a pig by the volunteer in the kitchen, a device that kept salt dry. The pig looked like the progeny produced by breeding a fireplug to an urn. Near the lid the right side of the pig spread open mouthed into a pipe. While the body of the pig was red as a Duroc, two yellow squiggles spiraled down each side of the handle looking like curly tails. In the Scottish Museum was a salt bucket that probably should be called a bird. Made by the Cumnock Pottery in 1871, the body of the bucket was brown. Instead of squiggles, however, a creamy feather decorated each side. Atop the bucket a speckled hen squatted on a ratty nest. She was alert, and her head twisted to the side, watching for foxes and weasels. Poking their heads out from under their mother's wings were four small white chicks, one peering out from the front of each wing and two peering out at the back.

Unconsciously I had slipped from the world of Worcester and Hepplewhite almost into the eccentric. I left the Georgian House and walked along Queen until I came to the National Portrait Gallery. There

I caught the art bus and rode to the Dean Gallery. As I had fled Donald's shop and the low road, so I was now tired of heights. A dollop of Dada, I decided, would help me climb down from the highlands. I studied Magritte's *The Magic Mirror.* Written in black in cursive across the recess of a white hand mirror were the words "corps humain." The mirror stood on tiles and leaned against what appears to be a brown wall. After looking at the painting for four or so minutes, I walked into the café and bought a cappuccino.

Although days inside are often quiet, for a reader hours never sag. If a person leaves the door ajar, books whisk in, quotations from their pages ruffling thought. "There were no books in Eden, and there will be none in heaven; but between times," Augustine Birrell wrote in *In the Name of the Bodleian* (1905), "it is otherwise." "It requires almost more courage to write about games nowadays than it does to write about the Decalogue, because the higher criticism is tending to make a belief in the Decalogue a matter of taste, while to the ordinary Englishman a belief in games is a matter of faith and morals," A. C. Benson wrote at the beginning of the twentieth century. "Amen," I said, after reading the paragraph.

Stacks of books push through the crack in my door. I read at breakfast, at dinner, and when I wake up in the middle of the night. During the day when I am away from the flat, quotations pop into mind. On returning to the flat I shuffle through the piles of books beside my bed and on the table in the sitting room. Often I cannot locate the quotations. Later, when I wedge them into conversations, I leave them unattributed, letting auditors assume they sprang spontaneously from my mind. "Far be it from me," I said the other afternoon, "to deprive good Christians of their right to eternal damnation."

Books often bring companions with them when they're checked out. Inside the university library's copy of *The Private Papers of a Bankrupt Bookseller* was a sheet of brownish paper, 7 1/4 x 8 1/2 inches. Ostensibly the book was a collection of papers discovered in the shop of an impoverished bookseller after his death. The bookseller committed suicide, decorously stretching out in the back of his store, an oven serving as a pillow. The papers consisted of short essays on literary matters. The bookseller's neighbor on Princes Street found the body and the papers. The neighbor owned a clothing store. Indeed, the bookseller often referred to his neighbor, always critically. The clothier proved a generous editor, however, and did not remove the unpleasant remarks about his person or business. *The Private Papers* was published anonymously in 1931. Will Y. Darling wrote the letter I found in the book on February 2, 1933. In the letter he confessed to having written *Papers*. "Sir," Darling wrote, his script inelegant, letters bounding high and fast to the right but words often stumbling and breaking at syllables, "I have the pleasure of the acquaintance of the assistant Librarian and as suggested to him I am sending with this letter a copy (First Edition) of the 'Private Papers of a Bankrupt Bookseller.' I hope you will do me the honour of accepting it as the more so as I was (for a short time) a student in Your University." In the book Darling was the neighbor criticized by the bookseller. Darling's literary career was short. He owned a ladies' store on Princes Street, profits stitched together from stays and gussets confining future essays to his mind, their pages uncut. Corsets supported Darling so well that in the 1940s he was lord provost of Edinburgh. He met the great; Winston Churchill called him "my old friend" in 1942. By the time Darling died in 1962, he had become Sir, the old bookseller forgotten and yellow in the library, readers never resurrecting his pages.

"The fate of all books," I thought and the next morning set out for the Edinburgh Zoo and fresh air. I began carefully, taking a taxi, the first ride I'd had in a car since arriving in Edinburgh. The zoo was built on the south slope of Corstorphine Hill, enclosures rising steeply up the hill. A "safari" hauled people to the top of the hill. The safari consisted of a Land Rover with an open trailer fitted with seats attached to it, both vehicles striped like zebras. Because I arrived early, Sandy cleared the seat next to him and, turning the Land Rover into a private car, drove me to the top of the hill alone. The sky was blue and white. To the south snow covered Capelaw, Allermuir, and Gaerketton Hills in the Pentlands like scarves, wrapping the peaks and sliding down into valleys. In the east the North Sea flared into a fan. In the north across the Firth of Forth the Lomond Hills bumped upward into blue. Near the top of the hill gorse was yellow and cornelian cherry lemon. Six magpies flew overhead. Ravens growled, and crows squabbled. A blue tit landed on a twig, the top of its head a fairy cap. Zoos delight and depress me, and I hesitated to leave the hilltop, knowing that walking downward would be both a metaphorical and literal descent. No matter how the animals intrigued me, I wouldn't escape awareness of man's inhumanity to the inhuman and the melancholy corollary that most inhabitants of earth would fare better if a plague swept man from the globe.

Under the lip of the hill a Mishmi takin, a goat antelope found in the high bamboo forests of western China and Bhutan, scratched his head, rubbing against the trunk of a Christmas tree that a keeper had tied to the lower branch of a beech. The antelope studied me, probably wondering if I had brought food. A lioness tore meat from the leg of a cow, the sound not ripping but shaking like a comforter pulled rapidly from a bed. A pair of Amur tigers grumbled over shanks of flesh. The tigers had churned the grass of their enclosure into mud. In a corner lay a white ball, a toy to help them endure days on a road leading to a real nowhere, not one of the fictional nowheres on my pages. Nearby a bush dog paced clockwise around an oval. Twice he called, the sound a squeaking "yeek, yeek," and once he sprayed a stump, throwing his hind legs up behind him so fast that he didn't seem to pause. He had run the round for a long time, and his feet had worn a lane into the ground. In practically every zoo, exhibitions of chimpanzees make me sad and splenetic. A few animals at a time are allowed to romp across an outdoor playpen. The rest are confined to cells like old people warehoused in nursing homes. Indeed, although the capillary lives of chimpanzees in zoos can be long, they endure mental death, their expressions frozen like those of people in the final stages of dementia. While bands of children shouted and whacked the cages confining the chimpanzees, the animals themselves rarely moved.

I was the only person at the zoo who was alone. Most patrons were families consisting of one or two children and a mother and a father, these last two often little more than babies themselves. Sometimes parents rolled children about in strollers. Other times they buckled offspring to their chests. Often children hitched rides on their fathers' backs, spending, so far as I could tell, more time grooming their parents than looking at animals. Being by myself made me more irritable than I would have been had I explored the zoo with family. Then I would have been ebullient for the sake of others. On this day, though, I avoided clumps of people. The shrieks of children and harsh scoldings of the adults repulsed me, so much so I practically bolted myself into a mental cage. I watched an Egyptian tortoise pull itself out of a pool until a boy beside me banged on the aquarium, causing the tortoise to slip back into the water and the boy's father to belch laughter. For a time I gazed at a group of king penguins, the orange splotches at the back of their heads reminding me of earmuffs. The penguins made me happy, and warmth rippled through me until three children shouted at them in hopes of startling them and making them dive into the water.

I looked at animals others ignored, two tapirs feeding on greens and winking their long snouts, a raven perched on a log nearby, occasionally swooping down to filch a leaf. People avoided the tapirs, I think, because their pen appeared unappetizingly muddy. Few patrons paid attention to owls, probably because the owls looked like fluffy baskets, swivelling their heads only occasionally. I spent much time looking at the owls: the scops, a black line circling and framing its face; the Bengal eagle owl, the feathers along its back coins gathered in change purses; and the great gray owl, a mustache white under its beak.

The zoo was tatty and needed money. Still, keepers accomplished things. Although the reptile house was practically empty—I saw only two snakes, both the same species but unidentified—the penguin enclosure looked like a land of small lakes. Keepers conducted breeding programs for endangered species, most small: among others, poison arrow frogs; a species of snail; and birds, the Waldrapp ibis, a black handbag, its bill a curved pink handle, and the Bali starling, this whiter than coconut, the tip of its tail black and cut like evening dress, blue around its eyes and tight over its neck like a choker, giving the bird an Egyptian appearance, making it look like an escapee from a tomb in the Valley of Kings. Although I roamed the museum for four and a half hours, I had energy enough to walk back to the institute, taking seventy-six minutes. For most of the time, I walked on the sidewalk on the left side of the Corstorphine Road. A wall towered above me on the left. Occasionally the wall bowed out and pushed me toward the road. Trains of buses clamored along the road, spraying diesel fumes and grunting as if they suffered from indigestion. At an Italian bakery on Brougham I bought a chocolate tart for ninety pence. A rind of pastry covered the tart, and the filling was heavy and rubbery, "tasting," I thought, "like something dug out of an urn in a cemetery." Still, I'd skipped lunch, so I ate the tart, taking sixteen bites, each costing me 5.6 pence.

Later I walked home. For dinner I toasted Irish soda bread and opened a can of sardines. Afterward I read Max Beerbohm's *And Even Now* (1920). I have received only fourteen letters since arriving in Edinburgh, all mailed to the institute. Nevertheless, I have left my door and mind ajar, and on this night the mail was startling. In the second essay in *Now*, Beerbohm discussed *How Shall I Word It*, a how-to book purporting to be "A Complete Letter Writer for Men and Women." The

"Letter Writer" was, Beerbohm noted, written for people anxious to please and loath to wound. No letter contained a harsh word or an ignoble thought. Faced, Beerbohm wrote, "with all this perfection, the not perfect reader begins to crave some little outburst of wrath, of hatred, of malice." In the essay Beerbohm satisfied any cravings I had for a little outburst and for mail as well, his book containing six wonderful letters. In one of the letters a young lady responded to an invitation from her old schoolmistress. "My Dear Miss Price," the letter began, "How awfully sweet of you to ask me to stay with you for a few days but how *can* you think I may have forgotten you for of course I think of you so very often and of the three ears I spent at your school because it is such a joy not to be there any longer and if one is at all down it bucks one up derectly to remember that *that's* all over atanyrate and that one has enough food to nurrish one and not that awful monottany of life and not the petty fogging daily tirrany you went in for and I can imagin no greater thrill and luxury in a way than to come and see the whole dismal grind still going on but without me being in it but this would be *rather* beastly of me wouldnt it so please dear Miss Price don't expect me and do excuse mistakes of English Composition and Spelling etcetra in your affectionate old pupil." Emily Therese Lynn-Royston signed the letter, after which she added a postscript: "ps, I often rite to people telling them where I was edducated and highly reckomending you."

Things That Interest Me

IN THE 1920S ARNOLD BENNETT, the British man of letters, published three collections of occasional pieces, all the volumes entitled *Things That Have Interested Me*. While the first collection contained 121 short essays, the second and third each contained 38. Almost nothing Bennett wrote about interested me: being a tourist in Portugal, "Unknown Southern France," "Theatre Finance," the League of Nations, saccharin's disappearance from pharmacies, and "Manslaughter by Shipping Directors," this last a criticism of lax safety conditions aboard ocean liners. In writing about the opera, Bennett noted that overweight male singers could be borne "with relative equanimity." On the other hand, he stated that "the obesity of women on the stage is a real affliction for the sensitive opera-goer." Nevertheless, he continued, "Stout sopranos are not criminals though I know several opera-goers who would violently refer to them as such." For my part the music of most operas lifts me beyond feed lots and cuts of shank and brisket. Still, a couple of the Mimis I've seen caused the floorboards to thunder and the First Circle to quake when they flopped onto the couch at the end of *La Bohème*.

Additionally, Bennett had little patience for biography, writing, "Where is the sense of reading biography unless it is going to affect what people say about *you* after your funeral?" I suppose some people dose themselves with biography as others bolt shelves of self-help books in hopes of changing their lives. Unlike Bennett, however, I don't care what people say about me—alive or dead. The truth is that when I fall off the twig, libraries will be silent. In any case I read biography to while away time until my funeral. Few people enjoy acknowledging their limitations, and after I finished Bennett's third collection, I felt discouraged. While his interests ranged through valleys and over the hills, mine, alas, stretched across vast emptiness. My discouragement was short lived, however. Biblical doings have long intrigued me, and as I sat on the couch, Bennett's three books piled on the table in front of me, Noah's wife came to mind.

I wondered about her name. Was it, I thought, Millamant or Mopsie, Pamela or Priscilla? Perhaps it was Dolly, pink-cheeked Dolly skipping with a milk pail and singing while she churned, a woman who deserved a better mate than Noah, that bull-necked, roistering chosen one. The next time saints-in-the-know rewrite the Bible they should treat Dolly better and make Noah thin hipped and kind. Turn his voice into a talking harvest and ripen his smile with autumnal wisdom. The Great First Cause could freeze-dry and shrink-wrap the animals, then Dolly and Noah, known to his friends as Bud, could glide through stormy weather in a slender bark instead of wallowing between waves in a manure skip. Damask roses could grow in the gunnels, and pearly nets drape across the thwarts, breezes singing through them, transforming them into harps. Satin sails would gleam and billow from ivory masts, these last decorated with carvings of fabulous creatures: centaurs and unicorns, emerald dragons, a scarlet turtle with silver wings, golden comets, and mysterious black stones that glowed and spread their sweetness on the night air, fragrances of lily and myrrh, honey and frankincense.

Mucking out the ark in the old story were Noah's children, Shem, Ham, and Japheth. In days gone by, time rumbled along at a different pace. Methuselah lived for 969 years, and Noah himself was 600 when he boarded the ark. Although he and Dolly supposedly stayed on the ark for 365 days, they might have lived on the boat for years circling the globe, sailing over the Rocky Mountains and above Cape Horn. As I sat on the couch, I wondered how many children were born on the ark. Not two, I thought, because two is a harmonious number, bending and curtseying, and man is a quarrelsome, combative creature, polite only when manners serve an ignoble purpose. Not eight, I concluded, because eight is also harmonious and balanced, consisting of four and four, each of which can be divided into two and two. Three was possible, half-manacled and resembling a claw. Seven, also, was possible, bent like a scythe but at a cursory glance appearing upright. Eventually

I decided six children were born on the ark, the number smoothly round, obscuring a self-serving, hypocritical nature raised on three and three, just the stony DNA for patriarchs, the Witches of Endor, and politicians in Freetown, Pyongyang, and Washington.

What interests me differs greatly from what interested Bennett. I wonder what sort of earrings Eve wore when she fled paradise. Did lapis lazuli cicadas or jasper salamanders decorate them? Perhaps they were gold, carved in the shape of Smokey's cloven hoof. "No," an acquaintance from Georgia said to me, "engraved on them was Satan's profile." "Whom does he look like?" I asked. "Ulysses S. Grant," the man replied. Related to and almost as interesting as biblical speculations are doubtful family reminiscences. The great-grandfather of a friend in Nashville spent some time in the Civil War on Robert E. Lee's staff. After the battle of Gettysburg, my friend recounted, his great-grandfather overheard Lee mutter, "Damnation. I made a helluva mistake when I accepted command of the Confederate armies. I should have fought for the Union." The problem with this story is that it is plausible, indeed probable, except, of course, for the curse words. In school all Southern children learned that Robert E. Lee never swore, not even when he was boy and stepped on a honeybee while running around barefoot playing "Kiss and Chase."

The great-aunt of another friend from Nashville was born in St. Louis and attended kindergarten with the poet T. S. Eliot when he lived at 4446 Westminster Place. When Eliot was a boy, according to the great-aunt, he had a pet opossum named Hank. Hank slept in a closet off Eliot's room, hanging from a coatrack. Hank was an omnivore, but he particularly enjoyed, the woman recalled, turnips and cherries, swallowing these last whole. One afternoon when Eliot's mother returned from her bridge club, she found her son and Hank in the kitchen playing war, the opossum a casualty lying on its back feigning death and the poet-to-be a soldier in half uniform, a kitchen pot pulled down over his brow. Unfortunately, Eliot had butted a strut in the kitchen wall, not simply cracking plaster but forcing the pan so far down his head that his mother could not pry it loose even though she basted the lip with bacon grease. Consequently she had to take Eliot to the emergency room, where a surgeon sliced the pan off his head.

Although Mrs. Eliot forced her son to see "a nerve doctor," Hank fared worse. She blamed him for the incident and banished him from the house, driving him to East St. Louis and dumping him on a garbage scow. She stood by the dock until she saw a barge push the scow out into the middle of the Mississippi River, insuring that Hank could not imitate those packs of literary dogs who, though separated by leagues from their masters and mistresses, managed to find their way home, inevitably staggering up to screen doors, thin and footsore, ticks hanging from their ears like buttons, but ever, ever faithful. The behavior of Eliot's mother deprived the poet of the chance to outgrow Hank and thus had artistic consequences. Eliot sentimentalized his pet. In later years he associated the marsupial with the gay years of childhood. In 1939 Faber published Eliot's book *Old Possum's Book of Practical Cats,* the title of which celebrated Hank. In 1981 Andrew Lloyd Weber wrote *Cats,* basing the musical on Eliot's volume. "Aren't the windings of life astonishing?" my friend said after recounting the story. "I'll bet Hank is grinning from ear to ear."

Many things that interest me appeal to the imagination and enable me to trip past smutty reality: oafish boozers hunched into walls outside pubs, splattering sidewalks with their dinners; the sirens of fire engines whiplashing the ears; smokers who have transformed themselves into chimneys and bus stops into smelters; and the Lothian Road at night, scabby men staggering, words bursting methanic through their lips, in doorways beside windows neon with advertisements for lap dancing, mortarlike men with cannonball heads and barrel necks, their ears touchholes stuffed with radios.

I am an urban spelunker. I explore shops whose fronts open like caverns but whose backs quickly slam down into impenetrable brick and stone. One afternoon I dug through Mr. Wood's Fossils on Cowgatehead. I unearthed marbleized sheets of orthocone nautiloids from Morocco. Three hundred eighty million years old, the nautiloids were slender and nine inches long, looking like pods, from the top halves of which seeds had been gnawed away. A trilobite resembled a saucer that had slipped sideways in a kiln and had been baked lopsided. Browns, greens, yellows, and blues twirled through a 120-million-year-old nautilus the size of my fist. Hyena teeth from China cost £10; dinosaur coprolites from the Jurassic period £10; and the 2-million-year-old fossil of a sand crab from Java £36. The shop was a tar pit. In the window lay the fossil of a crocodile skull, a native of Morocco 70 million years ago. I coveted the lower jaw of a cave bear from the Siberia of 15,000 years ago. A sharp canine jutted from one end, while five molars slumped together in a lump below the jaw joint. Priced at £1,500, the most expensive fossil in the shop was that of a nothosaur from China, a lizard that flourished 220 million years ago. The nothosaur lay pressed in stone, looking like a question mark turned backward, its head an arrowhead turned down to the right, behind the head the neck curving upward to the left like the circumference of a circle before it slid straight downward through the spine, finishing in a tail that bent to the left, legs branching out into five sharp tendrils.

Interests don't necessarily make a person interesting. They can just as easily turn one into a bore. My mind works by association, and from Cowgatehead I walked to the Harkess Funeral Home on East Preston, one batch of skeletal beings bringing another bony group to mind. Two women greeted me. Despite my being down-to-earth, I must have seemed too lively to be a prepaying customer, and they did not have time to bandy words with me. Of course, what we three actually had was time, unlike the home's patrons. Sitting atop a table in the hall was a selection of wooden boxes for ashes, round handles dangling from the ends of the boxes, the boxes themselves approximately ten inches in length, six in width, and seven in height. I had a ruler with me, but the women were so funereal that I didn't remove it from my backpack. In truth the women startled me. Undertakers in the United States are jovial. The last time I attended a funeral in Carthage, an undertaker told me he had a friend who taught his dog to play poker. "Gee," I said, "the dog must have been a dachshund or some sort of smart hound, certainly not a Labrador." The dog was a dachshund, the man said, but he wasn't smart. "Every time he was dealt a good hand," the man continued, "the dog wagged his tail."

In any case the boxes looked like small vaults, just the thing to discourage grave robbers, be they termites or the larvae of long-horned beetles. In a compartment in the middle of the table sat a shellacked jar, shaped like an urn but vaguely Chinese in appearance. The jar was also for ashes. I tried to unscrew the top. "The jar is sealed," one of the women explained, "so that if a person drops it on the floor, the top won't come loose and spill her loved one." I asked where relicts put boxes and urns. "On mantles or on bedside tables," the woman said, opening a ledger and closing the conversation. People do not escape me easily, however. "Before I go," I said pausing at the door, "I have a favor to ask." "What's that?" the woman answered, not looking up from the ledger. "I wonder if you could direct me to the single man's graveyard." "What?" the woman said, her head popping up. I danced out the door without answering. In the next block I stopped at Peckham's and bought two chocolate croissants. "This is a good day," I said to the boy at the cash register. "I have been talking to undertakers." "What?" he said, as he handed me my change.

Next I went to an art gallery in New Town, eating the croissants as I walked. Unlike the paintings, conversation in art galleries is often unframed, words falling from palettes in thick dollops. The most valuable oil in the gallery was a Victorian narrative, painted just after the end of the Crimean War, depicting the return of a weary soldier to his rural cottage. In the picture the soldier slumped in a chair, the left sleeve of his jacket sewed together, the cuff attached to the armpit, a doctor having lopped off the arm in the Crimea. The man's mother leaned over his left shoulder, her hands pressed tightly together, fingers intertwined as if in prayer while the man's wife knelt in front of him, eyes closed, arms wrapped around him. Behind her a baby slept in a cradle. The man himself was so tired that he was almost expressionless. "We think we have a buyer for this picture," a woman told me. "The soldier is Scottish, and the buyer is almost certain to donate the painting to the National Gallery." "Really," I said. "Yes," the woman said, "he can't keep the picture at home. His wife doesn't like paintings of poor people."

Occasionally the contents of a shop nauseate me. Fair meadows, as the expression puts it, often hide quagmires. Not the dusty and mildewed but the new often repulses me. One morning I explored a costume store on Grassmarket. Wigs and mustaches hung like moss from a wall. Policemen's helmets sat on racks; white parasols draped from a beam; noses floated across a shelf in red bubbles; green duck feet waddled along a table; and rubber firemen's axes shared an umbrella stand with canes, some of these last blue but most red. Costumes could transform purchasers into Elvis or Batman. People could become urban sheiks or sidewalk cowboys. On the front of a packet containing a bloody doctor's coat, a doctor waved a knife in his left hand, his coat splotched with red. The doctor's hair was parted in the middle and, spilling over his head in white falls, made him look insane or perhaps poetic, having, as versifiers put it, killed the thing he loved. "I'm not sure I like this place," I said to a clerk. "Go around the corner to West Bow," she said. "The woman who owns this store owns a fun shop there. You might like it better." I didn't. Plastic body parts covered one wall, most organs that people my age label "private." Dog coprolites filled two buckets by the door, all brown and plastic, none resembling the fossilized dinosaur droppings for sale at Mr. Wood's, these being conglomerates radiating yellows and blues, greens, and whites.

Happenstance often constricts my interests. Three weeks ago I went to the Traverse Theatre with a group from the institute to see *Knives in Hens,* a play written by David Harrower, the institute's "creative fellow." Translated into a dozen languages, the play had been staged by twenty-two professional companies around the world. "What did you think of the play?" a fellow asked me the next morning. "Agonizing," I replied. "Yes, wasn't it?" the fellow said. "Harrower really probed the sad heart of things." Alas, my use of *agonizing* referred to a physical, not mental, experience. Before the play began, another fellow treated me to a pint of beer, the first beer I drank in Scotland. Liquids race through males my age. Because an intermission did not break the play, I spent the last twenty minutes of the performance ignoring the stage and praying the end would come before I suffered an unfortunate accident. "Agonizing," I repeated, wincing in recollection, "absolutely agonizing."

Life often knocks interests out of mind almost before I acknowledge them, much less slap them onto pages. Last week I ambled up Middle Meadow Walk toward Forrest. I was coming from George Square, where I'd idled away minutes studying restoration of the old buildings on the west side of the square and mulling constancy, wondering why wayward thoughts more often than not shored up belief and personality instead of confusing and leading one astray. Why didn't a person lose himself as he followed thought through crescents and circuses, along rows, loans, and the hints of paths into shadowy closes and dark mews? "Here's the reason," I said, starting to talk to myself. I got no further. On the edge of the Walk, a beggar sat in a wheelchair, legs tangled underneath him. On my approach he dropped a water bottle on the ground beside the wheelchair. The man could not lean over to retrieve the bottle. I crossed the walk, bent down, and picked up the bottle. Before I could hand the bottle to him, the man stuck his cap into my face, brushing my chin. "Any change?" he said. I reached into my pocket. I had only one coin, a pound. I dropped the pound into the hat, then leaned over and placed the bottle in the man's lap. "Dropping the bottle was a ploy, a gimmick for attracting my attention," I thought as I turned back toward Forrest. I hated the idea, and so I snapped the thought off at the stem and walked up the hill mechanically, my mind barren, all buds wilted.

I am constitutionally incapable of being interested in some things. No matter the occasional hankering, sports don't intrigue me, in part because the verbal link forged between war and sports repulses me. Of course, sometimes the tie is real, not metaphoric. Pasted to a wall in the National War Museum was a recruiting poster for the Scottish Rifles. "Why be idle?" writing on the poster asked. "The Regiment has vacancies for sound young men." The Rifles will, the poster stated, "TRAIN YOU EDU-CATE YOU FEED YOU TEACH YOU how to play football, box, and swim." Depicted on the poster were two members of the regiment in military kit, one in a kilt, the other in tartan trousers, both standing straight as curtain rods, watching recruits play soccer, the game being refereed by a third soldier in trousers. Also on the wall was a smaller poster, probably measuring 12 x 20 inches in comparison to the Rifles' 2 x 2¹/₂ feet. "HEY LOOK," red letters declared before the line changed to turquoise. "Willie's off to Singapore with the Queen's Own Highlanders" (the print returning to red for the last three words). Although the poster did not mention sports, Willie was clearly a robust athlete. He strode across the poster in crisp shorts, a duffel bag bouncing like a feather on his left shoulder, a rifle over his right, his socks pulled high over swelling calves, and his right sleeve rolled above the elbow exposing a muscular forearm.

I only like games in which skill is not involved and that one plays simply for fun. The Museum of Childhood owns a copy of an old favorite from my academic days of writing about children's literature, "The New Game of Human Life," published in 1790 by John Wallis, located on Ludgate Hill, and Elizabeth Newbery at the Corner of St. Paul's Churchyard. Printed on rough paper, the game came folded into a pack of twelve squares. Unfolded, the game was 26 x 18¹/₂ inches. Stamped on the paper was an oval looking like a nautilus, the shell being divided into eighty-four compartments, all containing illustrations, most about 1¹/₂ x 2 inches, beginning with "The Infant" and ending at "The Immortal Man." The game was, the publishers stated, "the most agreeable & rational Recreation ever invented for the Youth of both Sexes." "To avoid introducing a dice box into private families," the publishers advised parents to purchase a teetotum and number the sides 1 through 6. Children could twirl the teetotum twice, "which will answer the same purpose" as dice. All players had markers, which they moved after spinning the teetotum. Thus if a child got a five on his first spin and a two on his second, he would move his marker forward seven spaces. The markers landed on compartments containing diverse characters. At eighteen "The Gallant" held a rose in his hand. At forty-two "The Orator" wore a wig and a long black gown. At four a waterfall of feathers tumbled out of "The Darling's" hat. At fifty-six "The Good Father" bent over, extending his arms toward his small daughter. At forty-seven "The Geographer" rested his right hand on the top of a globe. At twenty "The Lover" pressed both hands to his breast, and at fourteen "The Indolent Youth" lounged on the edge of a bed.

Accompanying the illustrations were rewards and punishments. The player who landed on "The Romance Writer" at forty had to return to "The Mischievous Boy" at five, while the player who landed on "The Drunkard" at sixty-three was sent back to "The Child" at two. In contrast, one skipped ahead from "The Temperate Man" at fifty-eight to eighty-two, "The Quiet Man," and from "The Assiduous Youth" at fifteen to fifty-five, "where he will find a patriot." If a player landed on "The Tragic Author" at forty-five he, the instructions stated, "shall go to the Place of Immortal Man at 84 & win the Game by succeeding him."

I rarely drink, but once or twice in life I've landed on sixty-three. Moreover, since childhood nature has delighted me, so much so that the out-of-doors often seems the greatest interest in my life. On Good Friday I returned to number two and if not "The Child," at least to "The Ambler." Just south of Holyroodhouse is Holyrood Park, some 650 acres topped by Arthur's Seat, the remnant of a volcano. The Seat is 251 meters high and looms over Edinburgh. Unless a tourist's legs are weaker than the stems of dandelions, he is obligated to stand atop Arthur's Seat. Certainly on returning home, friends will ask if he has climbed the Seat. If he hasn't, they will pinch their lips into seams and, like the sanctified confronting the woebegone, shake their heads, implying he was negligent and might as well have dozed days away at home.

I had put off climbing Arthur's Seat until, I told fellows at the institute, hours warmed and pages piled up on my desk. The truth was that occasionally and inexplicably I suffer from shyness. Although I owned several maps of Edinburgh, I wasn't sure how to approach Arthur's Seat, or indeed, where to climb. Almost every day I spotted hikers atop the summit, and rationally I knew finding my way to the top would be easy. Still, I dreaded wandering astray and having to ask strangers for directions. Only when thinking about climbing Arthur's Seat did I become diffident. Normally I am brazen and will push in where even imbeciles fear to tread. After breakfast on Good Friday, however, I tackled the Seat. On the Monday after Easter, Eliza was arriving to spend school vacation with me. Eliza is formidable. She does not tolerate shilly-shallying, and I set out to blaze a sensible trail to the summit, one that I could guide her over when we climbed the Seat together.

I walked up Blacket, crossed Dalkeith, then strolled up Holyrood Park Road until I turned east on Queen's Drive. On Blacket garden-center yards were blooming. Mahonia, quince, cherry, viburnum, and bundles of forsythia swelled into and over the sidewalk. Beds by front doors were brighter than chintz, stitched with daffodils, primroses, racks of pieris, grape hyacinth, and tulips, these last always red, their petals tapering into arrowheads. In the park magpies bounced over the Lion's Haunch. Jackdaws rode the air high above the Windy Goule or frittered about building nests, beaks wormy with twigs. Below the drive a colony of herons nested at the western end of Duddingston Loch, a bird sanctuary. A swan floated across the loch, his wings raised into sails, the wind pushing him. Near brambles pink and white with clusters of flowers a man told me he was dying. The next morning he was flying to Barcelona to say goodbye to his son and his grandchildren. On walks strangers often talk to me. Atop the Seat a retired teacher from Inverness quizzed me about the American Civil War. His son was working in Australia, but, he said, pointing to a brown-headed girl gazing dreamily at Edinburgh, his daughter had climbed the peak with him.

I stayed on Queen's Drive until I passed Dunsapie Loch, a small man-made lake, bustling with mallards, coots, eiders, great black-backed gulls, and a pair of swans. After passing the lake, I climbed Whinny Hill. Sweaters of tatty gorse covered the slope. In the distance ships plied the Firth of Forth, some tankers riding low and looking waterlogged, others freighters, high and barky with containers. At my feet queen bumblebees lumbered across paths. Small birds swooped like waves, breaking and landing on weathered spines of gorse. Around my head the wind droned, stripping all noise away, except the sound of its own orchestration. I walked along the high lip at the western side of the hill and started to climb Arthur's Seat. Rocks bearded the Seat like lichens, gray and red and stacked in wrinkles. Often I paused and watched people walking dogs, most dogs black and most walkers women. Later I descended the steep face of the Seat. The trail was damp and slippery, and worried that I might stumble into a sprained ankle and ruin Eliza's visit, sometimes I sat down and slid, stopping once to study a black slug pulling itself across a flat stone. At the bottom I turned north and walked along Hunter's Bog. In the shelter of the ridges grew small birches and pines.

In the bog a crow stood amid down and called, the feathers probably ripped from a wood pigeon by a hawk. Days are mosaics, their patterns determined by personality, not purpose. After leaving the park I hiked the Royal Mile until I reached the Huntly House museum. I climbed to the top story and, sitting on the floor, studied a mug manufactured at Prestonpans by Watson's Pottery in the 1840s. Baked across the middle of the mug were the words "NO CORN LAWS." The makings of a wreath wound around the mug. The wreath was red and green, sprouting in the middle of four green leaves a three-petaled red flower. At the tip of the flower four more leaves grew, these in turn opening into another flower, all the leaves and flower petals looking like mittens, some three-fingered, others two or four.

A slow drizzle fell through the next morning, and at midday fog was steamy over the ground. Nevertheless, I set out on another walk in hopes of discovering matter for a traipse with Eliza. This time I walked south of Holyrood Park beside the Duddingston bird sanctuary, following the cycle path built over the right-of-way of the old Edinburgh and Dalkeith Railway. High walls enclosed the path. The Prestonfield golf course lay beyond the wall on the right side of the track, and occasionally I heard the soft metallic sound of a driver hitting a ball. Brambles grew beardy along the wall, sunken berries clinging to canes. Ivy fell over coping stones, while lichens spread gray and white and sometimes orange across rocks. Often I climbed atop mounds of refuse and searched the sanctuary for birds. But all I saw was garbage and in greasy wastes yellow daffodils starved into lethargy and senescence. At the Duddingston Road I turned north to walk to Old Church Lane. Shoulders of the road were sewers running with trash. For that matter every unattended plot in Edinburgh bulges proud with urban waste. Still, the trash vanished once I stepped onto Church Lane. Had it not been for the constant slap and thrum of cars, Duddingston would have seemed a village, not a suburb.

Duddingston Kirk sat on a mattress of ground overlooking the loch below the west end of the causeway. Although the church dated from the twelfth century, most of the building was constructed in the seventeenth and eighteenth centuries. Unlike churches that soared into sharp, uncomfortable Gothic steeples, Duddingston Church was modest and comfortable. Its tower was low and square, and the whole building hugged the ground, seeming to draw sustenance from the soil, the dirt on which people actually live, not aspiring upward to some unattainable, ultimately brutal abstraction. Beside the front gate stood a tower in which, so story relates, parishioners spent nights observing the cemetery in order to thwart body snatchers. Or at least they hid there for the three weeks immediately following a burial. At the end of three weeks, bodies had decayed beyond marketability.

The gate to the churchyard was locked when I arrived. But as I turned to leave, Robert Darling, the treasurer, drove up. His wife, Muriel, was decorating the church for Easter Sunday, and he let me in to browse. The Darlings were my age and understood that flowers should spill from vases in sunbursts on Easter, goblets of vanilla lilies, in this case accompanied by yellow daisies and baby's breath, all pouring through laurel. While the Darlings arranged flowers, I roamed the churchyard. I leaned against a wall and, looking over the loch, saw greylag geese, feathers sweeping combed along their necks and wings, their bills, however, orange and feet and legs pink, dandifying them. Near the front door of the church stood a cenotaph commemorating lifesavers, people who rescued sailors from shipwrecks. Time had smoothed much of the engraving on the monument back into stone. Moreover, rings of newly planted flowers surrounded the monument, so I was forced to study the cenotaph from a distance. On the right side of the carving, however, was the profile of the Wind, its face worn monstrous, eyes broken sockets, brow receding, but its cheeks and jowls tempests of air. Before the Wind waves ran, their tops rising into shrieks. Amid the waves a three-masted ship bucked and tilted. Approaching the ship from the left was a long boat containing six men, the men at each end waving, the four men in the middle rowing.

Many tombstones were broken and had sunk into the turf. On the side of one stone, bones bracketed a skull while sands ran through an hourglass. On the other side the fat legs of cherubs bracketed another skull, to the right of the skull one leg and foot and part of a haunch, to the left both legs and the buttocks, the legs dancing mindlessly, the upper body that was once above them having vanished. Built into the wall of church were other tombstones. "David Scot and Margaret Gourley His Wife they Have eight children interred in this place," one marker declared, adding that Margaret died at forty-eight on April 20, 1693. After some time in the yard, I had to use a lavatory. "The church doesn't have one," Robert told me. "Just pee in the graveyard. Some of the inhabitants have lain there since the seventeenth century, and very little bothers them nowadays."

After visiting the grave of Michael Watson, a farmer who died in 1803 at eighty-three, his age, I am sure, making him sympathize with my need, I crossed the lane and walked east along the causeway. Tall walls pinched the causeway, for some reason making me feel good. Because the walk was narrow, I stepped off the pavement to let an aged man leading two aged dogs pass, all ten of their legs trembling. I walked to the end of the causeway and glanced at a nondescript cottage in which Bonnie Prince Charlie held a war council before the battle of Prestonpans in 1745. I'm not sure why I didn't pause longer in front of the cottage. Perhaps it is because royalty is distasteful to me, their doings usually leading to disaster. A friend told me that swans were protected birds, "royal birds belonging to the Queen." "Starlings would suit that family better," I said.

I turned around and, walking back to the west of the causeway, approached the Sheep Heid Inn. Although the building dated from the nineteenth century, the pub was famous, the license for an inn on the property dating from the fourteenth century. I stood outside the door for some time. Earlier I had almost entered the pub but had turned away. I had not been in a pub since arriving in Edinburgh. Neither had I bought a beer, knowing that the best way to avoid bad endings was to avoid good beginnings. Still, Eliza liked regular meals, and I realized that she'd want to eat soon after climbing Arthur's Seat. If lunch were delayed, she would become grumpy. Consequently I entered the inn and at the bar bought a pint of pale ale, "the lightest we have," I was told. I took the beer upstairs and, sitting at a table by a window, ordered lunch. The ceiling was low and white, and shellacked beams quartered it in veins. Green holly speckled with red berries decorated the napkins. "We've had them since Christmas," a waitress said. "We need to get rid of them before summer." I had eaten less than a handful of lunches since arriving in Edinburgh, so I ordered a starter, black pudding, this made from oatmeal and beef blood and bathed in goat cheese and sweet onion relish. The pudding was so good I topped the meal off with apple pie and ice cream. After a cup of coffee I started home. I did not return the way I came, however. I climbed steps leading from the causeway up toward Holyrood Park, thinking I had to find a simple way down from Arthur's Seat. The steps stopped at the edge of a field, and the fog was so thick I could not see beyond the field. "North," I said aloud, "will take me to Queen's Drive." I was right.

"What a good morning," I said later as I strolled along the drive, not a morning that would have interested Arnold Bennett but a good morning for me. As I walked, I recalled another family reminiscence, this, too, told to me in Nashville. My friend Lionel's great-uncle Peruna lived in Oxford, Mississippi, and knew the writer William Faulkner, becoming at one time his favorite drinking companion. When Faulkner was a child, Peruna recounted, he had a pet blackbird named Darling. Darling lived in the chicken house and every morning crowed like a rooster. What was more significant, though, was that whenever a hen became fatally ill with sorehead or bluecomb, Darling stood beside her nest as she lay dying and "sang her," as Peruna put it, "to a golden roost in paradise Gallus domesticus." Years later, Peruna stated, Faulkner would reduce Darling to the diminutive Darl and "immortalize him in fiction."

Peruna told Lionel many stories about Faulkner, most of them influenced, I suspect, by spirits. Faulkner, of course, drank too much. On one occasion, Peruna recounted, a Baptist minister advised Faulkner that the best way to control his consumption of alcohol was to leave glasses half full. "I can't do that," Faulkner replied. "Every time I raise a glass I see Jesus's face beneath the whiskey, and because I want to get to know our Lord better I have to drink every drop." "The Devil's in the drink, not Jesus," the minister said. The minister had purged the demon bourbon from many of his parishioners, though, he later admitted, never from such a hardened sinner like Bill Faulkner. In any case Faulkner always drank from a special glass when he visited the Oxford Country Club. Knowing this, the minister enlisted the help of his least sanctified deacon, a man who frequented both country club and country stills. The minister drew Satan's face on a paper circle the size of the bottom of Faulkner's glass, turning Satan's horns into smokestacks and nostrils into coal mines. He instructed the deacon to tape the picture to the underside of Faulkner's glass when they were together at the club. The deacon did as he was told, and the following day when the minister met Faulkner outside the post office, he asked him if he was still seeing Jesus in the bottom of his glass. "Hell no!" Faulkner replied. "Last night before going to the club I decided to follow your advice and leave my glass half full. But then when I lifted the first drink to my lips and saw the devil at the bottom of the glass, I changed my mind. I didn't want to leave that smoky bastard a drop, so saying 'get thee from me you son of a bitch,' I drained the glass, scooping out the dregs with a napkin."

Out

ELIZA FLEW FROM BOSTON LATE Easter afternoon. She traveled to Frankfurt, cramped between "two gigantic German Goths who spilled over their seats and smothered the arm rests." Because she bought an inexpensive ticket, she had an eight-hour layover in Frankfurt, after which she flew to Edinburgh, arriving at noon on Monday. The apartment was ready. I raised a cot in the sitting room and cleaned the shelves built into the walls. Eliza is a picky eater. At the grocery I bought skimmed milk and a choice of breakfast cereals, hoping she would eat one: Tesco's Malty Flakes with "red berries"—freeze-dried cherries, strawberries, and raspberries—and two brands from Jordans, Organic Swiss-Style Muesli and Country Crisp Four Nut Combo. Eliza is also a vegetarian and likes meals heavy with salads and chocolate. At Thorntons I bought the Continental, the biggest box of candy the store sold, containing 112 truffles packed in two layers in a round box wrapped in gold cloth. Since Eliza would be in Edinburgh a week, she had to eat 16 pieces of candy a day to finish the box. She started well, getting through 9 pieces the first day, but then she slumped, managing only 49 during her stay, an average of 7 a day, forcing her to pack the other 63 pieces in her suitcase when she left.

I adore Eliza, and I wanted to stock her mind with memories that might pop up decades later and brighten a rainy day. I so wanted her to enjoy herself that the week before she came I slept poorly, often waking at two in the morning and getting out of bed to read about restaurants or plan activities. Monday morning the North Sea swept over Edinburgh, wind cresting then breaking and running heavy over the ground in currents, the rain not a drizzle but waves pounding, the fog so thick I could barely see the top of the house in which I lived, much less Arthur's Seat or the castle. For the first time I used an umbrella. I rode the bus to the airport. All the passengers were soaked, the young smiling because they were young, the old resigned, their expressions stolid and unchanging, anticipating nuisances ahead. My feet were cold, and my friend Raymond came to mind. On dark days in Storrs sometimes he greets me by making slicing motions along his forearm starting at his wrist, all the while saying "the time has come for the warm tub."

When Eliza suddenly appeared in the terminal, forty-six bracelets jingling on her right arm, I felt gloriously happy and for a second wondered how I'd endured the months away from family. Eliza deserved better than the bus, and from the airport we took a taxi back to Blacket Place. While she showered, I heated a can of Baxters soup. On a plate I laid half a baguette and from the Iain Mellis shop on Victoria five cheeses, all cheddars, Eliza's favorite. She brought one suitcase and few clothes, magazines and books taking up most of the space in her bag. I worry about colds and fevers, so much so that Vicki calls me "Mama Bear," a phrase my mother applied to herself. I fetched a sweater and fleece from my closet and gave them to Eliza. The only socks she brought were thin and pink, so I handed her a pair of bed socks and seven pairs of walking socks. On damp days I urged her to change her socks twice, and the washing machine ran often during her visit. In fact I started the machine while she was in the shower. Because her nightgown was too flimsy for basement living, I washed a sweatshirt and a pair of baggy sweatpants in which I slept and gave them to her.

After Eliza finished lunch, topping the cheese off with five truffles, we set out. During her visit we were on our feet, with the exception of this first half day, for at least ten hours a day. Fog remained thick and webby until Thursday, but we blazed ahead, sometime during the week walking almost every street in the downtown from Strathearn and Beaufort Grange in the south to Lothian and Queensferry to the west, from Inverleith in the north around Calton Hill to Queen's Drive to the east. We ranged out along the Old Dalkeith Road to Craigmillar Castle then up to Duddingston. We walked along Cowgate through Grassmarket to Fountainbridge. We circled Castle Hill several times. We investigated every close we saw. We strolled New Town, ambling around squares and circuses like orb weavers inspecting webs for holes, both streets above and below the Queen Street Gardens. Often my thighs throbbed, and my left knee ached, especially when I walked downhill, forcing me to hobble. After four hours my feet burned. At night they were swollen and purple as eggplant.

Our first stop was the institute, where Eliza e-mailed Vicki, telling her she had landed safely. We e-mailed Vicki every day in hopes of making her think herself part of our experiences. Except for two hurried lunches with Steve Neff, a friend from Nashville who teaches law, and a dinner with Ronny and Christie Jack, whom I had known in Storrs, I hadn't eaten in a restaurant in Edinburgh. When I dine by myself in a restaurant, I eat quickly, always thinking how much better the meal would be if I were at home, a book in my hand, shoes off and feet raised, resting on the seat of another chair. Moreover, since the pound is strong and the dollar has lost so much value that it ought to be dubbed the Republican peso, Edinburgh is expensive. Even on nights when the prospect of sardines and cereal or beans with bread and cheese did not appeal to me, I ate in the flat in order to temper expenses. Chatter about finance undermines vacations, and while Eliza was in Scotland, I pushed money out of mind and we ate out often, something Eliza enjoys. Almost every day, and sometimes twice a day, we took cappuccino breaks, drinking "doubles," Eliza cutting the coffee with a chocolate croissant or carrot cake, one of her favorite sweets.

The first night we ate at Ann Purna, a vegetarian restaurant. Near the institute on St. Patrick Square, Ann Purna may be the best vegetarian restaurant in Edinburgh. Tablecloths were blue and white. Napkins were folded into scallop shells. On every table stood vases brimming with pink carnations. Beaded bowls sat on shelves, the beads shimmering, almost making the bowls revolve. On the walls hung small drawings, depicting Indians snuggling on couches, dancing, and galloping on horseback. Eliza and I ordered thalis, platters of Gujarati dishes. I don't know what I ate, but I cleaned my plate. "You receive a mark of 100 out of 100," Mr. Pandya, the owner, said. Mr. Pandya had come to Scotland in 1972 when Idi Amin banished people of Indian descent from Uganda. Mr. Pandya abandoned three petrol stations and a sugar-making business, arriving in Edinburgh with practically nothing except membership in the Rotary Club, something more useful than a bank card in helping establish him.

Mr. Pandya noticed my taking notes. After I explained that I was writing about Edinburgh, he brought a stack of papers to the table, most reviews and postcards praising the restaurant. "You made one weary journalist and his wife exceedingly happy," B. R. wrote on behalf of himself and his wife, Jane. "Wow!" Alice wrote from Hampshire. "I was in Edinburgh a few weeks ago and stumbled upon your restaurant. It's great—quite simply the best meal I have had in a long time. Just writing to say THANK YOU!" After dinner Eliza and I walked back along Clerk and Newington to Blacket Place. Within eight minutes of entering the flat she was asleep. I stayed up, washing dishes from lunch and putting out plates for breakfast. Almost every night I puttered about after Eliza went to sleep, cleaning the kitchen or laying out clothes for her to wear the next day, not merely socks and sweaters but also long-sleeved shirts that would keep her warm.

Twice more we ate at vegetarian restaurants, both times at lunch, once at Susie's Diner, again not far from institute. We sat at a worn table with a plywood top. People around us looked weathered and worried. "The result of being vegetarians," I told Eliza. "They are just healthy," Eliza said, eating carrot cake for dessert. One day after roaming New Town, we ate a late lunch at Henderson's on Hanover Street. I washed a goat cheese tartlet down with a huge glass of wine, afterward becoming garrulous, informing two women sitting next to us that I had aged into peculiarity. "Carry on," one said. "Carry on. The world needs peculiar people." Eating out was a fresh experience, and I tried different dishes. After we climbed Arthur's Seat I ate venison sausages at the Sheep Heid Inn. Against my advice Eliza had vegetarian haggis. She said she enjoyed the meal, but haggis without meat is bland, and to get through the meal she buried the dish inside a mausoleum of ketchup. Another day we ate lunch at the Café Royal on West Register, one of Edinburgh's best-known pubs, noted for an oval bar and a wall covered with portraits of famous Victorian inventors, all made from Doulton tiles. We sat at the bar. On the wall behind us Michael Faraday, famous for studies in electromagnetism, held a test tube in his right hand. Behind him an assistant poured a liquid into a beaker. Behind both men shelves bent under burdens of buckets and oddly shaped bottles.

Never had I eaten at a bar. Before me the top of a Corinthian column burst into a hat wild with gold ostrich feathers. On my right a brass stand rose into a molded lightbulb resembling flames. Lunches broke trudges. Not only did they give us something to talk about, but they let us relax. Unfortunately the woman who waited on us was unpleasant. She scowled, and when I paid, queried my charge card, the only person in Edinburgh to do so. "Did you steal this?" she asked. Few sixty-three year old men dressed in neckties and khaki trousers and accompanied by college-age daughters traffic in stolen charge cards, much less eat crab cakes for lunch. I looked around. Suddenly the café appeared tarty. Behind me bleary drinkers slumped against the wall. On the other side of the bar a rough couple sat in a love seat, the woman twirling her right hand in her companion's hair, pulling it up like someone plucking detritus from a bathtub drain. I felt like slapping words across the waitress's face, but I kept silent, not wanting to undermine Eliza's good spirits.

Two people form a contained unit. Unlike one person, they talk more about others than with others, observing, for example, that parents dressed little girls like adults in formal coats and dresses while they themselves wore jeans and dirty shirts, looking, as the old expression puts it, like something the cat sucked. Only rarely during the week did a stranger address us. At the Sheep Heid Inn a welder talked to us, but on our part the conversation consisted only of smiles, nods, and expressions like "you bet" and "that's right," the man speaking with a burr and stuttering so terribly that I could hardly understand three words in a paragraph. On most days we ate lunches in restaurants and dinners in the flat, these last consisting of soups, breads, and cheeses. Before Eliza's visit, I avoided lunch, and by the middle of the week I had gained weight. Twice we went to the theater, coming home first to shower and eat. One night we saw a dramatization of Tolstoy's novel *Anna Karenina* at the Royal Lyceum. Since Eliza was majoring in Russian, I purchased seats in the fourth row of the stalls. I dreaded going, however, knowing that Anna killed herself by stepping in front of a train and thinking the production would make me gloomy. I was wrong. The play was first rate. Alas, the woman sitting on my left wore soiled clothes, sourness oozing from her even when she was still. "Ignore her," Eliza whispered. "Imagine yourself in a cheese store."

Today, churches seem havens only on rainy days. Music greeted Eliza and me when we walked into St. Giles Cathedral on the first afternoon of her visit. A choir from Queen Margaret of Scotland Girls' School was singing "Were You There When They Crucified My Lord?" Before the nave stood arrangements of Easter flowers, the bundles trumpets, yellow and white with viburnum, forsythia, and lilies, their colors, like the spiritual, sweeping through sight, softening mood into appreciation and longing. The arches, piers, and vaults woven with ribs appeared visual echoes of themselves, rippling soundless and hypnotically, making one long to believe the old dream. Impressions, to paraphrase Yeats, come like swallows, and alas, like swallows they go. This time, however, war memorials did not batter thought into tears. Repeating experiences does not deepen awareness; it simply creates new layers of awareness, beneath which the old layers molder but still exist like the shops buried under the City Chambers on the other side of the Royal Mile. Still, in Eliza's presence I noticed St. Gaudens's memorial to Robert Louis Stevenson and a plaque celebrating Dr. John Brown, a doctor, the author of *Rab and His Friends,* and an essayist, two of whose books I read in February. Stevenson lay propped up on a daybed, each of the two pillows behind his back thicker than the side of his body. A blanket covered the writer's legs, and he held a pen in his right hand and a sheaf of papers in his left. For a long time I looked at the stained-glass window designed by Burne-Jones and manufactured by William Morris. The glass swelled into an arch so pagan that it seemed a turban, angels swathed in scarlet feathers, beneath them swords, the blades not honed by theology but soothingly springlike, roses and improbable daisies blooming red amid tassels of green leaves. In frames under the swords lounged figures so fleshly they seemed inhabitants of an earthly paradise. Beneath the window the statue of John Knox shrank, as evil often does before beauty.

Vicki says that Eliza and I resemble peas from the same pod, "from different ends but nevertheless from the same pod." In truth, Eliza and I are alike. We worry, we enjoy absurdity, and we like graveyards, relaxing in the quiet and reading tombstones searching for stories. During the week we wandered the cemetery behind Canongate Church, where I showed her the memorial to Adam Smith, whose books she'd read at college. From Canongate we walked to the Calton Burial ground. This time instead of looking at the statue of Lincoln, I studied the giant obelisk, ninety feet tall, modeled on Cleopatra's Needle in London, and erected in 1844 by the Friends of Parliamentary Reform in England and Scotland in honor of Thomas Muir, William Skirving, Thomas Fysche Palmer, Maurice Margarot, and Joseph Gerrald, five Scots convicted of sedition and sent to Botany Bay in 1794 for advocating parliamentary reform.

Good people and the good they do are usually forgotten, while history scrubs the bad, transforming them into the stuff of schoolboy tale, words like *glory* and *patriotism* obscuring truth. In 1792 a group of Whigs founded the Society of Friends of the People in London. Later Muir and Skirving established the Scottish Association of the Friends. Branches spread rapidly. Frightened that the French Revolution might jump the channel, the British government had the men arrested and charged with sedition. The jury was rigged, and despite Richard Sheridan's presenting a petition to Parliament in which the treatment of the men was called illegal and Charles James Fox's declaring that the men had done no more than William Pitt, the prime minister, in advocating reform, the men were transported. Engraved on the side of the obelisk were two quotations, the first uttered by Skirving in 1794: "I know that what has been done these two days will be RE-JUDGED." In August 1793, Muir said, "I have devoted myself to the cause of THE PEOPLE. It is a good cause—it shall ultimately prevail—it shall finally triumph." "Daddy, do you think the cause prevailed?" Eliza asked. "Yes," I said, adding "momentarily" under my breath. Aside from us the graveyard was empty. "Yesterday," I said, thought slipping the bit of sensible restraint, "there were so many tourists in the War Museum that we could hardly move. I wonder how many have heard of these men. Most people prefer guns to butter." "That's too harsh, Daddy," Eliza said. "Yes, it is," I said, putting my arm around her, "let's climb Calton Hill."

Climbing does not better intellectual perspective. Instead the physical effort distances one from thought. From atop the hill, buildings above Market and the Mound glowed gray and yellow and appeared inviting, unlike skyscrapers that rise into heavy doors, formidable and inhumane, not hives bustling with people but vaults, only admitting the corporate. I don't know what makes man climb—not aspiration, maybe just the feeling that shaking loose from others, if for a moment, betters life. Perhaps similar feelings motivate hermits and people who inhabit the edges of society. In any case Eliza and I climbed the 170 steps of the Nelson Monument to the lookout. The monument resembled a telescope, the eyepiece not pointing up but down toward the ground, the perspective from top distancing me from rancor. We wandered the hill for a while, trailing a group of Arabs, shells from pistachio nuts marking their windings. On Arthur's Seat eggshells, many painted, marked paths taken by children on Easter. While Eliza rested on a bench, I walked to the cairn raised by supporters of a Scottish parliament at the eastern lip of the hill. Among a miscellany of things embedded in the cairn were a memorial to a nurse who died at Auschwitz and a paving stone from Paris "used for defending democracy." No one is consistent. Despite my admiration for Muir and Skirving, I'm sure I would have disliked the people who built the cairn.

I knew the warder at the monument. Earlier I chatted with him in City Art Centre. Two of the nicest groups in Edinburgh are warders and volunteers. Many of the former recognized me when I visited with Eliza, often saying things like "Good to see you again, sir" and "Is this your daughter? She is awfully pretty." "We have changed some of the paintings upstairs," a warder in the National Gallery said when I introduced him to Eliza. "You will like them." In the Portrait Gallery, a warder told me that she and her husband had made seven trips to Elvis Presley's birthplace in Tupelo, Mississippi. "We are going to Boston this year," she said. "Do you think we will have a good time?" "A fine time," I said. "But next year," she continued, brightening, "we are going to Nashville and Memphis. I can't wait."

Because I thought rain suited the melancholy canvas of Greyfriars Kirkyard, the cemetery was one of the first places I took Eliza. Despite the weather, the light was different from when I first explored the graveyard, and the carvings on tombs were more prominent and intriguing: hourglasses; scales; skeletons kicking up their bones in dances macabre; keys in locks; an adder wrapping an urn like a thin scarf; crossed coffins, from the end of one coffin an arm sticking out as if from a sleeve, bending back at the elbow, the hand ringing a bell; a sword slicing through gravedigger's tools; behind skulls tools themselves crossed, mattocks jutting outward, pointed both right and left, a shovel behind both of them; and death's-heads wearing crowns, bony fingers interlaced atop rib cages. On the tomb of Thomas Bannatyne, an angel trod death underfoot, her breasts exposed, a Bible or prayer book in her left hand, her right arm pressing her chest above her right breast, her right leg bare to the loin, her foot on death's pelvis. On the pediment of the monument a cherub sat atop a pile of bones, in his left hand an hourglass, his right lifting a cloth exposing a skull. Behind the cherub a group of buildings opened like a manuscript on a book rest. Time had obscured the buildings on the right. On the left, however, was a six-story building, two windows in the side of each story, three in the front, a skull grinning in the entrance. In the middle stood a tower with what looked like a teapot on top, steam rising from the spout. On another monument an angel perched on a cornucopia overflowing with fruit. Religion and justice flanked the monument of George Foulis of Ravelston, both figures decapitated. Along the bottom of William Carstares's monument stretched a life-sized carving of a skeleton, its winding sheets unraveled, exposing a ragged chest.

Before Eliza came I had become almost housebound. Entertaining her forced me out the door, so far outside that on the Tuesday after she left I returned to Greyfriars and read inscriptions, near the Flodden Wall avoiding a man hunched over sniffing glue from a plastic bag. After his coronation in 1633 Charles I established the bishopric of Edinburgh and, citing divine right, tried to impose an Anglican-style prayer book upon the Scottish Church. To oppose the King Scots signed a covenant. On the reestablishment of the monarchy in 1661, Charles II tried to reinstate the Episcopal governance of the Scottish Church. The Coventers opposed him, and blood gushed, an estimated eighteen thousand dying in Scotland from 1661 to 1688. "About an hundred of Noblemen, Gentlemen, Ministers and Others noble Martyrs for JESUS CHRIST," the Martyrs' Monument stated, adding, "The most of them lie here." "Halt passenger," engraving on the monument commanded, "take heed what you do see, This tomb doth shew, for what some men did die. Here lies interr'd the dust of those who stood 'Gainst perjury, resisting unto blood; Adhering to the Covenants, and laws establishing the same." The prosecution ended with the accession of William and Mary and a settlement that recognized the Church of Scotland in its Presbyterian form as the national church. "Enough injustice," I muttered, and turning away from the East Wall, I walked west, stopping at the grave of Henry MacKenzie, author of *The Man of Feeling*, a sentimental novel wildly popular in the eighteenth century. "Just the thing to raise spirits," I thought. After noting that MacKenzie's "beautiful and pathetic fancy," "ingenuity and justness of thought," "elegance and delicacy of style," and "refined moral sentiment and religious purity" raised the literary reputation of Scotland, the inscription declared that the stone was erected not for the public man but the private man—"as a memorial of the love and affection of the widow and the children he left behind to lament his loss: who saw in all the relations of his life the practice of the virtues his writings inspire." William Dunbar died in 1788. He, his epitaph noted, "Supported his Rank in life with probity and Honour. Felt and practiced true Religion and must long be remembered as an example of the warmth and sincerity of Friendship." "His Sorrowful Widow," the tribute continued, "has raised this humble monument as an inadequate mark of Gratitude which she must feel to his memory till Heaven shall mingle her ashes with those of her Husband." I cannot rise above thinking about my life as I read the world. "What," I wondered darkly, "would my family put on my tombstone?" "His Death Was a Blessing. He Left an Inheritance, Dying before Medical Bills Stripped His Bank Account."

Moods never last long in graveyards. Carvings on tombstones are various and if not stories are the matter of story. As such they distract people from themselves, making cemeteries healthy places. Next to MacKenzie's stone was that of his son Joshua Henry, who "was led during the two years of suffering which closed his life to lean more securely on the pardoning love of god as a reconciled Father in Christ Jesus." Two years of suffering is everyone's nightmare. I dream of, nay, pray for, a quick end, the slamming of a door, the shutting of a book, lightning's slicing a branch from a tree. At the edge of the South Yard stood the Adam Mausoleum. Neoclassical, its architecture promised an ordered world, continents removed from gothic suffering. Only at a distance do imagination and pleasing fiction flourish. Attached to the wall of the mausoleum was a memorial to John Adam, who died in 1825 while returning to England from India. He had enjoyed a distinguished career in the East Indian Service, having first sailed for Bengal in 1795, becoming a member of the Supreme Council in 1819, and for eight months in 1823 acting as governor-general. What mattered to the Adam family was John Adam, not his success. "His surviving parent and his family," the engraving testified, "expected to have seen, in ripened manhood, what early youth had promised; to have beheld his benign countenance; to have enjoyed his enlightened discourse; to have been soothed by his warm affection; to have witnessed his active benevolence."

I walked into the West Yard. Ivy hung over the Flodden Wall, and Oxford ragwort flourished between stones high above the ground. Alas, many plots had grown weedy. D. Patterson Rollo, the spouse of Alexander Wallace, died in 1801 at forty-four. She was, her epitaph noted, "A loving and Conscientious Wife, An Affectionate Mother, and a Steady Friend." The tribute notwithstanding, on her grave someone had dumped a dozen cans of Carlsberg Special Brew, at 9 percent alcohol a fortified beer. At the edge of the yard I found a trash barrel. I carried it over to the grave and weeded the plot. "Be careful," a man walking past said, "the grass is full of needles." "I will," I said, suddenly hearing a chaffinch calling "weet, weet."

Before leaving the graveyard, I explored Greyfriars Church, open longer hours now that the tourist season had begun. Much of the church was built in the nineteenth century then refined in the twentieth. In the eighteenth century, gunpowder stored in church's tower exploded, blasting the west end of the building into ruin, and in the nineteenth a fire starting in a boiler flue gutted half the church. Still, I liked the building. Its walls were mulled white and comparatively bare, most of the memorials peaceful, celebrating ministers and benefactors, and the occasional artist, such as Robert Adam, the famous eighteenth-century architect buried in Westminster Abbey and the designer of Charlotte Square and Old College in Edinburgh. Nine pillars ran along each side of the nave, rising into six arches, the other arches having disappeared behind rooms and a gallery for the organ. In contrast to the graveyard the church was clean and well lit, a refuge from the clutter of life. A kindly docent insisted on showing me the church. She was old and deaf and to whatever I said responded, "I am glad you liked that. Now let me show you. . . ." Accordingly, I saw the Stool of Repentance, on which sinners knelt to pray for forgiveness for enjoying life too much. For my part I felt like kneeling and asking to be pardoned for trying to escape the kind but firm grasp of my guide. The organ was comparatively new, first being played in 1990. Decorating the front rank of pipes were two ovals, a friar appearing in one, Greyfriars Bobby, the dog, in the other. "That is really tacky," I said without thinking, pointing toward the dog. Thank goodness, the woman was deaf. "That is Bobby," she said. "We have a pamphlet about him, and you can buy a stuffed replica of him at the Visitor Centre. On the other side is a grey friar. On the pipes behind are four Scottish animals: a red squirrel, a pine marten, a black grouse, and a capercaillie." "The grouse and capercaillie are game birds," I said. "I would like to see them in the wild. I am a bit of a birder." "People hunt the grouse and the capercaillie," she continued. "But I don't suppose birds interest you."

I hesitated to leave Greyfriars. My guide was charming, and in its non sequiturs our conversation was more sensible than most chat. From the church I walked north along King George IV Bridge to the Elephant House Café, where I bought an almond croissant and a cappuccino. Had Eliza not come to Edinburgh, I wouldn't have entered the café. Eliza broke the rhythm of my days, and after she left, I became, in my terms, adventurous. Would that I had been to the café before her visit. J. K. Rowling, the author of the Harry Potter novels, wrote some of her first book in the café. Eliza and I both had read Rowling's books, and we would have enjoyed going to the café together. In any case I carried my coffee to the back room and sat at an empty table. Cirrus clouds of smoke streaked the air. Students leaned over tables, some scribbling, some typing rapidly on laptop computers, others reading. A boy walked in carrying a tray loaded with a cappuccino, a can of Diet Coke, and a pack of cigarettes. He sipped the cappuccino, then opened the can and drank some of the Coke. Next he lit a cigarette. He inhaled, then sipped the coffee again. A woman sat by herself talking into a recorder. Two homely men sat alone smoking and occasionally glancing around in hopes of seeing people they knew. From a compact disc player came the sound of funky, adulterous jazz, punctuated now and then by moaning. Clippings describing elephants papered a wall. Elsewhere naive art decorated walls, a number of the drawings nudes, one woman rolled into a nut, another heavy, sausages of fat rippling over her, the artist clearly familiar with Lucien Freud's paintings.

On shelves stood herds of elephants—tall, short, wooden, plastic, blond, and black—so many they bored me. Carved on the back of a chair and facing outward was the head of a male African elephant, the trunk low and tight against the animal's jaw so passersby would not trip over it. In contrast, the bulging forehead rose lumpy above the back of the chair, from the opposite side of the table looking like a woman's bust, one stuffed with boulders of silicone. What the café needed was the elephant's skull that hung above the stairway leading from the first to the second floor of the Thorn Exhibition at Surgeons Hall.

Beside windows stood pots containing tall, spiky plants. Beyond the windows rose the castle, half-moon battery curving in front of it like a buckler. Atop houses along Victoria stretched rows of khaki chimney pots, four, seven, ten, and fifteen in the rows I counted. Against the wall stood a case divided into three bookshelves, all containing books in which elephants appeared, among others, Agatha Christie's mystery *Elephants Can Remember; Elephantastick! A Trunkful of Unforgettable Jokes;* and Ken Brown's *Nellie's Knot,* on the cover of which stood a forlorn little elephant, her trunk knotted. Across the book jacket of Gerald Sparrow's *No Other Elephant* swayed a Conestoga elephant, a man and a woman sitting across from each other in what resembled the body of a covered wagon mounted on an elephant undercarriage, in front of them a turbaned chauffeur. I studied the library; Babar, the most famous elephant in literature, was missing. "Has Babar been poached?" I asked an employee of the café. The café was popular enough to sell T-shirts. The shirts were dyed one color, some orange, others red or green. Printed on them was a white elephant holding a coffee cup in his trunk. A line of elephants even paraded across around the walls of the men's lavatory, the animals not linked trunk to tail like elephants in a circus but grasping cups.

On leaving the cemetery Eliza and I walked down Candlemaker to Grassmarket, an area that aside from the buildings does not appeal to me, striking me as honky-tonky. We went into a couple of shops I like, Bow Well Antiques on West Bow, then up and around the curve on Victoria, the Iain Mellis cheese store. During Eliza's visit we explored several shops, most of them clothing stores on George Street in New Town. The Sunday before she returned to Boston was her twentieth birthday, and I wanted to buy her a small gift, the trip itself being her big present. After leading me through several stores, she bought a skirt at French Connection. Music blared in the store, the sound cacophonous and so loud it was rude. Clerks in the store were young and dressed as if they had been interrupted taking off their clothes. A boy's trousers sagged so low off his hips that his buttocks protruded, looking like halves of unripened cantaloupes. The brush strokes of a Chinese letter ticked the crease splitting a girl's backside. A cross shiny with zirconium dangled between a girl's breasts, the latter loose under a blouse as thin as a blue ribbon. A garden of flowers bloomed like summer across Eliza's skirt. Still, I didn't think the skirt fit. "Mommy's going to think that's too tight," I said. Later that night Eliza said, "You're right. I think the skirt fits, but Mommy won't." The next morning we hiked back to the store, and she exchanged the skirt for one a size bigger. "Mommy will really like that," I said. "I think so, too," Eliza said.

Eliza and I rarely rested, and the visit exhausted me. For half a week afterward my mental marbles rolled out the door. At breakfast two days after Eliza left, I dumped my tea bag into a cereal bowl, then tried to pour my cereal down a long cardboard tube, the kind around which paper towels are wrapped. That afternoon I went to the National Gallery to buy a book describing the work of Phoebe Anna Traquair, an artist whose paintings Eliza admired. The author autographed it. "Would you inscribe the book 'To Vicki,'" I said to the author, confusing daughter with wife. "She was just here, and she really liked Traquair." "Won't Vicki be surprised and pleased when I give her the book," I thought, hiking back up the Mound toward the institute.

During the first hours of Eliza's visit we went to art galleries. Vicki's father and mother collected eighteenth- and nineteenth-century English watercolors. From them Eliza inherited an eye. A day after visiting the National Gallery and viewing Sir Joseph Noel Paton's *The Quarrel of Oberon and Titania,* an extravaganza of fairies cavorting in flimsy dress, she flipped though a catalog on my breakfast table, stopping at a Victorian narrative painting. "This painting has to be by Paton," she said. "What?" I responded. "Look at the arm," she said, pointing to the forearm of a young woman. "The flesh and muscle tones are the same as those in the painting of Oberon and Titania."

During damp days we visited the National Gallery, the Portrait Gallery, the Dean, and the Gallery of Modern Art. Eliza wanted to start at the Dean, Dada and surrealism appealing more to youth than to age. For the old, ordinary life often becomes so habitual that the unfamiliar seems disquieting and threatening. For youth, which dreads settling into convention, Dada offers hope, the realization that one doesn't always have to live according to platitude or express one's self conventionally. Moreover Dada's apparent nonsense can provoke wonder and sometimes awareness of the possibility of regeneration, even spiritual awareness. Outside the gallery we looked at Eduardo Paolozzi's *Master of the Universe,* a rendition of mechanical modern man sitting on a stool and leaning forward, his left hand holding an isosceles triangle upright, the index finger of his right hand pointing to the ground. Beneath the finger a wag had slipped a penny. In three months in Scotland I had found little money on the ground, only two pennies and a five-penny piece. "The penny won't be there long," I said. I was right. By the time we left the Gallery of Modern Art an hour later, the penny had disappeared. In galleries Eliza and I always pick out favorites, hers being Yves Tanguy's *Never Again,* on which bits of things stretched across a distance looking like mirages in a desert.

Much like revisiting established ideas, returning to a museum can disquiet. Items one liked a month or a year earlier may have lost their appeal, making life seem evanescent, forcing a person to question not simply taste but at the extreme beliefs on which social life itself is raised. To me inconsistency seems vital, a natural and healthy response to the riches of life. That aside, however, the paintings I envision lifting from galleries and hanging at home fit a pattern. Almost always painted in the late nineteenth century or early twentieth century, they depict country or village life. If they show life in a city, the section of the city resembles a village.

At the Gallery of Modern Art, I coveted Utrillo's *La Place du Tertre,* a canvas depicting a square in Montmartre in 1913. A white building with blue shutters bracketing its windows stood on the left side of the canvas. Beside it an uneven row of buildings stretched to a street corner. On the corner of the street stood the Hôtel du Tertre, six windows visible on the front. A small square ran along the front of the building, twenty bare trees twisting up from the ground. In front of the hotel a woman wearing a shawl walked toward the corner. A couple walked the opposite direction along the road separating the square from the buildings. At the National Gallery, I imagined hanging a painting by Pissarro in the living room, *Kitchen Garden at l'Hermitage, Pontoise 1874.* In the foreground of the painting grew plots of what looked like lettuce and onions. Behind them a man hoed mustard. Behind the mustard were five buildings. In back of them a hedgerow of poplars ran along a field. To the left of the plots a woman pushed a donkey loaded with sacks, while another woman stood by a fence, a cloth tied around her head. On the right two women stood under crooked trees, one bent over, the other with a basket hanging on her shoulders. "Looking at this painting would never tire me," I told Eliza.

Not until Eliza's visit have I ever wanted a medieval painting, but she and I both liked *Madonna and Child,* a late-fifteenth-century painting by the Master of Embroidered Foliage. The madonna sat in the middle of the painting on a seat that resembled a carpet decorated with floral designs, among the flowers the lotus blossom. In her lap she held the child. She wore red, and the child white. From their heads halos rose upward in sunbursts, the gold delicate and spun, turning the mother and child into lamps, their brightness illuminating the green earth, not lighting a path to a distant world. On both sides of the carpet and beneath the pillow on which the madonna's foot rested, greenery spread in a luminous U, one of the plants wild strawberry, its leaves promising sweet redness. On the upper left side of the U stood a large house; on the right a mill, its wheel turning. Amid the greenery bloomed iris, violets, columbine, lilies, and white buttercups. A butterfly perched on an iris, wings raised, five eyes dotting and a sweep of bluish white meandering like a shallow stream across its hind wing. "You like that, do you, sir?" said a warder, adding, "So do I. It is rich but somehow comfy."

The rain stopped on Wednesday, and although fog hung like a lid over Edinburgh, we set out for Holyroodhouse early in the morning. In February when I visited the palace, I was the only person in each room beside the warders. Now crowds milled, most people trudging glassy eyed and weary. The arrogance oozing from the expressions of the Stuarts in the portraits momentarily made me a leveler; yet, in the gift shop I bought a cup commemorating the marriage of Prince Charles and Camilla Parker Bowles as a present for Vicki. After two hours in the palace, we started up the Royal Mile, stopping at every museum along the way: Huntly House, the Museum of the People, and the Museum of Childhood. All were crowded. At Huntly House I didn't push through people. Instead I looked closely at only one object, a piece of Wemyss Ware, a three-handed loving cup made around 1900. The cup was four inches in diameter. Cattle decorated the outside of the bowl. In one scene a brown and white bull, not polled, gazed over a wooden fence at a cow sitting on her haunches.

People were packed three deep in front of the display cases in the Museum of Childhood. The day I went to the museum in January I was the only visitor. "The crowds get worse," a warder told me. "During the festival in August," a man said, "a person can't get into a coffee shop. Many people leave town." When friends in Storrs discovered that I was only going to spend winter and part of spring in Scotland, they urged me to extend my stay. "You can't leave before the festival," an acquaintance said. "It is so exciting." As I breasted the crowds in museums, I was glad to be leaving Edinburgh in May.

For five days Eliza and I explored at least one museum a day, on Charlotte Square the Georgian House, at Surgeons Hall the Sir Jules Thorn Exhibition and the Menzies Campbell Dental Museum, and on Lawnmarket, Gladstone's Land, which opened at the end of March and which I had not visited previously. A six-story seventeenth-century building, the lower story being an arcade, Gladstone's Land was managed by Scotland's National Trust. The trust furnished rooms with period and reproduction furniture, the time frame running from the seventeenth through the eighteenth centuries, mirroring changes in the house. I wanted to meander the rooms, but bolts of people swept me forward, pressing the volunteer guides into drill sergeants directing the wheels and turns of tourist battalions.

I glimpsed furniture that interested me: in the Inner Hall a seventeenth-century oak chest, the smaller of the two chests in the hall, and in the Green Room a William and Mary walnut kneehole desk. The ceiling in the Painted Chamber had been decorated around 1620, but as I studied it, my eye plucking grapes and apples and snipping hollyhocks, a small boy raced into the room and banged into me, causing my left leg to buckle and my neck to snap. I stumbled against a gate-legged table.

The boy's parents smiled, and by way of an apology the mother said, "he's so energetic." After steadying myself, I smiled while muttering "imbeciles" under my breath and, walking back into the kitchen, hovered beside a close stool in hopes of letting the family get so far ahead they wouldn't bump into me again.

Scottish parents don't discipline small sons. In the National War Museum, two boys swung on the railing that protected *The Thin Red Line* from the public. While the boys kicked their feet up within inches of the frame surrounding the picture, a warder stood by looking overwhelmed until I barked, "For god's sakes, stop them. They will wreck the painting." I should add that I have aged into giving strangers advice. Yesterday while I was drinking a cappuccino in the Elephant Café, a young woman asked to take the ashtray on my table over to her table. "By all means take it," I said, adding, "but you should stop smoking. Cigarettes will turn you into a miasma of disease." "I smoke," said a boy sitting near me, an employee of the café who had recently moved to Edinburgh from Nottingham and was reading George Orwell's *Down and Out in Paris and London*. "And you should listen to me," I said, turning toward him. "In spite of having good taste in books, you are clearly foolish. Not only should you stop smoking, but you should move to Australia. Go to Perth."

The Royal Museum and the Museum of Scotland are joined, the buildings occupying two-thirds of the south side of Chambers Street. Their collections are so astonishingly various that the museums constitute Edinburgh's Smithsonian. Eliza and I spent two afternoons rambling through them, the exhibits exhausting us, stuffing our minds until everything tumbled out, making it difficult to pull a particular object out of the clutter into sight. "Everything in the world is here except cave paintings and automobiles," Eliza said late the second afternoon. "Yes," I said, "skulls from a herd of Aurochs; enough Roman relics to outfit a cohort; a treasure chest constructed in the 1690s, under its lid so many iron arteries and capillaries that Paolozzi's sculptures seem naive in comparison; a guillotine retired after lopping off heads for 145 years; flocks of stuffed birds; a red telephone booth filched when Dr. Who vanished from television; a tar pit of fossils; a seventeenth-century Dutch cabinet big enough to contain our whole family, including dogs, both dead and alive; from Glenfiddich a copper still that looks like a huge mushroom; and crawling up the back of a display case sundry crabs, coconut, coral, a Japanese spider, great spiny, and a giant shore, props from a B movie."

"Enough," Eliza said. "Do the crabs bother you?" I asked. "Maybe you would be more comfortable with nineteenth-century Chinese ivory animals. You could carry them in the palm of your hand. The museum owns a zoo: snakes, rabbits, tigers, rats, horses, monkeys, cicadas, turtles, dragons, water buffalo, and, of course, the legendary baku, its appearance a composite of other creatures, its body that of a dog or a cat, its nose sometimes a trunk, other times a snout."

"Enough," Eliza said again, turning toward the museum shop, irritation underlining the word. I stopped, although I wanted to describe my favorite object in the museum, a horse-drawn wooden hearse that saw "active" duty from 1783 to 1844. The hearse was black, the sides decorated with skulls and hourglasses, tears falling beside them in silver drops and wreaths unfolding and flowing upward around them green with new leaves. The roof of the hearse rose into a high crown, then sloped into a brim. Sides and the back and front of the hearse were open, and the roof rested atop yellow posts, seven on each side, eight in the rear, and four in the front. The driver sat on a black box, crossed bones decorating the front. "How I'd like to travel to a picnic in that, champagne, fried chicken, potato salad, and a tin of fudge in a hamper at my feet," I thought, provided, of course, that I was able to eat and was not simply a course to be savored by sundry members of the creeping and crawling generations.

Eliza wanted a postcard depicting a snuff mull, manufactured in Edinburgh early in the 1880s. Medusa-like, the mull was probably the ugliest object in the museum. The head of a blackface ram formed the front of the mull, its horns shellacked and twirling out from the skull, the ends tipped with silver. Behind and attached to the head was a wool-covered box in which could be stored the accoutrements of masculine after-dinner dipping or smoking. The lid of the box was silver and studded and resembled a targe. From the center of the targe rose a setting, in which rested a dark agate. Snuff mulls were rolled around at the ends of banquets. Indeed, the mull was so grotesque that only someone blinded by drink could look at it.

We could not find a card showing the mull. I asked the clerk in the museum store if any pictures of the mull were in stock. I described the mull and explained that its ugliness appealed to me. "We do not exhibit ugly things," the clerk said, "and we do not carry a card showing the object you described." Shrugging, I said, "Well, then I'd like to buy this," and handed her a card on which appeared two figurines manufactured at Thomas Rathbone's pottery early in the nineteenth century, one a piper, the other sitting in a chair, a flask in his hand. Before she took my money, she stared at the card. "Now these," she said, "are disgusting. I cannot understand why anyone would like them." I almost urged the woman to commit an unnatural act. But Eliza was standing beside me, and so I simply handed her forty-five pence, took the card, and walked away.

The rain stopped on Wednesday, and the next morning Eliza and I set out for Arthur's Seat, following the trail I blazed on Good Friday, walking along Queen's Drive to Dunsapie Loch then ascending Whinny Hill. The day was overcast, and fog hid the Firth of Forth. Predictions about the weather for the rest of the week were contradictory, and so we seized this break in the rain. A thin haze drifted across Edinburgh, but we could see the city from the summit. Indeed, while we were atop the Seat, rails of sunlight slipped through the clouds, so cheering us that we almost skipped along. On Crow Hill we watched a stoat scurry between rocks, periodically standing on his hind legs to assure himself that we weren't dangerous. As I had planned, we drifted down the Windy Goule to Duddingston and ate lunch at the Sheep Heid Inn. Afterward we walked back to town along the cycle path built over the old railway right-of-way. In the damp few-flowered leeks spread across the ground in green salads. Beneath Samson's Ribs two brown rabbits shuffled across the grass. We walked through the tunnel at the end of path. On the walls people had sprayed sentences, some advice or commands, others absurd, still others comments on the states of their minds, many idiosyncratic, reassuring me that individualism was not endangered: "Cynicism Is Death," "Please Use Adverbs," "Meat = Murder," "Sometimes I Want to Die," and "Only Pirates Sail the Red Sea."

The next morning was sunny, and we went to the castle. Despite the rain and fog, we had circled Castle Rock several times, viewing it from different perspectives, looking at it from Ramsay Gardens and Heriot Place. We had walked through West Princes Street Gardens, marveling at the daffodils yellow under the north slope of Castle Rock. We had roamed southeast along King's Stable Road and southwest along Johnston. From the outside, the castle was wonderfully appealing. History drifted out of mind. The batteries and towers, guardhouses and gates lost their functions and became the building blocks of paragraphs, darkened only by print, not blood. Of course, print can rip veins like a dirk. I grew up in a world flickering with celluloid cavaliers, all bastardly, loosely descended from Walter Scott's pen. How, I wondered, if at all, had growing up amid such romance affected the ways my friends saw and acted?

Eliza and I got to the castle just after it opened. Cars and buses already crammed the parking lot, and a switchback of lines had formed before the ticket office. In January there had been no line. We spent two and a half hours in the castle, and although I enjoyed exploring with Eliza, nothing I saw changed my early impressions. The National War Museum sickened me. Display cases were magnets drawing crowds of children. "Look at this machine gun," a twelve-year-old boy shouted to his friends. Kindergarten children ran about waving plastic swords. A mother photographed her two little boys having a sword fight in the Middle Ward on the sharp slope opposite the Governor's House. A case contained gas masks from World War I. In one the eyes bulged, a rubber hose trailing below, making the mask appear cartoonish, a prop from a satirical horror movie. Above the mask hung a precursor, an anti-gas hood from 1916, constructed from cloth dipped into chemicals in order to filter out gas. The hood floated through the case like a nightmare. I watched people approach the exhibit. Most turned away quickly, preferring rifles, their bayonets flickering like the northern lights, and old pistols looking like big silver hasps torn from medieval cloaks. At two o'clock we heard music coming from the Great Hall. "An orchestra of Japanese high school students," I said to Eliza. "No," she said, pointing to a bulletin board, "the San Marino Wind Ensemble." I studied the group and this time noticed two members whose ancestry was not Asian. The students played well and looked good, the boys dressed in dinner jackets and the girls in long black dresses. Unfortunately the adult who directed them wore a black leather flyer's jacket and corduroy pants. "A man his age should know better," Eliza said. "Thank goodness you've never worn a leather jacket. I would have been so embarrassed."

Saturday was sunny, and Eliza and I set out for Stockbridge and the Botanic Garden. We broke the trek at Circle Café on Brandon in order to stoke our furnaces for the day's wanderings, Eliza ordering her usual, a cappuccino and a slab of carrot cake. Just beyond the East Gate and at the start of the path to the Rock Garden, a Yoshino flowering cherry was blooming, the pink flowers sweet and clumpy like bowls of rice pudding. Below heather, platters of spring starflowers blossomed, their petals white and sharp. The leaves of Pyrenees cotoneaster glistened, looking like green metallic beads. Western trillium sprayed open above a dark border at the edge of the Woodland Garden. Tips of the trilliums' petals were starched, but the centers were sudsy with yellow. Rhododendrons flowered through the garden. My favorite was the macabeanum, a round bush sometimes familiarly called camellia bay. The yellow flowers piled atop each other, individual blossoms fluted and resembling vases, a stack of vases sometimes five blossoms high, a flower head consisting of more than twenty blooms, the whole looking like an epergne.

Small English daisies dappled the grass of the arboretum, turning the lawn into Minton. The leaves of Japanese poplar unfolded and stretched upward like liquid fingers; below them dangled tassels yellow with blossoms. Darwin's barberry was bright with racks of orange cups, pink splattering their bottoms. While kneeling to look at white butterbur, I saw a long-tailed tit, my first. I wanted to point the bird out to Eliza, but she was on the other side of a beech hedge, sitting on the grass, leaning backward, sunning. Our paces were different. The journey to Scotland was my last long trip. Never again would I spend so many months away from home. The beauty of the garden elated me. The elation was momentary, however, and melancholy set in as I imagined places I'd never visit. I lingered over plants, not wanting to move on because I knew I would not see them again. Eliza was young and didn't ponder limitations. Before her the future stretched endlessly blooming, and she bounced through the garden, the thought that she might not see some of the plants again not disturbing the moment.

While she bustled through the glasshouses, explaining the humidity exhausted her, I dawdled, covering my palm with the resinous fragrance of liverwort and imagining sitting beneath a jade plant, the turquoise blossoms hanging over my left shoulder, in my right hand a small purple teacup baked from a blossom plucked from glory bush. While the length of my life was finite, the variety of plants seemed infinite. As Eliza dozed outside absorbing sunlight, I stood in front of plants, vaguely hoping to absorb an awareness of infinity, not something that would extend life but something that would comfort and enrich: flat-flowered aloe, its limbs spiraling, covered with pods of yellow blossoms, then the strangest flower I have ever seen, tiger whisker, or, as varieties are called in some places, bat plant and devil flower. Chinese herbalists use the plant to treat ulcers, burns, hepatitis, and high blood pressure. I thought the flower resembled a crab shell. Instead of two antennae locks of filaments dangled from the flower. Buds replaced the crab's eyestalks and antennules in the middle of the shell. Before they opened, the buds looked like small candies wrapped in paper, the papers crimped together at the tops. Upon bursting into flowers the buds became pipes, their edges rolled. My favorite plant was familiar and brought the past, not the future, to mind, the two years I spent in Western Australia. Bridal veil broom is a close relative of white weeping broom, a weed established north of Perth that threatens the biodiversity of the region. The glasshouse, however, restricted the shrub's spread but not its jasminelike fragrance. Strands of thin limbs wept downward, all ringed by small white flowers. Amid the perfume, happy times almost forgotten hovered at the edge of thought, days when the children, and I, sailed across hours, the sky above us always blue. "Gosh," I said, standing and walking away from the broom, "I really want Eliza to remember this trip."

That night we went to a play. We got home at eleven, and Eliza quickly fell asleep. I didn't. When she woke the next morning, Eliza would be twenty years old, and I wanted the day to be happy and, if not exciting, sweetly memorable. We'd explored a guidebook of sights, and I thought about going to the zoo. On Sundays, though, throngs of children crowd the zoo, many of them thumping on glass outside cages, no matter instructions to the contrary, their parents often joining them, others dashing about in high spirits, disturbing not only the animals but people looking at them. Moreover, experiences at zoos are mixed, as one cannot escape awareness of man's inhumanity to animals, including his own species.

I plan carefully when responsible for others in hopes of rooting the spontaneous in the expected. Once I decided against going to the zoo, not many new sights lay within walking distance. With misgivings I decided to take Eliza to Craigmillar Castle. On the map the castle seemed about a mile and a half away from Blacket down the Old Dalkeith Road. In the walking the journey seemed to last forever and practically melted icing off the birthday. Cars rushed past in hot cloudbursts, roaring and spewing dark fumes. On the Craigmillar Castle Road garbage ripened in a ditch, looking like overflow from a third world country that had experienced an unexpected leap in population. Moreover, shoulders rose steeply from the pavement. Along the top of the shoulders a path wound crazily, dipping down into the road for a few steps then rising again only to vanish and reappear some yards ahead on the other side of the pavement.

Suddenly we walked around a bend. The garbage vanished, and the castle appeared beyond a farmhouse, its walls light gray and clean, buttons of speedwell and lesser celandine blue and yellow amid tidy cardigans of grass. An old dog slept in the sun outside the curtain wall, and along the east range a mother and father played hide-and-seek with two young children. Except for the family and the dog, pigeons nesting in the tower, and two baby rabbits foraging the brambles below the east garden, the castle was empty. Moreover, although Mary, Queen of Scots, took refuge in the castle during the difficult times after the murder of her friend David Riccio and was there while her advisers plotted the murder of her husband, Darnley, the castle, had not been the scene of the casual butchery that constitutes Scottish history. Eliza and I roamed the grounds slowly running hands and eyes over the inner curtain wall and imagining a banquet in the hall on the first floor of the tower. We stood atop the ramparts. We climbed every staircase and explored all the rooms. I watched a white horse grazing in a pasture south of the castle. In a quiet ruin moods are peaceful. When a pack of adolescents drove four-wheelers across a field, they seemed gnats, buzzing at the lip of consciousness.

After leaving the castle we walked north to Duddingston and ate our second meal at the Sheep Heid Inn. On holidays and weekends the upstairs dining room is open, and we ate lunch at the table at which I had sat on Good Friday. The table behind us was empty. On Good Friday two professional couples ate behind me, their conversation never straying from money. We each drank a big glass of red wine and for dessert had chocolate cake covered with chocolate icing, two scoops of chocolate ice cream on the plate beside it. "Not as good as Mom's," Eliza said, "but it will do." After lunch we returned to Blacket, walking along the railway track, this time avoiding the tunnel.

At the flat Eliza napped. I made a cup of tea then walked to Odd Bins on Newington and bought a bottle of champagne. Because I did not want to disturb the Phanjoos, who owned the flat and lived above me, I had not gone into the garden behind the house. The day after Eliza arrived, however, they left for their home in France. I found champagne glasses in the kitchen cupboard and woke Eliza, and we went into the garden and, sitting on a bench, drank the champagne, wearing sweaters because the day had become overcast. Nearby a Japanese magnolia bloomed, and we watched a goldcrest then a green finch pick ways under a rhododendron. "I don't want to forget Edinburgh," Eliza said when we finished the champagne. "Let's go for a last walk." We strolled for two hours. Afterward we returned to the Ann Purna and ordered thalis, this time with a bottle of red wine. "What a wonderful day," Eliza said as we walked back to the flat. "Yes, a wonderful day," I repeated, but looking off into the distance and feeling agonizingly sad.

When we got back to the flat, Eliza went to sleep while I washed and dried her clothes. Nagging me was the thought that I had left something undone. The next morning I realized what it was. While Eliza showered, I raced uptown to Blackwell's and bought a coffee-table book filled with pictures of Edinburgh. When Eliza described her trip to Vicki, the book would spur conversation. At ten o'clock we took a taxi to the airport. Before her plane left, Eliza drank a cappuccino and ate a huge chocolate cupcake. "I wouldn't eat that," I warned, "you'll get sick if the flight is bumpy."

The week had come full circle. I rode the bus back from the airport to North Bridge. I felt lonely, and so instead of going to the institute and writing, I walked down to Bernie's on Newington and got a haircut, my first in Edinburgh. I had looked through Bernie's window several times when walking to the institute. Bernie was an old-fashioned barber who had been cutting hair for over forty years. Moreover, his shop resembled a cell, the walls and ceiling a honeycomb of knickknacks. From the ceiling hung thirty-eight cups, many mustache cups, others varied, on the front of one, for example, a blue barber shop, a barber's pole white and crimson beside it. Parked on a shelf was a small yellow New York taxi. Roundabouts of automotive matters wound through the shop: a California driver's license with Marilyn Monroe's photograph on the front, plates from South Carolina and Arizona, and pictures of low, sleek cars, none of which I recognized. Bernie's name appeared in red in the middle of a souvenir plate from Nevada, "The Silver State," a line at the bottom of the plate declared.

On the walls hung a gallery of promotional shots of celebrities, their signatures printed on the pages—Fats Domino, Françoise Hardy, Frank Zappa, and Kid Creole, among others. Elvis Presley and Frank Sinatra stared from the ovals of dollar bills, next to them a bill for ten cents issued by the Bank of Tennessee. From a line swung a rubber fish, "The Fish That Swallowed Elvis," a caption declared. From a hook dangled a blue necktie, black musical notes wavering across it. Signs were more numerous than billboards along a highway. "Unattended children will be sold as slaves," one warned. "It takes a real professional to make a mess this big," declared another. Above a red oval with *Rinso* printed on it appeared the phrase "Soak the Clothes—That's All!" Below was the justification, "Saves Coal Every Wash-Day." Near the end of my haircut

Jock came into the shop. Jock noticed my floppy hat. "During the Korean War," he said, "when I landed at Pusan, officers took away our helmets and handed us soft hats just like that." He paused and shook his head before adding, "That's the British army for you."

Nobody was waiting when Bernie finished my hair, and so I stayed in the shop and talked. Soon Bernie and Jock and I were singing, first Tennessee Ernie Ford's "Sixteen Tons" and then a selection of Stephen Foster's songs. We stood and pranced about, not too high because none of us were young. "We should go outside," I suggested. "I'll put my hat on the sidewalk and people will think we are buskers." "They will think we are crazy," Jock said. "Then every so often I will scream and scare money out of them," I answered. "We'll make millions."

Our last song was "Old Folks at Home." After the chorus, a customer came into the shop, and I walked downhill to Blacket. I missed Eliza. The next morning I was at the institute before 7:30. Later in the day Eliza sent an e-mail. "I had a great time, Daddy," she wrote. "But I wish I had listened to you at the airport. The air above Frankfurt was really turbulent, and I threw up four times. All the way to New York I smelled like chocolate vomit."

No *Place* like *Home*

OCEANS SEPARATE CONNECTICUT FROM Scotland, only one geographical. In part I came to Edinburgh in hopes that different surroundings would affect my thought. My ideas were weary, and my metaphors dusty. Political doings blighted optimism, and instead of bouncing through days marveling at the wonder of fall and winter, I limped along, halt and so gloomy that I was partially blind. In Edinburgh I imagined new experience scratching my mind like heather, sharp but fragrant, ripping barky attitudes away, freeing both heartwood and matters of the heart so they could swell and throb. To a large extent I realized my hope.

Nevertheless, oceans are not as broad as they once were. When a person travels, home follows closer than his shadow at noon. Electronic mail is the contemporary clipper ship, crossing seas billowed by electrons. "Will no one," Josh wrote me two weeks ago, "toss the money-changers out of the White House and bundle them off to Beelzebub's Bosom?" Moreover, at times Edinburgh almost seems an American city. Packs of American tourists roam the streets, and hundreds of Americans attend the university, transforming foreign study into home study. And, of course, after a time a person becomes so acclimated that any place seems home. Eventually one ceases to explore, and living slips into a pattern. Days become regular, as if regularity were a virtue and not a failing, a sign that a person has vanished into convention. People treat timetable adjectives, *dependable* and *punctual,* for example, as praise. They associate with "regular guys," dullards who never disturb givens, no matter what the givens are. To be known as a good fellow costs life itself. So that one does not lose things, he finds places for them and puts them there every day, in the process losing the person he might have become.

Moreover, no matter how lightly one travels, he carries a mind stuffed with the familiar, in my case characters from Carthage, Tennessee. To some degree the characters live for me, enabling me to spend days simply, and dully. Last Monday Queen Mary II died in Carthage. Originally Queen Mary was a Sweedle from Maggart, second cousin to Puggie Sweedle, who after being arrested for bigamy got off by becoming a Mormon. Two decades ago Mary founded her own church, in the process christening herself Queen Mary II, for the record there being no Mary I. Within four months, she had collected a congregation of over a hundred people, in part because she had "a magic goiter." The goiter was as big as a honeydew melon. When she preached, it swung back and forth like a pendulum, hypnotizing auditors. Indeed, when Dr. Ramsbottom, dean of the Vanderbilt Medical School, heard about her death, he exclaimed, "Oh, dear, what a pity, we have lost the finest goiter in Tennessee and probably in the whole South."

Because Queen Mary preached as the spirit moved her, the sermons did not make sense. Still, she was worth hearing. In an age of conformity good nonsense is more difficult to produce than good sense, and in middle Tennessee Mary became better known than Ishbosheth, the second king of Israel. On sunny days her congregation worshiped outside on the top of Sugarsuck Hill. She required members of the church to shave their heads, leaving only a pigtail at the back. "So that," she explained, "when the Lord wants you, an angel can swoop down from the clouds and grabbing your pigtail tote you to heaven, bypassing expensive visits to the doctor and that unpleasant layover at the funeral home." During Mary's lifetime an angel fetched only one member of her congregation. Even then, doubters said he drowned on a fishing trip—high water, Hoben Donkin declared, sweeping the body out of the Cumberland into the Tennessee River, where gars converted it into appetizer. In any case other members of the church who died were buried in the Mountain Graveyard in Carthage, Queen Mary, however, forbidding family members to engrave dates on the stones, saying such things were trifling when the subject was eternity.

Of course writing about Queen Mary when a tree has already been chopped down for my coffin is also trifling. Still, the mind is not a valise, and a person cannot control its packing and unpacking. Queen Mary wrote hymns, all derivative and only one of which became popular, "What He Done." "For there's no sky but what he done: / No moon, nor star, nor earth, nor sun. / For there's no yard but what he made: / No weed, nor stone, nor tree, nor blade.* / For there's no body without his word: / No cow, nor toad, nor fish, nor bird. / For there's no water but what he said: / No rain, nor pond, nor lake, nor bed.** / For there's no pain without his lava: / No shriek, nor scream, nor devil, no bother." Attached to the first asterisk was "of grass"; to the double asterisk "before bed, creek." A refrain appeared at the end of each verse, the refrain introduced by a trumpet and the words "But then" repeated three times. Following the third *But then* were the words, "We'll come rejoicing bringing in the fire. Bringing in the fire, bringing in the fire, we'll come rejoicing bringing in the fire."

After two months in Edinburgh, my doings became habitual. As todays were yesterdays, so tomorrows will be todays, I mused. Early in the morning, seven days a week, I walked to the institute and wrote. Late in the afternoon, frequently after dark, I jogged around the Meadows, after which I returned to the flat and ate dinner. Once a week on the way back to the flat, I shopped at Tesco Express, buying the same things: soup and sardines; boxes of cereal; soaps, both for clothes and dishes; paper towels; milk; tea; sultanas; eggs for hard-boiling; and fruit, usually clementines. Once I bought a can of Tesco's low-fat rice pudding. Twice I bought digestive cookies and jars of Coleman's mustard. Two times a week I bought a baguette at Peckham's. During the day I took breaks from writing by going to the university library. On Thursday or Friday I bought cheese at Iain Mellis's shop on Victoria. At least once a week I roamed Edinburgh, visiting a museum or the Botanic Garden, but almost always ending at the institute and writing before jogging.

Eliza's stay at the end of March shattered routine. I didn't write or run for a week. I returned to museums I'd explored earlier, not something I would have done had she not come to Edinburgh. In them I saw things I hadn't noticed before, making the visits seem new. In the bedchamber at the Georgian House, needlework wound like a vine through hangings on a four-poster bed. Here and there and behind the bed, the needlework rose into bows, almost tying the vine to a decorative trellis. Behind the bed and on each side, two ends of the needlework trailed downward into pockets. Before falling asleep the occupant of the bed dropped his watch into a pocket, thereby keeping it comparatively warm and upright so that it wouldn't lose time overnight.

In Greyfriars Kirkyard I noticed Catherine Wilson's stone. She was, I read, the wife of Francis Jeffrey and had died on August 8, 1805, at twenty-eight. "Beside her lies," her epitaph recounted, "also the body of her infant son George who died 5th October 1802 aged six months." Thirty-five years ago I wrote about Jeffrey. He was one of the founders of the *Edinburgh Review,* and I had seen his grave in the Dean Cemetery. In the Dean he lay beside his second wife near the cemetery's south wall. Biography, alas, pares lives into distortion, stripping greenery away in order to expose trunk and limb. Catherine Wilson was Jeffrey's first wife and second cousin. What did he feel when she died? What did he think when an undertaker dug up the body of their son, dead for almost three years, and laid him beside her?

After Eliza returned to Boston, I wrestled routine. So that it would not pin me and press life out of days, I forced myself away from the desk. One Thursday I went to the Writers' Museum in Lady Stair's House off Lawnmarket. I had been to the museum several times, not to view exhibits, however, but to chat with identical twins who worked at the museum as volunteers. The women were literary, and quotations seasoned their conversation, usually quatrains of Wordsworth. They always brought books with them to the museum, this last time novels by Barbara Vine, the pen name Ruth Rendell adopted for her intellectual thrillers. The twins were not young, but if I had known them forty years ago, I would have married them both, differences in our ages notwithstanding. On this visit, though, I looked at the house, first built in the seventeenth century and changed over the years like all old houses, perhaps the greatest change coming at the end of the nineteenth century when a superstructure was added to the stairway that stood like a newel post at the southeast corner of the building. The superstructure looked like a helmet adorned with a spike. Inside the museum I returned to rooms devoted to Robert Burns. On July 27, 1796, on the front page of the *London Herald* appeared a notice of Burns's death. "His poetical compositions," the notice read, "distinguished equally by the force of native humour, by the warmth and tenderness of passion, and by the glowing touches of a descriptive pencil, will remain a lasting monument of the vigour and versatility of a mind, guided only by the light of nature and the inspirations of genius." The prose was balanced and regular, a conventional tribute among the lines of which Burns vanished.

Against a wall downstairs stood a rocking horse. Although wooden, the horse was vital, kicking life into the dry bones of Sir Walter Scott. The horse had been discovered in the attic of a house in George Street where Scott had once lived with his parents. Found under the seat attached to the horse and serving as a cushion was a pad of papers that had belonged to Scott's father. Scott was lame, probably suffering from polio when he was young, and the stirrup on the left side of the horse was higher than that on the right. Rough hewn, the toy was not a thoroughbred. Neither was it a jumper. Clearly Scott had ridden it at walls where it balked, so banging its head that its skull and neck resembled a spout, its muzzle battered, incisors, nose, and lips gone.

Exhibited in an upstairs room were sketches of local writers. Among the drawings was one of Alexander McCall Smith, whom I met at a reception celebrating the publication of *44 Scotland Street,* a book that had first appeared in the *Scotsman,* the local newspaper. Cabinets contained samples of the writers' handwritings. My writing twists into rises and falls. The ends of words level into lines, and letters disappear. Often I ignore margins and write from one side of a page to the other. In contrast Smith's writing was wondrously neat. He wrote down the middle of the page, on each side of his words the same margin, probably measuring one and three-quarter inches. He used black ink and wrote with an ink pen. I write with pencils and ballpoint pens, depending on what I find in the house. While Smith's letters listed to the right, mine stagger, most leaning to the right but some rearing up and standing at attention. My letters bounce like pogo sticks, some springing up into words above them, others sinking and scraping those below. Smith's letters never bumped each other. Between lines stretched rails one-quarter of an inch wide and looking whitewashed.

A gate separates Greyfriars Kirkyard from George Heriot's School. To protect students at the school from derelicts the gate is kept locked. While I stood in Greyfriars pondering Catherine Wilson's stone, I saw a teacher from the school unlock the gate. He was rushing to buy a sandwich from a shop on George IV Bridge. I asked him about the school. He suggested that I visit and gave me the telephone number of the school's main office. Two mornings later I went to the school. I wore a coat and tie, so I would not look like I had wandered off the street. Some 1,500 children attended Heriot, and employees patrolled the grounds. To save one the embarrassment of challenging me, I approached him and explained that I was going to see the headmaster. The main building is a quadrangle consisting of four equal ranges of buildings, each range three stories high except at the corners, from which rise four square towers. I think the building Edinburgh's finest, and although lying on flat land beneath Castle Rock, it towers, in my mind at least, above the castle itself. George Heriot was jeweler and goldsmith to James VI of Scotland. When James became James I of England, Heriot moved to London and kept his positions. He became very wealthy. He had no children, and on his death in 1624 most of his estate went toward endowing a hospital for fatherless boys. Although work on the hospital began in 1628, the first boys did not enter the school until 1659, the Civil War having slowed construction.

Old buildings are always young. They require so much maintenance and reconstruction that they are works in progress. I walked around the building before entering the courtyard, marveling at the decorative cornices, tall stacks of chimneys, and buckled quoins. Even in tarnished light the stones glowed. Carved above windows were stars, goblets, roses, and flagons. Later I learned that there were 202 sculpted windows in the building, only 2 of which were the same. From the top of the building stone cannons jutted out. On the sides were sundials. Gargoyles grinned and scowled, some pressing their hands to their lips, sealing their mouths as if their fingers were stitches. I stood for a long time in front of the clock tower on the north face. Carvings around the door were almost too ornate for the eye. Doric pillars supported an entablature. Above the door was a frieze consisting of four panels, each panel cluttered, the whole a comic strip. I read a frame. On the left George Heriot stood beside his forge squeezing a bellows. Behind the bellows rose a flame. To the right of the bellows was a workbench sagging with tools.

Being head of a school is exhausting. Few headmasters last ten years. Duties are never ending, not simply being responsible for children, but also being available and answerable to parents, sundry employees, to alumni, boards of governors, legislative and regulatory bodies, and then chatting with strangers like me, someone who might be who he says he is. I talked to the headmaster for eight minutes, then I toured the building. Engraved in stones paving the courtyard were numbers ranging from 1 to 180. Once students were assigned numbers and each morning stood on their numbers, easing the task of checking attendance. Now all the employees of the school could not stand atop the numbers, there being over two hundred. In a cabinet a book lay open to a page signed by Hans Christian Andersen. "I'll wager that a student forged Andersen's name," I said to my guide. "That's what I would have done." The fireplaces at each end of the Staff Common Room, once the Refectory, were bigger than my attic, their maws broad enough to swallow a forest in a single hot bite. Not wainscoted until the end of the eighteenth century, the Council Chamber was my favorite room. Blue and white tiles lined the fireplace. On the right appeared a cat; on the left a spaniel sat on its haunches.

The high point of my visit was literally high. Once every few years for the yearbook, the headmaster posed on the roof of the school amid a gaggle of students. I arrived at the school just in time to follow the group to the roof. We entered the northwest tower. Eighty-eight steps later we walked onto the top of the tower. Clouds had sunk low, but the view of Castle Rock was the best in Edinburgh, scraps of rough flannel seeming to cover hunks of the rock. Simplicity brought the castle to life, unlike, for example, the crown jewels that appeared glitzy, almost part of the tarty landscape of country music and pink Cadillacs. Once atop the tower we climbed six or seven iron rungs to a platform, from the other side of which a ladder consisting of twenty-three rungs descended to a main roof, the rungs trailing part of the way through an iron tube. Wind gusted, and the headmaster worried that students would frisk about carelessly and, turning themselves into kites, would tumble into the courtyard. "Did you enjoy that?" the woman who planned the picture asked me, adding, "heights must not bother you."

I'm not afraid of heights, but I worry that height undermines perspective, particularly if the height that someone thinks he has ascended is metaphoric, an achievement that elevates him above others. The day after I visited George Heriot School I explored part of the Water of Leith Walkway, a path following the course of the Leith River through Edinburgh, the current at times lounging along smooth forearms and dozing around quiet elbows, other times rushing muscular through gullies and over dams, spray roiling. I started at the Dean Gallery and walked east to Leith Row, where I turned around and retraced my steps, ending at Roseburnter. Red campion and wild hyacinth bloomed along the slope down to the path, blossoms of the latter delicate and weak. I preferred the hogweed that grew along the river, its leaves rough and hardy, its stems robust. Sweet cicely stretched across a flat. I crushed a leaf and rubbed the licorice fragrance into my palms. Although cones of butterbur still rose rude from the damp, its beams of pink flowers had dimmed.

Rugs of moss dressed walls. Low in the shade, honesty flowered, its blossoms so deeply purple that they seemed shadows within shadows. Leaf buds had burst on chestnuts. On some trees leaves had opened and spread; on others the leaves dangled in bundles, waiting for the sun to raise them into umbrellas. Ivy climbed many trees, wrapping trunks in turtlenecks. From walls hung handkerchiefs of ivy-leaved toadflax, the plant's small blue flowers embroidery. On a limb stripped of bark then tossed on a bank by high water, brown mushrooms thrived, looking like lapels, their texture soft as velvet. In dirt between walls and the path grew archangel and white dead nettle. As the ground warmed and season sank into gullies, Solomon's seal spurted green from the black edges of gardens. The brightest days of spring lay ahead, but here and there blossomed speedwell and dandelion, primrose and pink purslane, garlic mustard, green alkanet pudgy with blue flowers, comfrey and forget-me-not. Plush piles of ramsons thrived on sandy lips just above the water. I watched a song thrush forage the plush searching for worms. The bird was stunningly beautiful, along its back layers of rich brown, the feathers almost parqueted, beneath spots on its breast, caramelized and almost yellow.

Tits called from the scrub, flitting beyond sight, toying with my vision, their songs jingling like little bells. A robin perched on a twig; a wren scooted through leaves, and a magpie rowed past, the green on its tail flashing. Chaffinches rummaged bushes, and gray herons fished shallows. While mallards landed boldly, sliding into midstream, a moorhen hugged the bank as if hiding from the notice its red and orange bill attracted. Pigeons crouched in holes in the stone walls along the watercourse, plugging them like bandages. A gray wagtail clung to a snag in midstream, flicking its tail, a bandana of black under its bill, its breast and belly bright yellow.

Landscapes snagged me as I walked: rock gardens under houses along Coltbridge; Dean Village beside a raceway, the old mills standing but no longer grinding and converted into apartments; Miller Row so shady that the present vanished; and the Dean Bridge, its arches falling to the water a hundred feet below, walking through them, making the stroller imagine he was crossing into a different world, looping ahead of him a bluff of stony buildings; and then a rib cage of houses along Glenogle, the rows abutting then stretching away from the river. I stopped at the Circle on Brandon, a café at which Eliza and I once snacked. I intended to order a croissant and a coffee, but instead I ate lunch, the special: nan bread, a salad washed in lime juice, and the main dish, Thai green curry.

I did not chat with anyone in the restaurant; the curry seared my lips, and throughout the meal I sucked them into my mouth to cool them. On the walk throngs of joggers passed me. East of the Dean Bridge and across the river from the lushest part of the Dean Gardens a Doric temple stood atop St. Bernard's Well. In the center of the temple was Hygeia, the Greek goddess of health. Along with Panacea, Hygeia was a daughter of the great physician Asclepius. After Zeus killed Asclepius, striking him down with a thunderbolt because he worried Asclepius might make men immortal, Hygeia became the goddess of healing and health. Hygeia was often depicted feeding a snake, usually from a shallow plate, the snake clearly from the same den as the two serpents wrapping the caduceus, the winged staff of Mercury and the symbol of medicine. Because the temple was built above and commemorated a well, Hygeia held a bowl in her right hand, extending her arm and offering passersby refreshing drinks. On her left stood a small column. Atop the column a jug lay on its side, Hygeia's left hand locking it into place, pressing it against her left hip. Around the column a snake twisted upward in a wreath, its head at the mouth of the jug, sipping the healing water.

I didn't recognize Hygeia immediately, and I asked a smartly dressed couple walking a Labrador if they could identify the statue. The man said sheepishly that although he had lived nearby for eighteen years he had no idea who the figure was supposed to represent. The woman was bolder, harder, and surer than her husband. She was also more ignorant than a turnip. "The woman is Cleopatra," she said. "I don't think so," I said. "Cleopatra is usually depicted pressing an asp to her bosom." "Then it's Eve," the woman said. "She is tempting Adam to drink." The man looked at me and shrugged. "I'd rather be in hell with my back broken than be married to such an imbecile," I thought. Nevertheless, I said "maybe," adding "thank you" as the couple continued on their way.

On a walk never question the stylish or the overdressed. They are used to being seen indoors rather than seeing the outdoors. The best people to query about flowers or birds or even statues are gentlewomen of an advanced age. The most knowledgeable have white hair and eyes backlit by life. They wear comfortable clothes, loose skirts and sweaters, and unless they are trekking, soft shoes. Never are they taller than five feet five inches, and they are most informative when alone. Their husbands are pleasant, but like most men cannot own up to ignorance. As a result their identifications are inevitably wrong. One nice man labeled honesty roseberry willow herb. "I think it is honesty," his wife said tentatively.

"No, it is roseberry willow herb," her husband said. "I looked it up the other day." At the end of the walk I found Francis Jeffrey's grave in Dean Cemetery and rubbed my right hand over his name. Afterward I used the lavatory in the basement of the Dean Gallery. Bright tiles three inches square cover the walls: red, orange, blue, and green. As I left the building, I mentioned to the warder that the bathroom was my favorite lavatory in Edinburgh. "It is wonderful," he said, adding that "some people find it quite a shock." "A very pleasant shock," I said. "Thank you, sir. I am glad," he said, opening the door. "Come back and use it again soon."

After dinner that night I read *The Book of Aphorisms,* written by Robert MacNish, a Scot who died at thirty-five in 1837. "Great power of mind, and elegance of manners, are nearly incompatible," MacNish wrote. "It is difficult for a man of genius to be an adept in the graces of the drawing-room. Powerful minds have an originality and intractability about them, which render it extremely difficult for them to fall into that ease and conventional politeness, which are considered to constitute the finished gentlemen." MacNish got matters slightly wrong. Rarely is anyone a genius; some people, however, have a genius for living, something that enables them to avoid losing themselves in ease and convention and often makes them seem intractable. That something, of course, comes and goes. When it comes, however, it enriches life.

Fast Falls the Eventide

"ABIDE WITH ME, FAST FALLS the eventide," Henry Lyte wrote a month before his death. In three weeks I leave Edinburgh. As soon as my plane turns west, place and event will start drifting from thought. Experiences lodged along the shoreline of awareness will slide into the sea. Life is not shingled, and the tide will strip Scotland from mind. One or two memories will bob for a moment, but soon they will become waterlogged and sink out of consciousness, becoming an indistinguishable part of the past, that dark main under the present.

I'd like some things to abide or at least settle on a sandbar for a day or so: the Babel of English at the institute—Bulgarian, Rumanian, Turkish, Hungarian, and my southern American; lunch at the institute spent talking to Norwegian social scientists, my not understanding a word they said, their not understanding me, but the conversation animated; a hedge sparrow in scrub; and the elevator at the National Gallery, a cylinder resembling a transporter borrowed from *Star Trek,* with a voice saying "Doors closing" but then stuttering and repeating itself twice after the doors were closed. Memories wilt overnight. Along Lutton Place, Japanese cherries are blooming, the pink blossoms hanging over the sidewalk in ruffled clusters, green leaves above them in bows, candying the drab street. Beside St. Peter's Church is a garden shaped like a fireplug. Circling the garden in a metal rim are enameled patches of color: pink, purple, red, plum, blue, white, and a fan of greens. Between the beds are bushes, shoots shattering into leaves, the twigs themselves thin lines of paste gluing flower beds to each other in a mosaic.

As I pondered leaving Edinburgh, I thought about a beginning, not of my stay in Scotland but the introduction to this book. At the end of life's little day, to paraphrase Lyte, I wanted my experiences to mean something. I have not written a know-thyself book, one of those volumes in which the author strips off shoes, socks, shirt, and trousers, so that by the last chapter he stands naked before a mirror, not one that reflects flesh, however, but spirit, the stripping leading to understanding. I never strip. I suspect I was born wearing khakis and a sport coat. I wear socks in the shower. Indeed, if the house is not empty, and to be empty the dog must be outside, I bathe in underpants as well as socks. In *In a Green Shade,* Maurice Hewlett described my time of literary life, if not exactly my intention. "If ever there is a time for sententiousness it is when one is elderly, leisured and comfortable; that is the time to set down one's thoughts as they come, not inviting anybody to read them, but promising to those who do, that they will find a commentary upon life as it passes, either because it may be useful or because it may have been earned."

Leisured does not apply to my time in Edinburgh. My observations were earned. For the first fifteen weeks of my stay I was the first fellow to arrive at the institute in the morning, often showing up before Mary, the cleaning woman. I was also the last to leave, walking back to my flat after ten at night. Before going to bed I planned the next day's activities. Sleep did not come easily, and early in the morning I woke and read. When I return to Connecticut, friends will say they envied my vacation from teaching. I will nod, and soon time will sweep work out of recollection. Eventually I will remember the months in Scotland, much as my friends imagined them, as an extended rest.

I am not elderly, but fledgling readers, that is, those under forty, will not appreciate my writings. In *Sketches from Cambridge,* Leslie Stephen mulled the ending of Tennyson's poem "Ulysses." "When the crew of Ulysses obeyed his invitation to step in and 'sitting well in order, smite the sounding furrows,' they probably did not excite the admiration of Ithaca's youth," Stephen said. "Ulysses' own sentiment, that they were not then what in old times they had been, doubtless met with hearty concurrence from the bank. They must have caught a good many crabs before reaching the Happy Isles." Although a crab can stop an eight, sometimes swamping it, catching a crab is good for a person. Like defibrillators, handles of oars pound chests, making people gasp and restarting hearts deadened by routine.

As I mulled leaving Edinburgh, I altered my routine, not resembling an oarsman knocked off his seat but a sojourner stuffing his trunk with last-minute experiences. Two weeks ago I started running around Arthur's Seat. Not only had the weather brightened, making Arthur's Seat alluring, but I had grown tired of threading my way through people on the Meadows: clumps of students, arms linked in chains, cigarette smoke narcotic over them, their speech cavities of rotten English; couples stopping to pet; trains of women pushing strollers three abreast; runners in gangs breaking around me like aneurysms; people talking on cell phones, strides jerky and as unpredictable as their conversations; and packs of dogs, mostly unleashed and some unfriendly. Although I ran in grass off the pavement, I couldn't avoid dogs or their leavings, nubs of which always clung to my shoes and accompanied me back to the office. I grew tired of dodging bicyclists who sped down Middle Meadow Walk from Teviot and who raced along paths ignoring signs that said "No Cycling." I was weary of jumping beer cans and wine bottles and slipping sideways to avoid the landfills of trash that made running treacherous.

Sunny days brought out old people. Alone and usually female, they walked canted on the edge of falling, in one hand a leash, at its end a small, ancient dog, its muzzle white, hind legs akimbo, almost as if one leg had sunk into the grave. Why, I wondered, when I saw old women were they always alone? Didn't anyone care about them? Were the dogs their only friends? For a while I spoke to them, but then I stopped, the greetings of a stranger startling and frightening, not cheering, them. I also grew tired of cars, the endless whoosh that made me think I was rolling inside a washing machine, near me a zipper whacking the side of the tumbler.

Eventually the potted human wilts. Of course, I may have shifted from the Meadows to Arthur's Seat simply because I'm allergic to the habitual. In any case, the move brought spring to my legs. Instead of jogging in the evening, I ran in the morning. Comparatively few people ran around Arthur's Seat, and because climbing the hills involved a smidgen of ordeal, runners greeted each other, not as brothers or sisters but as friendly distant cousins. Moreover, the landscape changed as one ran, not simply the eroded slopes of the volcano but distant sights: Duddingston Loch, Craigmillar Castle, St. Anthony's Chapel, and fields sunny with rape, bright as clowns' trousers. Gorse was yellow, and petals fell from geam trees. I watched a kestrel fan the air and swans change places on a nest. Often I drifted off the road, climbing Dunsapie Hill or running beside the wall separating Meadowfield from Holyrood Park. Earlier in the year I'd occasionally left the Meadows and run through Marchmont. Because I had to dodge people and cars, I couldn't relax. I worried about tripping on slabs akimbo in the sidewalk. As a result I missed the neighborhoods through which I ran and might as well have stayed in the Meadows. On Arthur's Seat I gazed about, and because I could relax, I was paradoxically alert and energetic.

One Saturday before a long run I hurried to the institute and called the box office of the Hibernian soccer team. The night before I'd over-heard someone say that Saturday was Edinburgh's biggest soccer day—the Derby, when the town's two professional teams played each other. I had never been to a professional soccer game. Normally I wouldn't have considered going to the match, but circling Arthur's Seat made me want to explore. I bought one of the last seats in the stadium, in the upper deck in the executive section four rows from the top and slightly to the left of midfield. The woman who sold me the ticket said I should pick it up by two, the game starting at three. I left Blacket Place early, walking along the Radical Road under the Salisbury Crags then crossing Queens Drive and ambling behind Holyrood Place to Croft-an-righ. From there I walked on to Easter Road. Crowds milled, and life seemed rougher and more animated than in other parts of Edinburgh.

I turned east on Albion Road and picked up my ticket at one o'clock. Because gates to the stadium did not open for an hour, I roamed an enclosed parking lot behind the stadium. Two women in uniform stood in front of a door. I chatted with them. "We are family," one said. "The game will be ballet on grass," the other said, "and will top everything you've seen in Edinburgh." "Top it all," the other repeated. "You can't wear that scarf," one of the women said. "Joe had better get you another one." I had worn a claret and pink scarf, the colors those of St. Catharine's, my college at Cambridge. Supporters of the opposing team, the Heart of Midlothian, wore maroon and white scarves. After intro-ducing me to the president of the club, Joe, who was in charge of tourists, took me into a shop beside the stadium, where I selected a Hibernian scarf, green and white, the colors worn by Hibee fans. At each end of the scarf was a medallion, in the center of which appeared the club's crest and the date 1875. The white letters running along the scarf spelled "Hibernian Football Club." Almost every person who entered the stadium from Albion sported the colors, on a hat, scarf, shirt, or windbreaker. From the shop Joe took me in the stadium, and we walked along the runway outside the locker rooms to the field. Not since high school had I stood on a runway, and I wanted to race onto the field. I didn't. Instead I looked at the stadium. The eastern side of the stadium did not have an upper deck like the west. In the future Joe said the club hoped to add another deck so that the stadium could hold twenty-three thousand or twenty-four thousand people. For now, though, in my seat in the western stands I could look out at the Firth of Forth and watch seagulls swirl cursive through the air.

Parked near the ticket office was a white limousine. "Win Me for 1 Hour," a sign taped to a window said. "Just buy a ticket for todays Happy Hibee." Squads of Rock Steady event staff milled about the parking lot next to the stadium, all wearing yellow slickers. Two policemen rode past the ticket office on horseback, and I wandered back onto Albion Road. I had never seen so many police. I started to count them but gave up as more kept arriving. While most Hibee fans approached the stadium from the north end of Albion Road, Hearts fans approached from Albion Terrace, crossing a narrow bridge above a railway line and entering the stadium from a separate entrance. I strolled over to the terrace. Teenagers strutted along singing a song, the only word of which seemed to be "fuck" and variations thereof. Two hard-looking boys about twenty started at my scarf. The ears of both boys resembled jewelry stores, and a decoration almost as big as a syringe pierced the nose of one. I approached them and asked about Hearts. One said something I could not understand, after which the other reached into a sack and pulled out a beer. "Have one," he said. I thanked him but explained I rarely drank. "I am really looking forward to the game," I said. "So are we," the boy with the nose ring said, for a moment looking sweet and vulnerable and to my mind pitiful.

I asked a policeman if there would be trouble. "No," he said, adding that a "perfectly sane, rational person walks toward this ground and becomes a moron. Then he walks away and becomes sane again." When I took my seat, I read advertisements pasted on walls surrounding the pitch, for, among others, Festival City Cabs, Carling, Mackay White, and the Edinburgh Evening News. "To the Big Apple and USA," a sign for Continental Airlines declared. "Lochinvar Windows," I read, then recited the first verse of Scott's poem. "Oh! Young Lochinvar is come out of the west, / Through all the wide Border his steed was the best; / And save his good broadsword he weapons had none. / He road all unarmed and he rode all alone / So faithful in love and so dauntless in war, / There never was a knight like the young Lochinvar."

For me there never was an afternoon like the Derby. On my left sat a middle-aged man, beside him his daughter wearing a green and white jester's cap. The girl was one of a handful of females in the stadium, the crowd being at least 90 percent male. At the end of the game, when the police set up blockades and forced Hibee supporters away from Hearts fans, sending the former down St. Clair, the street was awash with men, their heads bobbing, some bald, others short haired, others long—a torrent of masculinity. Although the crowd was good natured, the mass of men made it almost frightening, causing me wonder what would happen if ill temper damned the stream.

On my right sat a good-natured electrical engineer from New Zealand. He had been born in Edinburgh and when little had watched the Hibees play. For fourteen years, he told me, he lived in South Africa. From South Africa he emigrated to New Zealand. He and his wife and daughter were spending two weeks in Edinburgh. While he came to the game, "the girls" were shopping. "On Princes Street," he said. Behind us sat four young men. The only adjective they knew was "fucking." They attached it to so many different people—Hearts fans, referees, players, the police—and shouted it so often that by the end of the game my neighbor and I laughed uncontrollably ever time they yelled.

The stadium pulsated with noise. Speakers blasted until the stadium filled, then the spectators provided the noise, the Hibs fans singing "Sunshine over Leith" by the Proclaimers and chanting "Hi-bees, Hibees," the Hearts fans countering with "Gordie Rules," Tynecastle Park, the home of the Hearts, being located just north of the Gordie Road in an area also known as Gordie. Hearts fans also shouted "Jam-bos," the team's nickname derived from a biscuit in the center of which was a heart stuffed with jam. Both sides waved their scarves, and at times stands seemed stormy seas, kelp tossing and flowing, green and white for Hibs, maroon and white for Hearts. Instead of deadening enjoyment, the noise lifted the spirits, and I spent the afternoon surfing the sound. I bought a cup of coffee and a steak pie. Both were terrible; yet the atmosphere transformed them into treats.

The afternoon passed like a smile. The Hibs were the better team, but the game ended in a tie, 2–2, the Hearts scoring their second goal just before the end after a Hibee defender made a mistake and pulled down one of the Hearts forwards. A few earnest fans muttered about the result, almost all being forty-five-year-old men, aging athletes or athletic pretenders with short hair and wearing leather jackets. Most people, though, left in good, effervescent spirits, having enjoyed the afternoon: the scrappiness of the players, the long runs, and the wonderful passes that curved like the rims of porcelain cups. I left wishing my stay was longer so that I had time for more football. After the game I walked back to Old Town along Easter and Abbeymount. At the foot of the Royal Mile three Hearts fans saw my scarf and shouted something. I couldn't understand them, so I approached and asked what they said. They repeated their remarks, but I still couldn't understand them. I shook my head and walked away, and they waved goodbye. I climbed the Royal Mile to George IV Bridge. After five o'clock the Elephant reduced the price of pastries to fifty pence. I ordered a cappuccino and an almond crescent. A waiter noticed my Hibernian scarf and rushed over to ask about the game. I told him the game was terrific. "I wish I had been there," he said, and for a moment we were almost buddies.

Jogging around Arthur's Seat changed my days. I wandered off paths and ran beneath wild cherries, their petals drizzling around me. I remembered lines from Housman's "Shropshire Lad": "Loveliest of trees, the cherry now / Is hung with bloom along the bough, / And stands about the woodland ride / Wearing white for Eastertide." I spent more time outside. One day after my run I repeated an earlier walk, wandering the Water of Leith from the Cauldron below the Gallery of Modern Art to the Deanhaugh Footpath in Stockbridge. Great periwinkle fell from walls in blue and green streams while double kerria burst into yellow like bales of hay exploding tight bindings. Tits gathered the makings of nests under willows, and a pair of song thrushes plucked twigs from a snag in the river. Near Damhead Weir a wren sang from an aspen, the song trilling and reedy. Ivy quilted slopes and clamored up the trunks of ashes and sycamores. At Deanhaugh I left the walkway and wandered north-west along Raeburn Place. People stirred along the street, comfortable to be in a neighborhood unlike the bludgeoning crowds on Princes. After two people recommended the shop, I bought lunch at Maxi's: a small baguette overflowing with cream cheese and smoked salmon, then a slice of passion cake, this really iced carrot cake. I carried my lunch back to the Water of Leith and picnicked on a bench. Across the river houses along Dean Terrace shone like knives.

How a person walks often determines how people react to him. The comparatively young distrust strollers, and when they come upon one, they pick up their pace and bustle past. In contrast older walkers stop and chat, invariably asking what I am doing in Edinburgh. As I ambled under the Belford Bridge, a golden retriever ran up to me, sniffed, then bundled on down the walk. "Oscar is only two years old," a woman approaching me said. "He's not trained yet, and he investigates everybody on the path to see if they are all right. If they are not, he hurries back to protect me. You passed the test." The woman and I walked together for half an hour, talking first about dogs and gardens. Gardens are intimate places, and conversation about flowers inevitably spreads to talk about lives, marriages present or past, then, as always with me at least, children grown and growing.

Despite struggling to break the shackles of habit, a walk routinely takes me to a graveyard. At Bell's Mill Weir, I rubbed my hand across Oscar's head, told my companion goodbye, and headed for the Dean Cemetery. Established in the 1840s, the graveyard was meticulously maintained. Alleys of laurel, yew, and holly wound through it, branching into paths then into limbs and twigs. Still, at first sight the graveyard looked like the remnant of an ancient wood, its stones the trunks of trees smashed by a storm. The trunks were various, some needles, others Celtic crosses, columns, and urns. Scattered among the trunks were temples and a pyramid. Here and there grew great copper beeches, their buds still tight, their limbs dangling, wrung-out joints making them appear arthritic. Battalions of profiles adorned stones, most of the faces looking like that of Robert E. Lee. Children knelt on other monuments; angels shouldered woodpiles of crosses; fetching females stared at the heavens, and lions dozed recumbent. Three sphinxes supported a triangle of stones on one monument. At the upper corners of the three stones appeared rams' heads; atop each head stood a stork, all the storks leaning backward, balancing a column wrapped in ivy and crowned by a platter.

After my run the next morning, I crossed Bruntsfield Links and strolled down Leamington to the Union Canal. I walked south on the towpath until an aqueduct lifted the canal above the Water of Leith at Slateford. Despite the water, the day was dry. Bicycles had crushed gravel on the towpath into dust. Brown currents seared the water itself, and along the banks reeds jutted up broken like tines on a dirty hairbrush. Rising behind walls on the eastern side of the canal were dreary autumnal housing estates. Behind the wall on the west were warehouses and the detritus of development: dirt humped into landfills, white trailers housing offices and watchmen, stacks of huge brown pipes, and bulldozers, cranes, and backhoes, giant insects, their thoraxes white or yellow, proboscises raised, mandibles spread ready to chew away a hill. Beside the wall grew thickets of nettle, stems acidic. A fisherman squatted on the towpath. I asked him if he had caught anything. "I no English," he said.

Beyond the blue bridge at Yeaman Place, the landscape greened a little. Homeowners dumped leavings from their gardens over walls behind their houses, and amid pincushions of nettles daffodils bloomed. A swan nested on a tablespoon of land, and a pair of ducks paddled beside the reeds, one a mallard, the other a white farmyard duck. The wall on the west side of the path ended and was replaced by a hedge of hawthorns. I looked across it and spotted Corstorphine Hill and the zoo. More people appeared, bicyclists and joggers, parents pushing baby carriages, raucous little boys throwing stones at ducks and waterlogged slabs of wood, elderly couples arm in arm, supporting each other, and lone men. Some of these last scowled and looked angry, and when approaching one man, I crossed to the far side of the path. On the fields at Merchiston, children played soccer, shouts from their fathers brackish in the air.

Beyond Merchiston, water in the canal turned blue. Moored on the east bank were small boats, a green houseboat trimmed in red and black named *Nola's Ark; Jubilee,* a red and blue houseboat; *Otter* and *Mooncatcher,* boats slightly larger than periwinkles but with motors attached for cruising; *Mischievous One,* a coracle with a roof, a titch of a boat, inviting to small boys and fun to own; and then, stacked like shells, rowboats for rent. In a mound of black dirt Solomon's seal grew as tall as young corn. Later on my return when I retraced my steps to Leamington, I passed a canal boat filled with tourists. The boat looked like a long green shoe, the brass around its portholes shined into eyelets. A bearded man stood on a deck at the rear of the boat and steered. Inside a woman with heavy arms cooked in the kitchen, steam spraying about her. In the lounge a party drank champagne. When I walked past, they raised bottles to the window and grinned. I waved, and the "captain" blew the boat's whistle.

At Slateford I left the towpath and joined the Water of Leith descending into the Colinton Dell, a shady luxuriant place, water racing frothy and almost joyfully through it, slopes rising steep above it, the undergrowth furry, the trees at times almost walls. Before descending into the dell, I noticed four women my age sitting at a table outside the Tickled

Trout, a restaurant. Piled around the women were binoculars, guidebooks, and beakers of red wine. I stopped and asked what I should look for in the dell. Dippers, they said, and a kingfisher. I saw neither. Nevertheless, the contents of the dell glittered like those of a treasure chest: gold nuggets shimmering atop green settings of saxifrage; ruby patches of pink purslane; wood sorrel, its leaves curtseying; red campion; wavy bitter cress; ground ivy, its blossoms sparking like sapphire; petals of wild cherry blowing like flakes of ivory; wood anemone; and hart's tongue fern spilling between stones in emerald seams.

I climbed out of the dell at Colinton. I intended to go farther, but the graveyard at St. Cuthberts, Colinton's parish church, seduced me. "How nice it would be to sleep though eternity here," I thought, "the Leith curving below the churchyard, the shushing sound soothing, the company old but probably good." I smiled remembering something Josh wrote me recently. "Remember," he said, "that Christians are also God's creatures." The graveyard was wonderfully tended. Someone had cut barrels in half and filled the halves with plants: primroses, pansies, ferns, and an assortment of small cedars, their shades various, yellow, green, blue, and almost red. A mortsafe lay atop a stone worn out of words, a skull and crossbones still visible on it, however. Death's-heads and bones endured longer than names. One stone must have long lain on the ground, for the carving on its back was clear while the name on the front had sunk out of recognition. "Hark from the Tomb a Solemn Sound," the engraving warned. "Prepare Prepare it crys / To drop your body in the dust / Your Soul to Mount the Skies."

I abided in the graveyard until late afternoon. Days had lengthened, and I could have trekked on. But I wanted to save the lower part of the Water of Leith for another day. The more I saw in one day the less I would remember. Also, I am by nature the kind of person who sometimes pushes present pleasure aside in hopes of saving it for the future. I should add that I am not quite so careful, however, as Agarista Sampson in Carthage. Agarista was a good and faithful wife. When her husband, Pobus, was dying, she never left him alone, spending days beside his bed knitting his shroud, "a good woolly one," she said, "for the cold days ahead." Late the afternoon just before he died, Pobus rolled on his side and, looking through the bedroom door, noticed a ham on the kitchen table. "Aga," he said. "I am on the way out, but I believe I could swallow a little ham." "Pobus," Agarista said, laying her knitting needles down in her lap. "I'd like to oblige you seeing as how you are almost dead. But you've got lots of friends and a mite of cousins, and I am going to need every bit of that ham to serve folks after the burying. How would a platter of watermelon rind pickle do? I have a jug of it in the pantry. It is about to go off, and I need to get rid of it."

Holiday

"YOU'LL REGRET IT IF YOU don't travel," my friend Jay wrote. "Go to St. Andrews and visit the Isle of Skye." Travel would have shattered both budget and me. Shouldering the anxiety caused by visiting strange places alone was too heavy a burden. If Vicki had accompanied me to Scotland, I might have traveled. When I became foot and mind sore, maybe she would have grabbed my belt and jerked me along.

In any case after a month in Scotland I confined myself to a stall, the better to mull the provender of daily life. To keep myself from kicking free, I raised rails at the back of my stall, deciding that I wouldn't leave Edinburgh, I would not write about places to which I couldn't walk, and I'd refuse invitations to dinner, this last not because glanders or wobbler syndrome frightened me but because evenings out exhausted me, causing colic before and laming me after. Even worse, I always said something boorish that twisted through recollection like larval cyathostomiasis.

For a week I had jogged around Arthur's Seat. The time had come to take a day off. Moreover, as I had become fitter and slipped into running stride I grew more assertive and prickly. Attached to elevators in university buildings are recordings. Before a door closes, a dull male voice warns, "Doors closing." Earlier in the week I rode the elevator in the David Hume Tower, coming down from the English department on the sixth floor. Classes were about to begin, and although I was the only person on the elevator, I knew a crowd of students would be waiting for the elevator on the ground floor. When the elevator reached the ground floor, it stopped, the doors closed for a moment, giving the voice time to say, "Doors opening." Shortly thereafter the doors began to slide open. When a gaggle of students thrust forward, I shouted, "Big man coming out." The students scattered like pigeons, making odd, almost cooing, sounds.

The smoother I ran, the more outspoken I became. As the end of my stay approached, I speculated about the Scottish character. Most people I met in Edinburgh had been gracious. Nonetheless, I decided rational men should never let Scotsmen snuggle into friendship. For generations Scots had butchered cousins, neighbors, and strangers. The claymore had sunk into their genes, and some peaceful, sunny afternoon it would inevitably jump from the scabbard into mayhem.

Also contributing to my "antsiness," if one can compare a human's formic behavior to that of an insect, was the remark of an acquaintance, a statement attributed to a third party. "Sam," the party supposedly said, "has a great ego, but he invariably has time for other people's egos." I have always taken pride in not being proud. In any case, wherever Maybe goes, Maybe Not accompanies him. People who write personal essays so enjoy quotidian events that they want to share them, on the page or in conversation, thus running the risk of being labeled egocentric. In any case an egocentric person is safe and usually well mannered and pleasant. Interested primarily in his own doings, he is tolerant. He is not a moralist, at least not a Pentecostal intent upon saving others from themselves. He rarely criticizes his neighbors, viewing their oddities with bemusement and their conduct with indifference, and if he is an essayist, wondering how he can fit people to the page without causing pain to them or himself.

Although remarks about one rarely cause epizootic lymphangitis, they can inflame. Paradoxically the aches produced by physical exertion make one forget himself. A throbbing ankle is an effective anti-mind, purging ulcerating notions from the cerebral cortex. Accordingly, this past Saturday I decided to walk to Balerno and back. The first part of the holiday was familiar, from Newington to the Meadows, from the Meadows down Leamington to the Union Canal then along the canal to the Water of Leith Heritage Centre at Slateford. At Slateford I followed the Water of Leith Walkway to Balerno five miles away. Retracing a familiar route stripped anxiety from the trip. I wouldn't have to worry about tickets and passports or rude native customs. I bounced out of my basement at 8:20. At 6:16, I returned scuttling crablike, my left knee lagging, throbbing with pain. I had walked eighteen miles and had molted into exhaustion's calm of mind.

For the trip I wore a floppy hat bought by Vicki from the Nature Company seven years ago, its rim loose and broad, protecting cheeks and nose from sunburn; high-topped hiking boots; and a long-sleeved blue shirt. Trailing down the left arm of the shirt was a white box, orange railings around it, inside the word *Princeton.* Six years ago Vicki bought the shirt for Francis, then a student at Princeton, to give to Eliza. Because Eliza was at that adolescent stage in which she thought tight clothes fashionable, she never wore the shirt, so I appropriated it. In case I slipped on the path or wanted to kneel and examine a flower, I wore jeans. I prefer khakis. Strangers treat a person dressed in khakis more politely than a person in jeans. Still, on this trip, trousers did not matter, as three people addressed me as "sir." I also wore a windbreaker. The jacket had four pockets. The two upper were small chest pockets, only large enough to hold an eyeglass case. The lower two pockets on each side of the jacket were large and opened into scoops.

On my shoulders I slung a backpack. In the pack's small pockets I stuffed wallet, keys both to the flat and to my office at the institute, and two ballpoint pens, one a Bic, plastic casing around the tube of ink six-sided, making using it uncomfortable, the edges slicing into my skin. The other pen was round and fat. I found it by the automatic book withdrawal machine in the library. The pen was white; printed in blue along the side was the statement "Make Scottish Co-op your fair trade store!" I did not know anything about fair trade, but the pen rested easily on my fingers, and I liked holding it. Into the pack's large pockets I dumped binoculars; a Mirror Ball notebook, twenty-four red mirrors on the cover; and three guides: a paperback copy of *Scottish Wildflowers, The Birds of Britain and Europe* in hardback, and lastly *A Guide to the Water of Leith Walkway,* a spiral pamphlet forty-two pages long.

When I reached the towpath, I shifted things about: putting the pens in the upper left pocket of my jacket, the guide to flowers in the right lower pocket, and the guide to birds in the left. I also hung the binoculars around my neck, removing them from the case, so that the case swung from my neck, becoming a pocket in which I could stuff flowers and in which I soon transferred my notebook and the guide to the waterway. Because these two pads were tall and pushed the flap of the case open, I worried that one would slip out and be lost. As a result I checked the case compulsively, running my hand across the top every minute or so.

Revision betters a book. In contrast revisiting a place often planes observation, filing the edge off prose. I did not enjoy my first walk along the canal, in part because I compared it with walks along the Water of Leith, the latter wilder and on the surface more natural and appealing more than a cityscape. Initially this walk also seemed bleak. Just past the brewery at Viewforth a stone bridge spanned the canal. On the north side of the bridge was a medallion depicting a castle with three black towers, soot having carried the day. Carved into the medallion on the other side of the bridge was a shaggy tree, probably an oak. "Maybe," I thought, "the Boscobel Oak in which Charles II hid from Cromwell after the battle of Worcester." Most of the sixteen thousand troops in Charles's army were Scots. Three thousand were killed in the battle; afterward another two thousand were deported to America. England, Scotland, and America would have fared better had the oak been lumbered before the battle, and Cromwell's troopers found Charles and pulped him, preventing his escape to France.

On the eastern side of the canal a chapel sank abandoned into weeds, its windows bricked, behind a child's blue pedal car. A stack of car doors slumped rusting against the back of a shed, and like vines black drainage pipes climbed the backs of liverish buildings, tendrils digging between bricks into kitchens and bathrooms. A man sitting on a bench broke wind as I approached him. The man looked as if more than indigestion bothered him. Nevertheless, the immediate often brightens a day more than the distant. Across the canal a black cat wearing a red collar sat like a doorstop atop a wall. From reeds moorhens called to each other, the sounds light metallic "queeks." A swan cruised down the middle of the canal. From each side of the bird's breast, a line of ripples spread in a V. Because I was far away, the ripples looked like oars, and at first I thought the swan a sculler. A green finch flew into a hawthorn. I stopped walking and noticed forget-me-nots and cuckooflower. A robin landed on a fencepost six feet from me. Its breast was the reddest I'd seen, and its small bill looked like a seed. A diesel engine blew its horn, and I watched a small freight clack south along Shandon Crescent, suddenly remembering childhood and sitting on the curb in Ashland, Virginia, counting the cars on passing freights.

I walked past eight fours manned by students from the George Heriot School. Two were quadruple sculls, and girls rowed two of the boats. The rowers were beginners, and members of the varsity crew cycled along the towpath shouting instructions. Because of cyclists, I couldn't relax. Packs of families romped by. Children had trouble controlling bicycles, and they swerved from side to side, forcing me off the towpath. Other cyclists were training for triathlons or dinner-table marathons and whizzed carelessly past, often startling me and once or twice almost spinning me around. I sway when I walk, the result of genes, not age. My father also swayed when he walked, and I worried that if I walked naturally and staggered, a cyclist would crash into me.

The canal crossed high above the Leith in an aqueduct built in 1822. Along the aqueduct, the towpath narrowed, and bicyclists dismounted and carried their bikes under their arms. Still the bicycles spread across most of the path, wheels waggling and pushing me to the edge of the water. I walked along the aqueduct, thinking I might feel Roman. I didn't. On reaching the south side of the aqueduct, I turned around, crossed back over the Leith, and walked down the steps to the Water of Leith Visitor Centre. A dipper stood on a rock in the middle of the river, his chest round and white, his upper body dark brown, the color of an old wooden floor, hard wear having ground dirt into the grain and polish having sealed and shined it so the boards looked clean.

On the walk I saw two other dippers, these after Currie Station, flying low above the water, their wings beating slowly. Below millraces gray wagtails perched on snags. Song thrushes scrambled under bushes; wrens popped off the ground into song, and jackdaws nesting in a broken tree glared at me. A tree creeper shuffled up a dead trunk, and choruses of blackbirds sang from low scrub while tits tumbled about singing high and low. A man noticed my binoculars and asked if I had seen any interesting birds. To him the birds I saw were everyday, but to me they were exciting. I almost shouted whenever I saw a blue tit. I followed a pair of bullfinches through brush, their heads capped with black, the male's chest a stunning rose pink, their white rumps flashing when they flew. To me they seemed lyrical, and I wanted to press them into mind in hopes that someday they would flutter out of memory, feathers sweeping shadows from mood.

Along the walkway I collected bouquets of flowers: dog violets; marsh marigolds; near Balerno ranks of wild hyacinths, most blue, but a few pink, and some ghostly white; carpets of ramsons; wild garlic; honesty; comfrey, most common comfrey, their blossoms creamy, but some plants Russian comfrey with violet blossoms; goldilocks buttercups; archangel; both red and white dead nettle; butterbur; red campion; sweet cicely, wings of white spreading from the middle of leaves; and water avens nodding in the shade, pink petals and yellow stamens set in lanterns of purple sepals. I arranged bouquets in bowls of ferns: maidenly filmy fern, forked spleenwort, its leaves combed upward, ends split, and hard-shield fern, spilling over in falls, the leaflets close and sharp looking like gauntlets made from chain mail. I couldn't identify most ferns, and when I returned to the Visitor Centre late in the afternoon, I suggested that the Conservation Trust publish a pamphlet describing ferns growing beside the Leith.

The pamphlet probably wouldn't sell, however. On the amble I saw scores of walkers and runners and a few bicyclists. No one aside from me carried binoculars, and I didn't see anyone bending over a flower. Most people trekked along, chatting with friends or family, leading dogs, and pushing baby carriages, enjoying the exercise, just pleased to be out of house or office. For my part I was glad to be alone. Instead of having to match a companion's words or pace, I meandered, stopping and starting for flowers and birds. Across the river from Redhall House, I walked through a laurel hedge. Although many blossoms had turned brown, some were fresh enough to powder the air, making it smell like a dressing table. Liverwort plastered itself to damp rocks, giving them a pitchy fragrance. Near Balerno I smelled manure and saw cattle and in a field five white draft horses.

The walkway followed the path of the old Balerno Branch Railway. The branch had opened in 1874 and remained in use until the late 1960s. The railway bed was close to the river, but frequently I shunted onto sidings, exploring corners of fields or climbing atop remnants of spillways that hung over the river like hips, some of the bones of which had become honeycombed, water eating at them like osteoporosis. On my previous walk along the Leith, I had slipped the rails at the Colinton. This time I pushed past Colinton and walked through the railway tunnel. The entrance to the tunnel resembled a giant horseshoe, and the tunnel itself curved like a cast stretching from a person's upper arm around his elbow to the lower arm. On the way back to Slateford, I counted the steps from one end of the tunnel to the other, starting in the middle of the walkway at the Easter Hailes Gate. I took 156 steps, more probably than I took on the way. Weariness shortened my stride and concentration, the sound of my feet making the numbers themselves resemble echoes.

Industrialism left boot prints along the Leith, and remnants of mills abounded: fulling, grain, paper, board, and flax, among others. Some remains resembled rock quarries; others were scenic, romantically broken into vaults, nearby stone channels flush with weeds, not water. A couple had been recycled into office buildings or housing developments. Along the banks were seventeenth- and eighteenth-century houses. In Connecticut I live in a clapboard house, a small Dutch colonial, the ceilings of which are so low my head almost brushes them. How wonderful it would be, I thought, to live behind the thick walls of Spylaw House. The exterior glowed green with age, and I imagined the inside, the ceilings high, moldings blossoming into topiary.

The church at Currie was built in 1785. On either side of the front door stood two tall elegant windows, the lower portions each divided into four smaller windows, each nine panes. The upper portion rose vaulted, pressed together at the top like ribs, the mullions curving, dividing the two lower parts into six panes apiece, the single upper part into nine panes—the total number of panes in a window, fifty-seven. The Kinleith Mill manufactured paper until 1966. Afterward the mill had been demolished, and the site was scabby with bricks, walls, burned timbers, knots of iron, and hunks of concrete. A fence surrounded the wreckage, and signs warned passersby to stay away. I wandered through a break in the fence, following paths made by adventuresome boys. I imagined finding a treasure, but I was too tired to study the grounds and to conjure up a discovery, say, the skeleton of a fox. In Connecticut I would have overturned rocks and boards and found baskets of snakes. In contrast to Kinleith was Woodhall Mill, a development in Juniper Green under the shadow of the Edinburgh Bypass and managed by Applecross, known for "the art of home creation." Although the houses were decorous, the development bulged fat against the Leith, pressing against walkers and irritating me. I couldn't imagine finding excitement amid the managed neatness of Woodhall.

After turning the wrong way on the Bridge Road at the end of the walkway and wandering for several hundred yards along the Lanark Road, I eventually reached Balerno. I was thirsty and tired and went into the Grey Horse, the first pub I saw, and ordered a pint of pale ale. I drink little, and normally a pint of ale would have made me tight. Aside from perspiration breaking out on my brow then vanishing like dew, I didn't notice the drink. The public room in the Grey Horse was very small, too small for me to stretch into comfortable conversation. Smoke was thick as asbestos, and nine men and two women were in the pub, all friends. Instead of speaking, I rubbed a long-haired dachshund who brushed across the floor cadging massages. I drank my beer quickly and left. Outside I noticed the menu for the Crafty Café, a small restaurant attached to the pub. As I read the menu, a man opened the door, and I followed him in, ordering the all-day breakfast, a plate overflowing with an egg once over easy, baked beans, tomatoes, toast, bacon, fried sausage, and black pudding. I also ordered coffee. The woman who waited bar next door took my order. "Get the big cup. It costs the same amount as the small," she suggested. The café was homey, consisting of a single blue and white room and six tables covered with red oilcloth. When the woman set my breakfast on the table, I said that I had walked from Edinburgh and wasn't sure I'd be able to make it back. "You'll be fine," she said. Never had a breakfast tasted so good. Only embarrassment prevented me from ordering it a second time. When I left the café, my step did not bounce, but neither did my feet drag. In the backyard of a house at the corner of Bridge and Bavelaw, a woman had hung out her laundry, fourteen pairs of underpants, all a healthy robust size, all white and waving like signal flags on a yacht. "A fortnight's supply," I said. "Doubtful; remember this is Scotland," an Englishman of my acquaintance said later, "that could be six month's supply." "That would mean that the woman wore a pair for thirteen days before swapping it for a clean pair," I said, figuring quickly. "Do you think that reasonable?" "Oh, no, certainly not," my acquaintance said. "I apologize. I miscalculated. That was an eight-month washing. No decent Scotswoman changes her undergarments until at least eighteen days have passed."

Would that I could have rigged the underpants about my spars and sailed back to Newington. By the end of the holiday I was listing, keel leaking, camber concave, rudder wobbling, and fantail dragging. On Causewayside I stopped at Tesco Express and bought three pints of orange juice for two pounds. Bolted to the front of the store was a cash machine. An inclined walk led to a platform in front of the machine. Railings surrounded the platform. When I left the store, I wedged my backside under the bottom rail and, leaning forward, drank a pint, being too tired to shed my backpack. Once home I stretched out on my couch and read, picking C. E. Montague's *The Right Place* out of a stack of books. "Outer edges of old holidays, the marginal bits that you may have looked upon at the time as mere unavoidable selvage," Montague wrote, "have a trick of waxing almost poignantly pleasant in recollection." "Maybe Not," I thought, "or Maybe."

Last Runaround

IN FEBRUARY I REGISTERED for the Great Caledonian Run, a ten-kilometer road race held early in May. Training, I told fellows at the institute, imposed structure on days, a necessity when one was away from home. I said I planned to finish in the last 5 percent of the runners. "Anyone can mimic youth and bolt from the start," I explained, adding that discipline and breeding separated a person from the brutish and vulgarly hormonal. Of course the truth was that I didn't care where I finished and that I entered the race in hopes losing weight and lowering my blood pressure. During the past decades I'd run races in Canada, the United States, and Australia. "If I tack Scotland onto the list," I wrote my friend Josh, "I'll be quite the sport, a four-country athlete."

"Shuffling is not a sport," Josh replied. "And you should fall to your knees and thank God for tweezing athleticism from your genes. The Lord loved you so much that he made you the most uncoordinated beast I've ever met." To be a sport, Josh declared, an activity had to meet several criteria, "not one of which applies to shilly-shallying around Edinburgh." When a person was young, Josh elaborated, sport interfered with studies. Later sport constricted the adult's life, causing him to fawn over the doings of adolescents, plucking out taste buds, making him salivate over meeting lumpy people more ignorant than parsnips. Thirdly, involvement in sport led to indiscretion and scrapes with the authorities. "Most importantly," he concluded, "a real sport corrodes morality and pits integrity. Almost as soon as an athlete dons his kit, he becomes adept at cheating. He gouges and bites. His head becomes a hammer, and his elbows and feet bludgeons. He lies and fakes injuries. He pretends to have caught balls that he dropped. His speech deteriorates. He uses syllables not words. He swears and behaves like a roustabout. Eventually the corrupt and the powerful cultivate him and call him a role model. Not only is his development as a human being stunted, but chances are good he will someday be confined, either in a prison or in a boardroom. The latter cell is worse. Fellow inmates will shackle him with conversation about things he did decades before he wore boxer shorts, if indeed he has matured enough to don proper undergarments."

Josh douses his paragraphs with curry powder, eschewing medium for vindaloo. For my part I prefer mild paragraphs. Often I have advised him to mix sweet with his sour. "Then," I said, "people won't become bilious and bother you." Still amid Josh's seasoning lurks a peppercorn of truth. Running has involved me with the constabulary. Last week as I tacked up Queen's Drive toward Newington breasting a headwind, I noticed a policeman on the far side of the drive. He held a radar gun in his right hand, aiming it toward traffic coming down the hill. "How fast am I going?" I shouted. He turned the gun my way, after which he jabbed his left hand down to his side and, pointing at the curb, yelled, "Pull over!"

The Caledonian corkscrewed through Old Town, starting on Melville across the Meadows from the institute. Beyond the Meadows, runners turned onto Lauriston, twisting through Tollcross and winding up King's Stables to Princes. On Princes the route meandered east until it turned up the Mound. From the top of the Mound the race bustled downhill along Market before slicing over Jeffrey to Canongate. At the bottom of the Royal Mile runners nipped past the new parliament building then pulled themselves along the cusp of Arthur's Seat to Holyrood Park Road. At the mouth of Holyrood runners turned north and trotted downhill, bearing west on Cowgate until they reversed themselves and climbed the hill at Candlemaker. At Teviot they turned west into a short dogleg that led to the Meadows and the finish.

During the race I intended to ponder a character that had recently come to mind, an activity that would straighten the course and prevent me from thinking about being tired. Tump Tump Gowdie was born in the hills of eastern Kentucky. He was named after both his father and grandfather, both of whom were called Tump, Tump Tump's Christian name being taken from his father, his middle name from his grandfather. T.T., as his friends called him, had gone into the coal mines when he was a boy. By the time he was twenty, he had become a union organizer. This career was short lived. Thugs hired by the coal company chased him into Tennessee, threatening to shoot him if he returned to Kentucky. Working for the union had given T.T. a stage presence, and in Tennessee he became an itinerant speaker.

Working in mines stunted T.T.'s growth, and he was barely five feet tall. When he spoke, however, his voice rumbled upward like a blast underground, and he seemed to grow two feet. He was not handsome. His nose twisted to the left, pointing to, as critics said, his politics. Sprouting from each ear was a thistle of hair. Both his eyes and a goatee were pale blue, the latter dyed. He always wore green trousers, a green checked shirt, wingtip shoes with thick black soles, and argyle socks, these last responsible for his name on the lecture circuit, the Duke of Argyle. He also wore a long blue overcoat that dragged the ground and that had big side pockets. The pockets bulged like watermelons, seedy, in his words, with notandums, scraps of paper covered with ideas culled from libraries. In the upper right-hand pocket of his coat, he kept a stack of library cards held together by rubber bands. Occasionally if he were speaking near a table, he pulled the cards from his pocket and, fanning them across the tabletop, said, "Pick a card, any card. You can't lose in a library."

The Duke was a good speaker, and groups booked him, paying him modest fees. Frequently, though, he spoke extemporaneously, usually outside courthouses, setting a black hat on the ground in front of his feet. In addition to money, listeners tossed a miscellany of things into the hat: sandwiches; cans of Vienna sausages; packs of chewing gum, Teaberry in Smith County, in Trousdale, Juicy Fruit; catfish; marbles; jewelry, once a string of pearls; rabbits' feet; pencils; flowers, predominately iris and zinnias; and in Lebanon on Christmas Eve a petrified baby opossum. In Pulaski, shortly after the Gideons left town, the Duke received seventeen Gideon Bibles.

Experience shapes people, and the Duke was a libertarian, distrusting government and wealth. "The law," he frequently declared, "traps honey bees but ignores hornets." "The more a man is worth," he said, "the more worthless he is." Often his language was poetic, just right for dusk in a country town. "Oh, ye cadaverous intellects, beware the roaming reptiles of right, rattling at neighbors but ignoring their own venomous behavior. Oh, ye obese intelligences don't fret about original sin. There's enough actual sin in the world to keep you going from Sunday to Sunday." The Duke believed that correct grammar, like proper table manners, separated people into classes and undermined not only communication but also reform and originality. "Don't worry about that and which craft," he said. "Grammar ain't a belt. It's only garters, purple suspenders, and fancy silk underwear. Spelling doesn't matter. Who cares how letters are arranged, just so long as most of them are there?"

Like Josh, the Duke often jumped fences before he reached them, unnecessarily irritating listeners. Still, occasionally I almost agreed with some of his ideas. "Once a year every minister should be examined by a psychiatrist." "The Bible teaches," he was fond of saying, "that the wise men came from the East, not the South. Vanderbilt ain't Harvard, and there's not a socialist at Sewanee. Don't be a puny conformist. Without individuality, liberty is tubercular. Without differences of opinion, education is propaganda. Inbred ideas weaken the brain and cause aneurysms." Like all good speakers, the Duke was often melodramatic. When speaking in a pasture at night, the only light provided by a torch or two, he'd suddenly become silent and, staring into the distance, would blanch and tremble. "The one-eyed lard fiend," he'd moan, and cover his eyes. No matter how spectators glanced around, he never described the fiend.

The Duke was also a little peculiar. After a talk someone usually invited him to dinner, more often than not serving fried chicken. The Duke only ate chicken purchased at groceries. Because most country people raised chickens and never bought a fryer, his meals were frequently vegetarian, always filling, being platters of greens, butter and string beans, biscuits, corn, tomatoes, and pecan pie, but vegetarian nevertheless. The Duke refused to eat a bird that had scratched about the yard, explaining that the chicken was liable to be the mother or father, grandfather or grandmother of many occupants of the henhouse. "I tremble to think what they would do to me if they discovered that I ate parts of their kinfolk," he said.

The route the race followed was familiar. I'd spent the week before the run jogging around Edinburgh, doing final errands and preparing my departure. One day I ate lunch with Ronny Jack and another academic at the Grain Store, a restaurant above Grassmarket on Victoria. The restaurant was at the top of two flights of stairs. On each landing stood a metal florist's can, perfume spilling out of pink lilies and sugaring the shadows. I had not met the other man before, but like Josh he'd aged into crisp speech and behavior. Eight years ago he switched off his electronic mail. "I've not looked at it since," he said. During the meal I mentioned a mutual friend who mysteriously became an alcoholic in his sixties. For decades the man had been at the center of literary studies in the Midwest. His fall was astonishingly fast. "Perhaps," I said, fumbling for an explanation, "the time for his kind of criticism passed, leaving him isolated and lonely, ignored by younger critics." "Nonsense," the man said, "it was all those whores in Ottawa."

For lunch I ate hake and kale, spiced with capers. The meal was tasty, but so was the lunch I ate the next day, a hamburger roll stuffed with haggis and awash with brown sauce that I bought for eighty-five pence at Preacher's on Lady Lawson Street. I ate the roll while walking along West Port. At West Bow I went into Bow Well Antiques to say goodbye to Alasdair, the son of the owner. The plates and figurines for sale in Bow Well were the best I had seen in Edinburgh, just right for conversation but too pricy for me. I noticed a new acquisition in a display case, a commemorative plate with Robert Burns's profile in the middle. Burns wore a black coat, and his face looked like porridge. Panes in the display cases shone like water, something I mentioned as I studied Burns's profile. "I clean them," said Mary.

Mary was over eighty. Although her back curved forward like the handle of a cane, her eyes were bright. She stared at the plate for a moment, then quoted "Tam o' Shanter." "But pleasures are like poppies spread— / You seize the flow'r, its bloom is shed; / Or like the snow falls in the river— / A moment white, then melts for ever; / Or like the borealis race, / That flit ere you can point their place; / Or like the rainbow's lovely form / Evanishing amid the storm."

The next morning I bought presents for Vicki. Earlier in the year I bought Vicki a cup commemorating the marriage of Prince Charles to Camilla Parker Bowles. On the cup appeared the date of the marriage, April 8. So the prince could attend the funeral of Pope John Paul II, the marriage was delayed a day, and I walked to gift shop outside Holyroodhouse in hopes of picking up a cup dated April 9, so that Vicki would have a pair of tacky conversation starters. After buying the cup, I strolled up the Royal Mile. In Canongate Crafts I bought Vicki a red throw, Celtic designs twisting through it in puzzles.

I carried the presents to my office at the institute. Three cherry trees bloomed in the courtyard. While the blossoms hung thick above the walkways puffy as cumulus clouds, patches of wild hyacinth bunched across the ground in rugs. For a moment I thought about carrying a chair into the courtyard and dozing under the cherries. Natural beauty disrupts plans and often leads to dislocating inertia—indeed to the kind of madness that provokes a person to absent himself from society, something of which I approve. Alas, I was in training, preparing for home and the end of my stay. I left the cherries and walked over Waverley Bridge to Princes Street and Jenners, Edinburgh's famous department store, first opened in 1838. The original building burned in 1892. Rebuilt in pink sandstone, the store reopened in 1895 and was a visual oasis, the only building attracting the eye amid a plain of undistinguished, almost invisible contemporary buildings stretching west along the north side of Princes Street to the Lothian Road. In the middle of Jenners was an open oblong hall, an arcade three floors high, above it a trestle of beams supporting a glass roof. Behind the balconies on the second and third floors were a series of shops. A protective railing ran around each of the floors, the top of the railing wood, the balustrades metal, colored gold and forged into thistles two and a half feet tall, 134 thistles to a balcony, this last a fact not known to the employees to whom I talked.

At Jenners I bought Vicki a silver bracelet, this, too, decorated with knots vaguely Celtic. I also purchased an apron, on which was printed Scots words and expressions, among others, *fankle, dreich, neep,* and *numpty.* My mind works by association. The apron made me think about kitchens and food, so I explored the food store. For a moment I considered treating myself to a smoked duck breast. But then I realized that I wouldn't know how to prepare it, so for £7.99 I bought Jenners Paradise Cake, a brick weighing 1,225 grams, among the ingredients of which were sultanas, whole eggs, pineapple, walnuts, cherries, almonds, praline paste, and demerara sugar.

Vicki likes the works of the nineteenth-century painter Edwin Landseer. At the Royal Scottish Academy was an exhibit Landseer's Scottish paintings, called *The Monarch of the Glen,* the title of the exhibition taken from Landseer's famous painting of a stag standing atop a tuft of land, posed like a statue on a column, mountains and sky purple behind him, his antlers a great rack spreading across the canvas, the animal's nostrils wide, his eyes bright, his expression noble Grecian. For Vicki I bought the catalog, after which I wandered the exhibition rooms. At times the walls seemed zoological gardens blighted with dead animals: flocks of birds and herds of deer, the bodies of these last collapsing, their heads thrown back, wringing their necks into burns.

As I have never been other than tamed and leashed, so I preferred domestic paintings in which dogs appeared: the famous *The Old Shepherd's Chief Mourner*, in which a Highland collie crouched beside his master's coffin, his muzzle resting on the lid, the scene wondrously sentimental; and *A Highland Breakfast*, in which a young mother suckled her child while five dogs lapped milk from a tub to her right. Latched onto a sandy terrier were puppies fat as sausages. To the terrier's right, a collie clutched a bone in her mouth while a white terrier looked up enviously and a deerhound wrinkled its muzzle. At times a scene drew me through the canvas, and I did not see the painting so much as memory. Last summer my dachshund George died, and when I looked at *Extract from a Journal whilst at Abbotsford*, I saw my old companion, not Maida, Walter Scott's deerhound. In the painting Maida lay curled on the floor, staring at a puppy chewing his tail, too tired to shoo the puppy away. Maida's shoulders collapsed inward, and his muzzle was ragged and pinched, just like George's was during his last summer. "Shucks," I said and, walking around the corner into another room, started counting animals in *Return from Hawking*. In the foreground were two horses, ten hawks, a mound of dead birds, one of which was a gray heron, eight dogs, and six people, one of these a boy, two, girls. In the background someone rode a horse down a lane, five or so dogs underfoot.

I have aged into feeling diminished when I see a dead animal. On rainy days I plucked hundreds of earthworms from sidewalks in Edinburgh and pitched them onto grassy mounds. Hunting repulses me, though it didn't when I was young. To hunt after a person reaches fifty seems indecent, staining character like the mark of Cain. I grew tired of rifles and game bags, muddy eyes and lolling tongues, and retreated to Landseer's landscapes, in particular *Glenfeshie*. High in mountains dyed orange by the sunrise, one could wander far from people and imagine the best of man.

Despite having an end clearly in mind, my joggings around Edinburgh wandered like the race itself. I explored closes I'd neglected, among others, Dunbar fragrant with boxwood, Bakehouse, and White Horse. In the seventeenth century the last was home to an inn. Now restored, the close appeared fresh and washed, its windows, however, at different levels, making it so irregular that it seemed shaped by time, not man. Chessel's Court was open, and light flooded in, turning an eighteenth-century building pastel. I liked the new parliament buildings from the outside, panels of gray and black granite hanging down their walls like moss, the roofs resembling keels of boats rubbed silver by barnacles, along Canongate a curving wall, set with fossils and inlaid with stones, quotations carved into them. My favorite quotation was from Gerard Manley Hopkins. "What would the world be, once bereft / Of wet and wildness? Let them be left, / O let them be left, wildness and wet; / Long live the weeds and the wilderness yet." I pressed my hands against the stone into which the quotation from Hopkins had been carved. The stone was so cold it felt wet, something that warmed my feelings.

After buying the cup for Vicki at Holyrood, I visited parliament. The cost overrun had been enormous, but the building was beautiful, ceilings, corners, even desks catching the eye, reminding one that life was various and irregular, not symmetrical like a warehouse. Warders were proud of the building. For them it was an emblem of Scottish independence. "I hope it comes," I said. Woven above the chamber were webs of wood and steel. Huge windows opened, letting in racecourses of light. Woods in the chamber were oak and sycamore, the colors blond and yellow. Seats of the deputies wavered like musical notes seeming to reflect natural rhythms rather than the strident, mechanical goose step of politics. "I think the room will elevate, maybe ennoble, people," a warder said.

While buying presents for Vicki, I visited the John Knox House on High Street, opened early in May after being closed for a year. Knox probably died in the house in 1572, the house having been confiscated from its long-term owner, the goldsmith James Mossman, because he supported Mary, Queen of Scots. To me Knox was unappealing, a zealous, righteous man so narrow that he affected history. At moments the appointments of the house rose above association with Knox and Calvinism almost to beauty. Lining the fireplace in the Mossman Room on the first floor were delicate blue and white Bloempot tiles manufactured in Rotterdam in the late eighteenth century. On the back and on both sides of the fireplace, the tiles formed a still life based on an engraving by Carel Allard, three vases overflowing with flowers, lilies, carnations, trumpet vine, daffodils, and perhaps peonies. I'd like to think peonies among the flowers. According to old lore, peonies shone at night protecting shepherds and their flocks from evil spirits. The peony seemed almost a New Testament flower, lifting the dark veil of the Old Testament and driving the malignant spirit of Calvinism from the room.

Certainly the Oak Room on the third floor was an earthly garden, this despite a painting on the wall depicting Cain and Abel sacrificing to God. Indeed, only the date of the painting, early seventeenth century, suited the room. The rich oak paneling of the room smacked of worldly success, sacrifices to and rewarded by Mammon, a deity driven from favor by the selfish excesses of his followers but one whose theology focused attention on this world, where, after all, people make hells and heavens for themselves and their neighbors. Above the ceiling of the room lurked a painted ceiling, once covered but now exposed, a ceiling whose wild profusion Knox would have found blasphemous. On the ceiling appeared rabbits, lobsters, pigeons, grapes, flowers, hawks, hounds, bows, drums, and stars, among whirling constellations of other things. Amid the designs squatted an hermaphroditic Pan-like figure, his body stretching over three boards. He was laughing, holding a deep tray of fruits and vegetables above his head. Asses' ears jutted from the sides of his forehead, and his legs ended in hooves. Firm breasts the size of grapefruit ripened on his chest, while between his legs his privates looked like a flower bulb, one that had sprouted, its leaves an unopened bundle leaning to the right. From his anus hung three stalks, their bed clearly fertile because below the creature's buttocks the stalks burst into roughage bigger than fans, among them fruit swelling like pears. "Just the thing to add a little bounce to my run," I thought, leaving the house and walking up High Street toward St. Giles Cathedral.

This morning at ten o'clock I ran. Since the race started near the institute, I changed clothes in my office. I wore clothes Vicki bought on sale, a pair of gray Nike shorts, white socks, a long-sleeved black "Head" shirt, probably made for skiers but which shed perspiration quickly, and pair of Asics Gel-Kayano running shoes with thick soles. When I arrived in January, the shoes were new. Months of trudging through rain and mud and of pounding sidewalks and asphalt had stripped elasticity from them. Still, they were comfortable. I also wore a baseball cap. Vicki bought it, too, before I left Connecticut. On the crown appeared UCONN, the letters blue surrounded by a gray border and a ditch of white. All the letters were capitals; the final three letters were slightly smaller than the U and the C, making room for "Huskies," the nickname of athletic teams at the University of Connecticut. On the left side of the bill appeared the head of a husky, the dog silver, its tongue hanging out. I thought that a spectator might recognize the cap and perhaps yell, "Go

Huskies." I was mistaken. The worlds people imagine as big are tiny. I have worn the cap on all my runs in Edinburgh, and not once has anyone said anything.

The race started according to plan. I lined up near the end of a long rope of seven thousand runners. Plans, as Burns wrote in "To a Mouse" and as Alasdair quoted in Bow Well after Mary recited "Tam," "gang aft agley." I felt energetic, and so instead of lingering at the end of the crowd, I started passing other runners, something not easy, as roads were often narrow. I hopped from runner to runner, comparable to jumping from one stone to another to cross a creek. Instead, though, of bounding across rocks, I leapt past backsides, many of them big as boulders. I looked ahead and picked out the biggest behind I saw. Once I passed it, I looked forward again and took aim at another rump. "So you ran from arse to arse?" Don, the secretary of the institute, said. "Yes," I said, "except on hills. Because of all that jogging around Arthur's Seat, I chugged past people on hills, many of them who, despite pulling only small cabooses, switched themselves on to sidings."

"You must have been moving right along," Josh wrote me, adding, "like the colt the Duke bred after he retired on the money he made from speaking." Foxcroft Farms in Kentucky bought the colt from the Duke. "That horse looks pretty fast," the owner of Foxcroft said, after observing the colt. "Fast ain't the word for him," the Duke replied. "Lightning struck his mama during a terrible storm. What was good for the mother, the lightning decided was good for the son. But no matter how that lightning chased the colt across the pasture, he couldn't catch him. The bolts were always two or three lengths behind." I didn't kick my heels up so high as the colt. But the run didn't tire me. I finished in fifty-seven minutes and one second, in the middle half of runners and passing at least three thousand people. Unlike runs in other countries, the race was silent. Runners did not chat with each other, and except for greeting a relative or friend, crowds on the sidewalk were quiet. Sponsors of the race hired bands to play at the halfway mark beside Holyrood and at the finish line, but no spectator blew a trumpet or played rock and roll music.

After the race, I changed clothes at the institute. Then I walked back to my flat, showered, and made a pot of tea and ate a fist of Paradise Cake. Two hours later I returned to the institute and started an essay. By six I had written 1,652 words. "Enough," I thought. The next morning my legs ached. By afternoon I felt good, and so I jogged around Arthur's Seat. I met only one other runner. "I'll finish the essay in two days," I thought, "then the last days will be mine. Maybe I will find something else for Vicki."

Afterword

THE COURSE OF A PERSON'S DAYS, to draw from John Addington Symonds, depends less upon intellect and planning than upon "sentiment, emotion, involuntary habits of feeling and observing, constitutional sympathy with the world and men," and "tendencies of curiosity and liking." Despite my intention, I didn't stop jogging after the Caledonian. With the end of my stay rushing into sight, I became more active. I sped up, not because I wanted to hurry across a finish line, but because I wanted to slow days down. To stretch hours I filled them with doings. The day after the race I ate lunch with Faith Pullin, a retired member of the English department. We ate in Home Bistro on West Nicolson. We sipped champagne and told stories about academic doings. Once Faith became so exasperated that early one morning she flew to Morocco. That evening she flew back to Edinburgh. The next day she met classes as usual.

Two days after eating with Faith, I had lunch with Steve Neff. Steve was my closest friend in Edinburgh. Forty years ago, when Steve was fifteen and a sophomore in high school and I was twenty-four and just back from Cambridge, he was in an English class I taught at Montgomery Bell Academy in Nashville, Tennessee. He was stunningly bright and nice. We kept track of each other through the years, occasionally sending Christmas cards or books, and once or twice meeting by happenstance in London. After high school, Steve marched through Harvard, law school at the University of Virginia, the International Institute of Human Rights in Strasbourg, and a fellowship at Christ College at Cambridge. Twenty-two years ago he joined the faculty of law in Edinburgh, over the years writing a shelf of articles and books, the most recent being "a general history," *War and the Law of Nations,* published by Cambridge University Press. At the end of my stay he was checking footnotes in a book for Harvard entitled *Justice in Blue and Gray: A Legal History of the American Civil War,* the only history of the Civil War, he said, that didn't mention Shiloh or Gettysburg.

We ate at the Grain Store on Victoria Street, my second visit. I returned because I liked the food and the place. Ceilings were smoky and arched, and the rooms had once been shops and cavernous bins. Thick pillars ran through the restaurant, rising from the floor below and supporting St. Columba's Free Church above on Johnson Terrace. The church was stony and heavy, although since St. Columba's advertised itself as "Presbyterian, Evangelical and Reformed," its theology may have been light, ponderous only in uplift. Steve and I ate pigeons and shared a bottle of merlot. Instead of billing me £34.50 as he should have, the owner charged me £27, not something I noticed until after I left. I ought to have retraced my steps to Victoria and paid the extra £7.50. Alas, I did not, the wine blowing me about wantonly, direction forgotten, both moral and geographical.

While Steve hustled back to the law school, I roamed streets above Grassmarket. Purpose can blind. In contrast, the ambler often stumbles upon things that intrigue him. I discovered Steve was a gourmand. Taped to the window of Sardi's, an Italian restaurant on Forrest, was a culinary review written by Alexander McCall Smith. Steve had accompanied Smith to Sardi's, where he started his meal with smoked salmon parcels priced at £6.50. Next he ate a fillet steak priced at £14.95, after which he said, "That was really good." "Dr. Neff," Smith wrote, "is very thin. He can eat whatever he likes and not put on an ounce of weight. In this area, as in others, genes reveal the fundamental unfairness of life."

In *Memoirs of a Polyglot,* William Gerhardie said that "unimaginative people were wont to rate" experience too highly. Gerhardie was right. In going back to Connecticut, however, I was returning to a place I knew so well that all new experiences, aside from those triggered by aging, would have to be imaginative. Consequently I spent two of my last evenings in Edinburgh at the theater cramming actual experiences, one night attending Tom McGrath's play *Laurel & Hardy* at the Royal Lyceum, another Monteverdi's *The Coronation of Poppea,* put on at the Traverse by the Royal Scottish Academy of Music and Drama. Both evenings I walked home along West Port, climbing the stairs at Vennel and ambling along Heriot. I slipped through shadows, avoiding scrums of drunken men. A few were aggressive, but most were so soused they staggered in and out of the streets, pausing only to urinate, vomit, or shout to friends.

I'd spent little time roaming Edinburgh at night, preferring to read in my flat. Walking home from the theater, I looked at the castle. Spotlights shone on the buildings, transforming the top of Castle Rock into a chipped brass ring, something that could bind but could also lift if one escaped history. The most beautiful building along my way was the George Heriot School. While light oozed golden brown through the windows of the chapel, the outside of the school resembled a chest rich with treasure: a bracelet found at Alloa, round across the south face of the Quadrangle, a hair ornament from Orbiston, its tines jutting up sharp through the dark west face, here a ring found at Buiston, there a gold collar from Coulter. "I have mined too little of this," I thought. "I should have explored night." The truth is that I've never roamed nights. In part I didn't go into pubs in Edinburgh because of habit. Rarely have I been in a bar in the United States.

During days I shopped and bought more knickknacks for Vicki. I returned to Jenners and bought a Royal Crown Derby figurine, a robin, its bill a gold needle, a red apron covering his breast. At the Scottish Museum I bought a paperweight with a Celtic design on the front and then a replica of one of the Lewis Chessmen, originally carved in the twelfth century. Four inches tall, the piece was a king. The king was the stuff of conversation, not of beauty. He sat in a carved chair, his hair falling braided down his shoulders. He was goggle eyed and, leaning forward, appeared humpbacked and imbecilic.

At Wemyss House, the home of the National Trust for Scotland, I purchased a pair of earrings decorated with thistles. On the first floor of the house was the Drawing Room Gallery, designed by Robert Adam and once the largest drawing room in Edinburgh, now partitioned into three rooms. Furnishing the drawing room were paintings and furniture owned by the architect Sir James Sterling. The furniture was horrific. Before a window stood a white radiogram, a combination radio and gramophone dating from 1965. The radiogram perched on thin black legs, its upper body a white box, dials on the lower half, on the upper half speakers, the sound coming through two hexagons, each punctured by thirty holes. A miscellany of books slumped sideways in a bookcase. "Why not slip a naughty book onto the shelf?" I said to the volunteer who showed me the room. I suggested *The Perfumed Garden,* a lively bit of erotology, composed in Tunis in the sixteenth century and translated in 1886 by Sir Richard Burton.

Fifteen years ago I shared an office with a man whose mother-in-law was puritanical. On the woman's death, her son asked my friend to mail her books to him, most of which were religious. My friend did so, not sealing the box before removing *The Perfumed Garden* from his own library and laying it atop her books, just beneath the flaps of lid. "A splendid book," the volunteer stated. "Chapters nine and ten have long been my favorites." The chapters resemble small guidebooks, providing names and descriptions for the privates of men and women, differentiating them by appearance and behavior. If the organs of generation and pleasure can be compared to birds, the doings of one set of parts might resemble the actions of the American kestrel, to quote Roger Tory Peterson: "Hovers for prey on rapidly beating wings, Kingfisher-like. Sits fairly erect, with an occasional tail lift."

The volunteer was the first person to whom I'd mentioned *The Perfumed Garden* who'd read the book. Clearly I awakened dormant interest. "We should put *Fanny Hill* beside it," he said, mentioning John Cleland's lively eighteenth-century novel. "Still," he said, "what's the point? No one who comes here would notice." "I would," I said. Later I stretched out on the floor of the drawing room to sketch a chair, the ugliest chair I have ever seen outside a cathedral. Made in France or Russia around 1810, the chair sat on an X frame, its feet cat's paws, its seat and back scooped out, looking like empty pudding bowls. At the end of each armrest perched a sphinx, hair bound in brass, tail twisting over its haunches. "Are you all right?" the volunteer asked, as he escorted a group through the room. "I'm doing exactly what I want to do," I said. "You're a laddie who will always do what he wants to do," the man answered.

Separating man from nature was Christianity's greatest sin. Instead of homes for hamadryads, trees are lumber. Naiads choke in irrigation ditches or die in swimming pools, poisoned by chlorine. Housing developments scour hills and valleys, driving fauns from the imagination. One afternoon I walked around Castle Rock. Red campion, wild turnip, chickweed, vetch, and valerian were blooming. The next morning I made my last visit to the Botanic Garden. To celebrate the Second Coming of the Good Samaritan, people will plant gardens. Rhododendrons had burst into pom-poms. While petals on "Susan" were purple and shrill as cheers, petals on "Roza Stevenson" were yellow and almost demure. As some leaves of plantain lily opened into light gold scoops, others gripped stalks, transforming them into leathery handles. Sea cabbage fluffed up silver and green on a dry slope. Beside a stream the tuberous roots of umbrella plant folded over each other in rocky clumps. Hairy stems rose glistening two feet above the roots, looking as if they had been stabbed into the roots rather than pushed out of them.

Big horse chestnuts loomed like hillsides, their leaves green plates of lichen-covered stones, their blossoms bleached evergreens. Spikes wrinkled out from Forrest's maple, orange and red flowers covering them like bunting, twelve blossoms on one spike, sixteen on another, and seventeen on a third. Four chicks followed a moorhen across a small pool. In brush a chaffinch called "weep, weep." Along a path blossoms on Siebold crab apples clustered teased above new leaves. Flowers so covered fothergilla that the bushes looked like heaps of ball fringe. Along Blacket Place, Japanese skimmia had bloomed since the end of March, its perfume lotuslike, slowing my steps and making me dozy. In the garden bundles of red berries clung to skimmia. Light shining through the translucent leaves of European beech turned the trees into candelabra, cool with lemony flames. I watched a breeze blow along the long beech hedge at the back of the garden, causing leaves to tremble in waves. Once a wave brushed past, the hedge became still and smooth, the sight bringing mortality to mind. "A slight rustling then quiet," I thought, "my life."

Thoughts about what lay ahead may have provoked my melancholy. When I arrived in Boston late on the nineteenth, I planned to take a bus to Framingham, where Vicki would meet me. Immediately we would drive northwest toward Middlebury, Vermont, to attend Edward's graduation from college, spending one night on the road. After he graduated, I knew Edward would not need me, Yale having awarded him a fellowship for graduate study. "Children are their parents' gravediggers," Josh once said. In any case moods are short lived in gardens, one plant leading to another, never letting the mind rest fallow and indulgent.

Suddenly I noticed a tree peony. The blossoms resembled yellow goblets, thicker than carnival glass but scalloped around the edges and fragrant with dregs of licorice and blood orange. A valance of perfoliate alexanders ballooned over an open space. Leaves of the alexanders pinched the stems in clasps, so that flowers seemed to rise from the center of the leaves before exploding into constellations of stars. A peacock butterfly landed on a leaf and spread its wings to gather the sun. The butterfly was commonplace, but I had never seen one before, the pupils in the eyes on its wings black, pouches of orange and blue sagging below and small strings of white tears dropping like pearls.

I lingered in the garden until early afternoon, then I walked west through Inverleith Park, eventually taking a path south to Raeburn. At Maxi's I bought a sandwich, Parma ham and olives on a baguette, a cup of coffee, and a slab of fudge cake. I walked to the Dean Gardens and ate lunch on a bench dedicated to a man who died in 1995. "Weep if you must. Parting is Hell," read a plaque on the back of the bench. "But life goes on, so all is well." After lunch I walked along the Leith. Near the Dean Bridge I met a mother and her daughter. The mother was in her late thirties, and the daughter was thirteen, that gangly age when everyone embarrasses, especially parents, though, to be truthful, this particular mother was a burden. She had dyed her hair circus red, and when the daughter noticed me looking their way, she winced and, glancing at her feet, pulled slightly away from her mother.

At Damhead Weir I watched a dipper swivel through the rushing water. I studied the bird for a quarter of an hour, on the one hand thinking I might not see a dipper again, on the other worrying that if I watched too long familiarity might turn a sight that thrilled me into the everyday. Hawthorn had started to bloom, and along the bank on the high bend above the weir cranesbill and pickaback plant flowered. A jogger slumped on a bench. He told me he was training for the fire brigade. He worked for a cell phone company. The job was good, he said, but his children were young and sometimes he was away from home for two weeks. "I could spend more time with the children if I belonged to the fire brigade," he said, before standing and lumbering toward Belford Bridge, adding, "I need to lose ten pounds."

On the way to Blacket I stopped at Thorntons and bought a box of candy. Because I got to the institute early in the morning, I came to know Tam the mailman. Two days earlier Tam had given me a green Celtics cap. "They are the best football team in Scotland," Tam said. "You can wear the cap in America, then when you come back to Edinburgh to live." A bachelor, Tam took care of his mother, and I bought the candy for her. "She is diabetic," Tam said, "but she can have one piece a day." For Susan, Anthea, and Don, who managed the institute, I bought bottles of Mumm's champagne. "Tomorrow is my husband Alasdair's birthday," Anthea said. "We will drink the champagne and toast you." "Swill the bubbly," I replied, "but don't mention me. Tell Alasdair you bought the champagne." Even though I did not know people well, leaving wasn't easy. "We hate to see you go," a librarian said when I returned my last batch of books. "We will really miss you," a warder at the National Gallery said, after asking when I was returning to the United States. "I am going back to school and get a certificate so I can teach art," Carl, a waiter at the Elephant, said, "and I am trying to stop smoking."

The closer my departure date, the more energy I had. I ran harder around Arthur's Seat, breaking off from the road to canter into Meadowfield Park and scamper up and down Whinny Hill. Three days before I left, two students tried to pass me as I jogged up Queen's Drive toward Holyrood Park Road. I forgot my age and, as the fleet of foot say, turned on the jets. That night I was restless, so at six I left the flat and spent two and a half hours roaming Arthur's Seat, climbing through rabbit warrens, following ravens across the burned dasses, and watching a pheasant as it picked its slow way down Dunsapie Hill. Fever flies flew low over the grass, whirling slowly like biplanes, and cuckoo flowers bloomed in wet seams atop Whinny Hill. At times I threaded my way through gorse tighter than a hair shirt. Near the end of the amble the outside of my left knee began to ache. The next morning my leg was stiff, and I could barely hobble.

Because walking was painful, I spent the better parts of my last two days close to the flat, leaving to limp up East Preston to Mr. Ding's Chinese takeout, buying fried rice for dinner both nights. I also purchased two books to read on the plane: Paul Johnson's thriller *Body Politic* and Alexander McCall Smith's *The 2 1/2 Pillars of Wisdom*, a comic trilogy about the author of *Portuguese Irregular Verbs*. The first two sentences of this last book made me snort with laughter. "Professor Dr Moritz-Maria von Igelfeld often reflected on how fortunate he was to be exactly who he was, and nobody else. When one paused to think of who one might have been had the accident of birth not happened precisely as it did, then, well, one could be quite frankly *appalled*."

I cleaned the flat thoroughly, mopping, vacuuming, polishing, and scrubbing. I brushed the air filter on the clothes dryer, fed plants, and flushed drains. I scoured the insides of the refrigerator and waste cans. I carried the oriental rugs into the garden and beat them. I washed and folded sheets and towels. I dusted the backs of pictures and the undersides of tables. I changed the page on the calendar in the hall, turning from January to May, above this last a reproduction of a painting depicting low tide at Mousehold. In the harbor fifteen masts stuck up like quills. Because the hall was dark even in the day, I may have miscounted, there being sixteen masts instead of fifteen. Still, I counted three times. Before leaving I took inventory. During my stay I did not use the microwave or the blender. On the stove I used only two of the four burners and did not open the door to the oven. During the months I used two pans, three cups, two saucers, two cereal bowls, two dishes, and a small brown pitcher in which I poured milk for tea. I only broke one item, the handle of scissors that had already been mended. Four times I used the toaster. I never rented a movie and consequently did not turn on the compact disc player. Similarly, I did not switch on a radio, although there were radios in three rooms. I found four electric alarm clocks in the flat. I did not plug in any of them. I never made a telephone call. On the other hand, I received four calls, three wrong numbers, two of these from a child with a Pakistani accent and one from a woman searching for Management Associates. The night before I left, Barbara, the owner of the house, made the last call, ringing from France to wish me a good trip home.

In the four and half months of my stay, I used three and a half rolls of paper towels, these doubling as napkins. I drank nothing but tea, 2 percent milk, and orange juice. I never brought beer or wine into the flat. Carrots were the single fresh vegetable I stored in the refrigerator. Only on the day before I left did someone aside from Eliza enter the flat, this another member of the institute hoping to better her apartment. I showered and shaved every day but used only one can of Gillette shaving cream, the 9-ounce size for sensitive skin. I used two razor blades and three bars of Palmolive soap, the sole of the last bar remaining when I left. I used one deodorant, a stick of Tom's of Maine natural deodorant weighing 64 grams and smelling like wood spice. Even though Eliza visited, I only went through three rolls of toilet paper plus four sheets of a fourth roll, all one-ply. I washed clothes often, changing trousers every three days, socks every day, and underpants and shirts every two days. Consequently, I went through three boxes of washing powder, each weighing 1.15 kilograms. My great extravagance was two 500-milliliter bottles of dishwater liquid, Tesco's bio-friendly liquid. Most nights I watched thirty minutes of news on television. Rarely did I glance at other shows, and when I did so, I turned them off quickly.

At 10:30 on the nineteenth I flew to London. That afternoon I took Virgin Atlantic to Boston. I sat in row 64, the last row in the plane occupied by passengers, the final row empty, taken by stewardesses during takeoff and landing. On my right was a door to a lavatory, the room occupied during most of the flight and the toilet growling incessantly. Near the end of the flight the sink became plugged and overflowed. I did not eat the meals served on the plane. I arrived in Framingham at six o'clock. Vicki showed up shortly thereafter, and I took the wheel of the car and drove to White River Junction, Vermont. The trip lasted almost four hours. We stayed in a Best Western motel. After dropping our bags in the room, we looked for a restaurant. Except for the McDonald's, which stayed open until eleven, every restaurant in town was closed. We ordered salads, but none were left, so I ate a Quarter-Pounder and shared a cup of Coca-Cola with Vicki. "Welcome back to the U.S.A. and your special homecoming banquet," Vicki said as we stuck our straws in the cup.